Workplace Communications

THE BASICS Canadian Edition

George J. Searles
Mohawk Valley Community College

K. M. Moran
Conestoga College

Pearson Canada
Toronto

Library and Archives Canada Cataloguing in Publication

Searles, George J. (George John), 1944–
    Workplace communications : the basics / George J. Searles,
    K.M. Moran.–Canadian ed.

Includes index.
ISBN 978-0-205-73647-8

    1. English language–Business English. 2. English language–Technical English. 3. Business writing–Problems, exercises, etc. 4. Technical writing–Problems, exercises, etc. 5. Business communication–Problems, exercises, etc. 6. Commercial correspondence–Problems, exercises, etc. I. Moran, Kathleen M., 1955– II. Title.

PE1479.B87S43 2011   808'.06665   C2010-905287-0

ISBN 978-0-205-73647-8

Vice President, Editorial Director: Gary Bennett
Editor-in-Chief: Ky Pruesse
Acquisitions Editor: David S. Le Gallais
Marketing Manager: Loula March
Developmental Editor: Megan Burns
Project Manager: Cheryl Noseworthy
Production Editor and Copy Editor: Colleen Ste. Marie
Proofreaders: Lenore Latta, Susan Adlam
Composition: MPS Limited, a Macmillan Company
Permissions and Photo Research: Dawn du Quesnay
Art Director: Julia Hall
Cover and Interior Design: Miriam Blier
Cover Image: AID/Getty Images

9 10 V092 15

Printed and bound in Canada.

CONTENTS

Chapter 10   Long Reports: Format, Collaboration, and Documentation

Chapter 11   Oral Presentations: Preparation and Delivery

PREFACE

WELCOME TO THE CANADIAN EDITION

- Greatly expanded treatment of electronic communication
- Many new visuals and examples throughout
- Increased coverage of documenting online sources, including the most current forms of MLA and APA documentation
- Canadian examples of documents

Workplace Communications: The Basics originated as the solution to the problem of accessible textbooks for students anticipating careers in such fields as welding, air conditioning, and electrical maintenance. Although some excellent texts had been written in the fields of business and technical communication, nearly all were aimed at the university level. Finally, George Searles decided to fill the gap and meet his students' needs by creating his own textbook. More than five years in the making, the first edition of *Workplace Communications: The Basics* was published in 1999. His students at Mohawk Valley responded enthusiastically, citing the book's accessibility, clarity, and pragmatic, down-to-earth emphasis as particularly appealing features. To his great satisfaction, it met with similar success at many other colleges, and new editions appeared in 2003, 2006, and 2009.

The first Canadian edition retains all the essential features of the earlier American versions while incorporating much new material. Short on theory, long on practical applications, and written in a simple, conversational style, this book is exceptionally user-friendly. It's appropriate not only for recent high school graduates but also for returning adult students and other nontraditional learners. It's comprehensive and challenging enough for trade school and community college courses and for similar introductory-level classes at most four-year institutions.

Like the earlier editions, this book includes many helpful features such as the following:

- Learning objectives and outlines for each chapter
- Numerous examples, illustrations, and exercises based on actual workplace situations
- Useful checklists at the ends of major sections
- Realistic exercises that reflect each chapter's focus

STUDENT SUPPLEMENTS

PEARSON mycanadiantechcommlab

This state-of-the-art, interactive, and instructive solution for technical communication is designed to be used to supplement a traditional lecture course or to completely administer an online course. See the opening pages of this text for details, and visit www.mycanadiantechcommlab.ca.

MyCanadianTechCommLab includes a Pearson eText, which gives students access to the text whenever and wherever they have access to the internet. eText pages look exactly like the printed text, offering powerful new functionality for students and instructors. Users can create notes, highlight text in different colours, create bookmarks, zoom, click hyperlinked words and phrases to view definitions, and view in single-page or two-page view. Pearson eText allows for quick navigation to key parts of the eText using a table of contents and provides full-text search.

MyCanadianTechCommLab offers videos, sample documents, and interactive exercises to improve communication skills. Throughout the textbook, icons highlight material where related activities or samples are available on MyCanadianTechCommLab.

Explore dozens of **writing samples**, from letters to emails to reports, that model effective communication.

Practise correcting ineffective communication using interactive **document makeovers**. Feedback guides you to understand problems and find solutions.

Watch **videos** of professionals from various fields talking about how their writing and speaking are vital components of their success in business and industry.

A student access card for MyCanadianTechCommLab is packaged with every new copy of the text. Access codes can also be purchased through campus bookstores or through the website.

CourseSmart for Students

CourseSmart goes beyond traditional expectations—providing instant, online access to the textbooks and course materials you need at an average savings of 50 percent. With instant access from any computer and the ability to search your text, you'll find the content you need quickly, no matter where you are. And with online tools like highlighting and note-taking, you can save time and study efficiently. See all the benefits at www.coursesmart.com/students.

INSTRUCTOR SUPPLEMENTS

The **Instructor's Manual** that accompanies the first Canadian edition of *Workplace Communications: The Basics* is intended for both experienced instructors and for those relatively new to teaching the course and includes the following:

- Supplementary commentary. Organized by chapter, this provides instructors with further insight into the subject matter and the methods of teaching as well as with an ability to build a lesson plan and effective teaching strategies.
- Reprints of selected visuals found in the book. This is to facilitate the creation of handouts and the use of visuals in the classroom environment.
- Answers to the exercises in the text, where feasible.
- Reprints of the checklists for evaluating assignments in the text.

In addition, **PowerPoint Presentations** cover the key concepts in each chapter.

CourseSmart for Instructors

CourseSmart goes beyond traditional expectations—providing instant, online access to the textbooks and course materials you need at a lower cost for students. And even as students save money, you can save time and hassle with a digital eTextbook that allows you to search for the most relevant content at the very moment you need it. Whether it's evaluating textbooks or creating lecture notes to help students with difficult concepts, CourseSmart can make life a little easier. See how when you visit www.coursesmart.com/instructors.

ACKNOWLEDGMENTS

I would like to thank Pearson Education Canada for the opportunity to work on this version of the textbook. I would also like to thank many of my colleagues and my family for their support while writing this.

I would also like to acknowledge those who reviewed this book in each stage of its development: Sue Ackerman, Nova Scotia Community College; Jim Catton, Algonquin College; Patrick Dawson, Algonquin College; Ryan Gibbs, Lambton College; Peter Lecour, Canadore College; Chris Legebow, St. Clair College; Richard McMaster, Ryerson University; Jessica Mudry, Concordia University; Lara Sauer, George Brown College; Bruce Watson, SAIT Polytechnic; and Shelley Zwicker, Nova Scotia Community College.

K. M. MORAN

INTRODUCTION

As even its title suggests, *Workplace Communications: The Basics* is in no sense a typical English textbook.

Appropriate as such topics may be in a traditional composition text, you'll find nothing here about how to write 500-word essays, and nothing about how to critique English literature. Instead, this text focuses on the purpose, audience, and tone of communications. Throughout, there is great emphasis on the essential features of effective workplace writing: concision, clarity, and proper formatting. In keeping with the book's highly practical nature, you'll work exclusively with nonacademic forms of writing, the kind done on the job. Among these are memos, email, electronic messaging, business letters—including the application letter and résumé—and both short and long reports.

In addition, chapters detail how to handle specific tasks: writing summaries, descriptions, instructions, and proposals; delivering oral reports; and enhancing oral and written presentations by using visual aids, such as tables and graphs. Every chapter includes numerous examples and illustrations, advice on using computers, and exercises that enable you to practise applying specific principles. Through the use of common-sense strategies, you'll learn to express yourself quickly and directly, with no wasted words. Once you begin to communicate more confidently and efficiently, you'll be better motivated to eliminate any basic mechanical errors that have weakened your writing in the past.

The communication skills you'll develop are important not simply for the sake of completing a course and satisfying an English requirement. Combined with specialized training in your major field of study, these skills will also help equip you for success in the highly competitive environment of today's workplace. In survey after survey, employers repeatedly mention good communication skills along with character, technical knowledge, and computer literacy when asked what they consider to be the most desirable attributes a job candidate can possess. Fortunately, you need not major in English to learn to communicate better. Anyone can. It requires only three components: desire, effort, and guidance. The first two are your responsibility. Coupled with your instructor's efforts, this text will provide the third.

The content of *Workplace Communications* is based on George Searles's experience of more than 30 years, not only as a writing teacher but also as a professional social worker, a widely published freelance journalist, and a communications consultant to numerous businesses, organizations, and social service agencies. This Canadian edition, written with K. M. Moran, includes Canadian examples and valuable suggestions provided by other college-level instructors. The emphasis is not on the abstract theory but on practical application. This text is designed specifically for *you*, the student. After completing the book you'll know a great deal more than you did before about written and oral communication in the workplace. You'll be better prepared to confront any communication challenges your chosen career presents. And if you decide to continue your education, what you've learned will provide a solid foundation for further study.

GEORGE J. SEARLES AND K. M. MORAN

The Keys to Successful Communication:

PURPOSE, AUDIENCE, AND TONE

LEARNING OBJECTIVE

When you complete this chapter, you'll be able to identify your communication purpose and your audience, thereby achieving the appropriate tone in every workplace writing situation.

PURPOSE
AUDIENCE
TONE
EXERCISES

EVERY INSTANCE OF WORKPLACE WRITING occurs for a specific reason and is intended for a particular individual or group. Much the same is true of spoken messages, whether delivered in person or by phone. Therefore, both the purpose and the audience must be carefully considered to ensure that the tone of the exchange will be appropriate to the situation. Although this may seem obvious, awareness of purpose, audience, and tone is the single most crucial factor in determining whether your communication will succeed. This opening chapter concentrates on these fundamental concerns, presents a brief overview of the basic principles involved, and provides exercises in their application.

PURPOSE

Nearly all workplace writing is done for at least one of three purposes: to create a record, to request or provide information, or to persuade. A caseworker in a social services agency, for example, might interview an applicant for public assistance to gather information that will then be reviewed in determining the applicant's eligibility. Clearly, such writing is intended both to provide information and to create a record. The purchasing director of a manufacturing company, on the other hand, might write a letter or email inquiring whether a particular supplier can provide materials more cheaply than the current vendor. The supplier will likely reply promptly. Obviously, the primary purpose here is to exchange information. In yet another setting, a probation officer composes a pre-sentencing report intended to influence the court to grant probation to the offender or impose a jail sentence. The officer may recommend either, and the report will become part of the offender's record, but the primary purpose of this example of workplace writing is to persuade. And finally, a technical writer may have to create a set of instructions that will be used by the purchaser of a new machine. The written document is created to help the customers understand how to operate the equipment properly and safely.

The first step in the writing process is to consciously identify which of the three categories of purpose applies. You must ask yourself, "Am I writing primarily to create a record, to request or provide information, or to persuade?" Once you make this determination, the question becomes, "Summarized in one sentence, what am I trying to say?" To answer, you must zoom in on your subject matter, focusing on the most important elements. A helpful strategy is to employ the "Five Ws" that journalists use to structure the opening sentences of newspaper stories: Who, What, Where, When, Why. Just as they do for reporters, the Five Ws will enable you to get off to a running start. Consider, for example, how the Five Ws technique applies in each of the following situations:

■ *Caseworker writing to provide information and create a record*
    WHO   WHAT   WHERE
    Carolyn Matthews visited the downtown office of the Ministry of

WHEN   WHY
Community and Social Services on May 15 to apply for public assistance.

■ *Purchasing director writing to request information*
WHO   WHAT
I'd like to know whether you can provide gaskets for less than
WHERE   WHEN
$100/dozen, shipped to my company on a monthly basis, because
WHY
I am seeking a new supplier.

■ *Probation officer writing to persuade*
WHO   WHAT   WHERE
Jerome Farley should be denied probation and sentenced to federal prison,
WHEN   WHY
effective immediately, because he is a repeat offender.

■ *Technical writer writing to inform*
WHO   WHAT   WHY   WHERE
You have just purchased an X200 processor. In order to use it effectively in your
WHEN
office, you will need to read the following instructions and, each time you

use the machine, follow them carefully.

AUDIENCE

Next ask yourself, "Who will read what I have written?" This is a crucial aspect of the communication process. To illustrate, consider these two examples. The first is from the *Toronto Star* newspaper, reporting a study released by the *Canadian Medical Association Journal*. The second is an excerpt from the abstract accompanying that article.

Mother's Vitamins Give Baby Good Start

Women who take a multivitamin during pregnancy are far less likely to deliver underweight or premature babies, says a study published today in the *Canadian Medical Association Journal*.

The finding should prompt the World Health Organization to change its prenatal vitamin policy, which currently distributes folic acid and iron to expectant mothers in developing nations, the study's lead author says.

"The WHO's policy suggests . . . there is no advantage to multivitamins," says Dr. Prakesh Shah, a neonatologist at Toronto's Mount Sinai Hospital. "We found that (multivitamins) will lead to a 17 per cent reduction in low-birth-weight births."

The Mount Sinai team pored through 13 previous research papers and synthesized data on some 30,000 births. They compared multivitamins to the health agency's folic acid and iron option, and to no supplementation. The team expected that most of the studies they reviewed used the recommended dietary allowance of individual vitamins.

It found that a one-a-day multivitamin—a pill that includes iron, folic acid and vitamins A, B1, D, E and zinc—reduced the incidence of low birth weights by 19 per cent compared with taking nothing.

Babies tipping the scales at less than five pounds, eight ounces, are considered low birth weight and are prone to many problems, including infections, feeding trouble and a higher risk of death. As adults, they are at greater risk of coronary artery disease and diabetes.

In an accompanying commentary on the study, however, Dr. Zulfiqar Bhutta and Dr. Batool Azra Haider of the Aga Khan University in Karachi, Pakistan, say further study is needed.

They contend, for example, that multivitamins have been reported to increase fetal head size, adding increased risks to infants and mothers at birth.

Shah, however, says vitamin supplements are especially important for women in developing countries, where normal diets may not provide enough of the micronutrients. Even in developed countries like Canada, a full vitamin package would lead to fewer low-birth-weight babies, he says.

(From Hall, Joseph. "Mother's Vitamins Give Baby Good Start." *Toronto Star*. 9 June 2009. Web. 11 June 2009. Reprinted with permission—Torstar Syndication Services.)

Effects of Prenatal Multimicronutrient Supplementation on Pregnancy Outcomes: A Meta-analysis

Prakesh S. Shah, MD MSc, Arne Ohlsson, MD MSc, on behalf of the Knowledge Synthesis Group on Determinants of Low Birth Weight and Preterm Births

From the Department of Paediatrics (Shah, Ohlsson), Mount Sinai Hospital and University of Toronto, and the Departments of Health Policy, Management and Evaluation (Shah, Ohlsson), and Obstetrics and Gynaecology (Ohlsson), University of Toronto, Toronto, ON.

Background: Reduced intake of micronutrients during pregnancy exposes women to nutritional deficiencies and may affect fetal growth. We conducted a systematic review to examine the efficacy of prenatal supplementation with multimicronutrients on pregnancy outcomes.

Methods: We searched MEDLINE, EMBASE, CINAHL and the Cochrane Library for relevant articles published in English up to December 2008. We also searched the bibliographies of selected articles as well as clinical trial registries. The primary outcome was low birth weight; secondary outcomes were preterm birth, small-for-gestational-age infants, birth weight and gestational age.

Results: We observed a significant reduction in the risk of low birth weight among infants born to women who received multimicronutrients during pregnancy compared with placebo (relative risk [RR] 0.81, 95% confidence interval [CI] 0.73–0.91) or iron–folic acid supplementation (RR 0.83, 95% CI 0.74–0.93). Birth weight was significantly higher among infants whose mothers were in the multimicronutrient group than among those whose mothers received iron–folic acid supplementation (weighted mean difference 54 g, 95% CI 36 g–72 g). There was no significant difference in the risk of preterm birth or small-for-gestational-age infants between the 3 study groups.

Interpretation: Prenatal multimicronutrient supplementation was associated with a significantly reduced risk of low birth weight and with improved birth weight when compared with iron–folic acid supplementation. There was no significant effect of multimicronutrient supplementation on the risk of preterm birth or small-for-gestational-age infants.

(Abstract from Shah, P.S., Ohlsson, A. "Effects of Prenatal Multimicronutrient Supplementation on Pregnancy Outcomes: A Meta-analysis." *Canadian Medical Association Journal* 180.12 (2009): n.pag. Web. 9 June 2009. © Canadian Medical Association. This work is protected by copyright and the making of this copy was with the permission of Access Copyright. Any alteration of its content or further copying in any form whatsoever is strictly prohibited unless otherwise permitted by law.)

Writing involves close audience analysis. Which person are you writing for?

Anyone can immediately recognize the differences between these two pieces of writing. Obviously, the *Toronto Star* coverage is general in nature, employs simple vocabulary and no technical terms, and is therefore easy to follow. The abstract, on the other hand, with its highly specialized content and terminology, is much more challenging. Even the titles of the two articles reflect these contrasts. The reason for the differences is that a mass-circulation newspaper like the *Toronto Star* is intended for the general public, whereas a professional periodical like the *Canadian Medical Association Journal* is written specifically for highly educated experts. Both articles cover the same material, and the purpose of both is to inform. But the two publications are targeted at entirely different audiences—hence the dissimilarity. This contrast makes sense. For the newspaper piece to be significantly more specialized, or for the abstract to be any less so, would be inappropriate. Each is well suited to its readership.

Workplace communications are governed by this same dynamic. An email, memo, letter, report, or oral presentation must be tailored to its intended audience; otherwise, it probably won't achieve the desired results. Therefore, ask yourself the following questions before attempting to prepare any sort of formal communication:

- Am I writing to one person or more than one?
- What are their job titles and/or areas of responsibility?
- What do they already know about the specific situation?
- Why do they need this information?
- What do I want them to do as a result of receiving it?
- What factors might influence their response?

Because these questions are closely related, the answers will sometimes overlap. A good starting point for sorting them out is to classify your audience by level: layperson, expert, or executive. The layperson does not possess significant prior knowledge of the field, whereas an expert obviously does. An executive reader has decision-making power and, one hopes, considerable expertise as well. By profiling your readers or listeners in this way, you'll come to see the subject of your planned communication from your audience's viewpoint as well as your own. You'll be better able to state the purpose of your communication, provide necessary details, cite meaningful examples, achieve the correct level of formality, and avert possible misunderstandings, thereby achieving your desired outcome.

In identifying your audience, remember that workplace communications fall into four broad categories:

- *Upward communication:* Intended for those above you in the hierarchy. (Example: An email reply to a question from your supervisor.)
- *Lateral communication:* Intended for those at your own level in the hierarchy. (Example: A voice mail to a co-worker with whom you're collaborating.)
- *Downward communication:* Intended for those below you in the hierarchy. (Example: An oral reminder to an intern you've been assigned to train.)
- *Outward communication:* Intended for those outside your workplace. (Example: A letter to someone at a company with which you do business.)

These differences will influence your communications in many ways, particularly in determining format. For in-house communications (the first three categories) the memo was traditionally the preferred written medium. Now the memo has largely been replaced by email. For outward communications, such as correspondence with clients, customers, or the general public, the standard business letter has been the norm. Business letters are either mailed or transmitted by fax machine. Even for outward communications, though, email is often the best choice because of its speed and efficiency. If a more formal document is required, a confirmation letter can always be sent later.

TONE

Your hierarchical relationship to your reader will play a major role in determining the *tone* of your communication as well. This is especially true when you're attempting to convey bad news (the denial of a request from an employee whom you supervise, for example) or suggesting that staff members adopt some new or different procedure. Although such messages can be phrased in a firm, straightforward manner, a harsh voice or belligerent attitude is seldom productive.

The workplace is essentially a set of individuals and relationships, busy people working together to accomplish a common goal: the mission of the business, organization, or agency. A high level of co-operation and collective commitment is needed for this to happen. Ideally, each person exerts a genuine effort to foster a climate of shared enthusiasm and commitment. When co-workers become defensive or resentful, morale problems inevitably develop, undermining productivity. In such a situation, everyone loses.

Therefore, do not try to sound tough or demanding when writing about potentially sensitive issues. Instead, appeal to the reader's sense of fairness and co-operation. Phrase your sentences in a nonthreatening way, emphasizing the reader's point of view by using a reader-centred (rather than a writer-centred) perspective. For obvious reasons, this approach should govern your correspondence intended for readers outside the workplace as well.

Here are some examples of how to creatively change a writer-centred perspective into a reader-centred perspective:

Writer-Centred Perspective	Reader-Centred Perspective
If I can answer any questions, I'll be happy to do so.	If you have any questions, please ask.
We shipped the order this morning.	Your order was shipped this morning.
I'm happy to report that . . .	You'll be glad to know that . . .

Notice that changing *I* and *we* to *you* and *your* personalizes the communication. Focusing on the reader is also known as the "you" approach. Another important element of the you approach is the use of *please, thank you,* and other polite terms.

Now consider Figures 1.1 and 1.2. Both emails have the same purpose, to change a specific behaviour, and both address the same audience.

The first version adopts a writer-centred approach and is harshly combative. The reader-centred revision, on the other hand, is diplomatic and, therefore, much more persuasive. The first is almost certain to create resentment and hard feelings, whereas the second is far more likely to achieve the desired results.

In most settings you can adopt a somewhat more casual manner with your equals and with those below you than you can with those above you in the chain of command or with people outside the organization. But in any case, avoid an excessively conversational style. Even when the situation is not particularly troublesome, and even when your reader is well known to you, remember that "business is business." Although you need not sound stuffy, it is important to maintain a certain level of formality. Accordingly, you should never allow personal matters to appear in workplace correspondence. Consider, for example, Figure 1.3, an email in which the writer has obviously violated this rule. Although the writer's tone toward his supervisor is appropriately respectful, the content should be far less detailed, as in the revised version shown in Figure 1.4.

Figure 1.1 Original Email

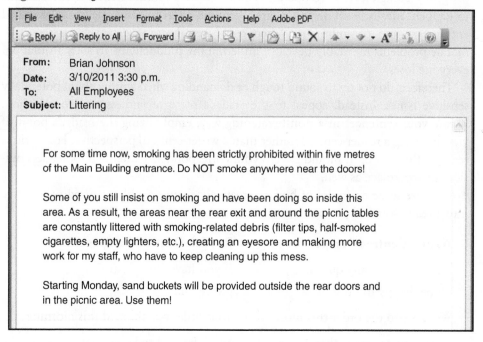

Figure 1.2 Revised Email

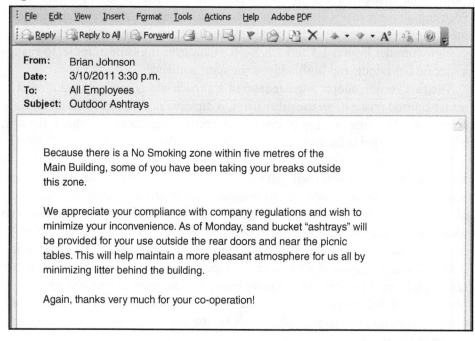

Figure 1.3 Original Email

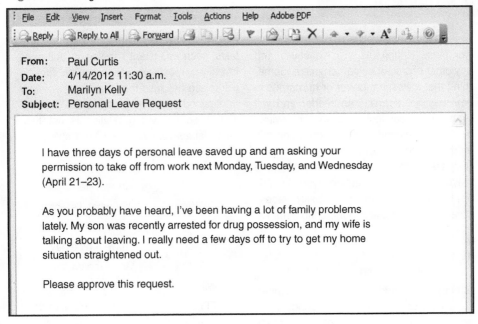

> I have three days of personal leave saved up and am asking your permission to take off from work next Monday, Tuesday, and Wednesday (April 21–23).
>
> As you probably have heard, I've been having a lot of family problems lately. My son was recently arrested for drug possession, and my wife is talking about leaving. I really need a few days off to try to get my home situation straightened out.
>
> Please approve this request.

Figure 1.4 Revised Email

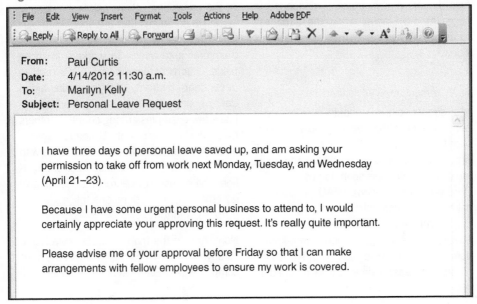

> I have three days of personal leave saved up, and am asking your permission to take off from work next Monday, Tuesday, and Wednesday (April 21–23).
>
> Because I have some urgent personal business to attend to, I would certainly appreciate your approving this request. It's really quite important.
>
> Please advise me of your approval before Friday so that I can make arrangements with fellow employees to ensure my work is covered.

Tech Tips

A slangy, everyday style is out of place in workplace writing, as are expletives and any other coarse or vulgar language. Something that may seem clever or humorous to you may not amuse your reader and will probably appear foolish to anyone reviewing the correspondence later on. Keep this in mind when sending email, a medium that seems to encourage a looser, more playful manner of interaction. Typical of this tendency are email emoticons, silly "faces" created by combining punctuation marks, like this:

:)   : (;)

Smile   Frown   Wink

Although intended to reinforce meaning, such devices just distract or annoy most serious readers, undermining the writer's credibility. These additions also vary between cultures, so they could just confuse readers. For example, Americans put noses in their faces, while the Japanese focus on the eyes (and their faces are not sideways.)

: -)   ^_^

American   Japanese

In a similar vein you should avoid overdependence on abbreviations and acronyms (words composed of the initial letters of a phrase or expression). Probably the most familiar are ASAP (as soon as possible), FYI (for your information), FAQ (frequently asked questions), NRN (no reply necessary), and SASE (self-addressed, stamped envelope). Although such well-known acronyms can be useful, a great many others—far less obvious—have hatched in internet chat rooms and other informal contexts, such as instant messaging. Although inventive, most are inappropriate for the workplace because they may not be readily understood—especially by older workers and those for whom English is not their native language. Here are 10 examples:

BTW:	by the way
IRL:	in real life
FWIW:	for what it's worth
OTOH:	on the other hand
HAND:	have a nice day
TMOT:	trust me on this
IMHO:	in my humble opinion
TTYTT:	to tell you the truth
IOW:	in other words
WADR:	with all due respect

At the same time, there exist innumerable technical acronyms that are specific to particular businesses and occupations, and are therefore quite useful to workers in those fields. Such acronyms as ADC (aid to dependent children), CAD (computer-aided design), and PVC (polyvinyl chloride) are just a few examples among countless others that facilitate efficient dialogue among employees familiar with those terms. As with so many aspects of workplace communications, the use of acronyms is largely governed by considerations of audience, purpose, and tone.

Note: Among the many websites devoted to acronyms, Acronym Finder is one of the most comprehensive. See www.acronymfinder.com.

A sensitive situation awaits you when you must convey unpleasant information or request assistance or co-operation from superiors. Although you may sometimes yearn for a more democratic arrangement, every workplace has a pecking order that you must take into account as you choose your words. Hierarchy exists because some individuals–by virtue of greater experience, education, or access to information–are in fact better positioned to lead. Although this system sometimes functions imperfectly, the supervisor, department head, or other person in charge will respond better to subordinates whose communications reflect an understanding of this basic reality. Essentially, the rules for writing to a person higher on the ladder are the same as for writing to someone on a lower rung. Be focused and self-assured, but use the you approach, encouraging the reader to see the advantage in accepting your recommendation or granting your request.

An especially polite tone is advisable when addressing those who outrank you. Acknowledge that the final decision is theirs and that you are fully willing to abide by that. This can be achieved either through "softening" words and phrases (*perhaps, with your permission, if you wish*) or simply by stating outright that you'll accept whatever outcome may develop. Consider, for example, the email in Figures 1.5 and 1.6. Although both say essentially the same thing, the first is completely inappropriate in tone, so much so that it would likely result in negative personal consequences for the writer. The second would be much better received because it properly reflects the nature of the professional relationship between writer and reader.

Figure 1.5 Original Email

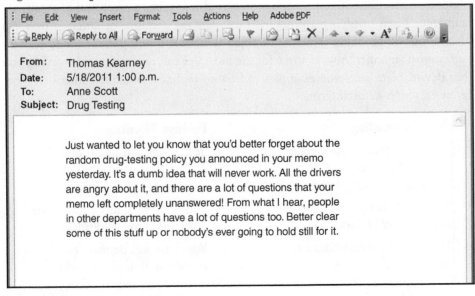

Figure 1.6 Revised Email

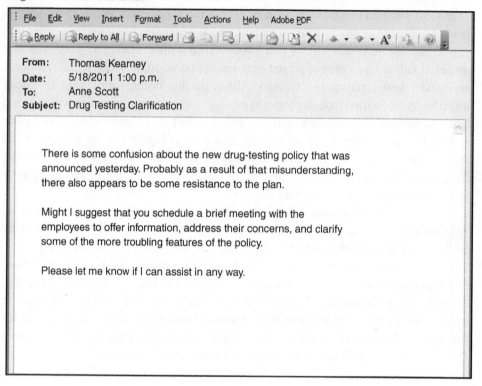

Communicating with customers or clients also requires a great deal of sensitivity and tact. When justifying a price increase, denying a claim, or apologizing for a delay, you will probably create an unpleasant climate if you present the facts in an antagonistic manner. Always strive for the most upbeat, reader-centred wording you can devise. Here are some examples of how to rephrase negative content in more positive, reader-centred terms:

Negative Wording	Positive Wording
We cannot process your claim because the necessary forms have not been completed.	Your claim can be processed as soon as you complete the necessary forms.
We do not take phone calls after 3:00 p.m. on Fridays.	You may reach us by telephone until 3:00 p.m. on Fridays.
We closed your case because we never received the information requested in our letter of April 2.	Your case will be reactivated as soon as you provide the information requested in our April 2 letter.

When the problem has been caused by an error or oversight on your part, be sure to apologize. However, do not state specifically what the mistake was, or your letter may be used as evidence against you should a lawsuit ensue. Simply acknowledge that a mistake has occurred, express regret, explain how the situation will be corrected, and close on a conciliatory note. Consider, for example, the letter in Figure 1.7. The body and conclusion are fine, but the introduction practically invites legal action. Here's a suggested revision of the letter's opening paragraph, phrased in less incriminating terms:

> Thank you for purchasing our product and for taking the time to contact us about it. We apologize for the unsatisfactory condition of your Superior microwave dinner.

Moreover, given the serious nature of the complaint, the customer services representative should certainly have made a stronger effort to establish a tone of sincerely apologetic concern. As it stands, this letter seems abrupt and rather impersonal—certainly not what the context requires. (For a much better handling of this kind of situation, see the adjustment letter in Figure 3.9.)

This is not to suggest, however, that workplace communications should attempt to falsify reality or dodge responsibility. On the contrary, there is a moral imperative to uphold strict ethical standards. The Enron scandal in 2001; Bernard Madoff, the Ponzi schemer, in 2009; and other individual and corporate misdeeds have put ethical questions under the spotlight and greatly increased the public appetite for investigative reporting by the media. The *Merriam-Webster Online Dictionary* defines ethics as "the discipline dealing with what is good or bad and with moral duty and obligation." Reduced to its essentials, ethics involves choosing honesty over dishonesty, requiring us to act with integrity even when there would be short-term gains for behaving otherwise. Ethical communication must therefore be honest and fair to everyone involved in the exchange.

By their nature, workplace communications can greatly affect people's lives. Accordingly, customers and clients, investors, taxpayers, and workers themselves should be able to consider such materials to be accurate, reliable, and trustworthy—in short, ethical. But those documents fail the ethics test if corrupted by any of the following tactics:

- *Suppression of information:* The outright burying of data to hide inconvenient truths. (Example: A company fails to reveal product-testing results that indicate potential danger to consumers.)
- *Falsification or fabrication:* Changing or simply inventing data to support a desired outcome. (Example: A company boasts of a fictitious enterprise to lure investors into supporting a new venture.)
- *Overstatement or understatement:* Exaggerating the positive aspects of a situation or downplaying negative aspects to create the desired impression. (Example: A

Figure 1.7 Letter to Customer

Superior Foods, Inc.

130 Maple Grove Rd., Kitchener, ON N2G 4M5 (519) 555-1234

October 13, 2011

Mr. Philip Updike
246 Alton St.
Waterloo, ON N2J 3B2

Dear Mr. Updike:

We are sorry that you found a piece of glass in your Superior
microwave dinner. Please accept our assurances that this is a very
unusual incident.

Here are three coupons redeemable at your local grocery store for
complementary Superior dinners of your choice.

We hope you will continue to enjoy our fine products.

Sincerely,

John Roth

John Roth
Customer Services Dept.

Enclosures (3)

public-opinion survey describes 55 percent of the respondents as "a substantial majority" or 45 percent as "a small percentage.")

- *Selective misquoting:* Deleting words from quoted material to distort the meaning. (Example: A supervisor changes a report's conclusion that "this proposal will seem feasible only to workers unfamiliar with the situation" to "this proposal will seem feasible . . . to workers.")

- *Subjective wording:* Using terms deliberately chosen for their ambiguity. (Example: A company advertises "customary service charges," knowing that "customary" is open to broad interpretation.)

- *Conflict of interest:* Exploiting behind-the-scenes connections to influence decision making. (Example: A board member of a community agency encourages the agency to hire her company for paid services rather than soliciting bids.)

- *Withholding information:* Refusing to share relevant data with co-workers. (Example: A computer-savvy employee provides misleading answers about new software to make a recently hired co-worker appear incompetent.)

- *Plagiarism:* Taking credit for someone else's ideas, findings, or written material. (Example: An employee assigned to prepare a report submits a similar report written by someone at another company and downloaded from the internet.)

Workers must weigh the consequences of their actions, considering their moral obligations. If this is done in good faith, practices such as those outlined in the preceding list will surely be avoided. Decisions can get complicated, however, when obligations to self and others come into conflict. Workers often feel pressure to compromise personal ethical beliefs to achieve company goals. All things being equal, a worker's primary obligation is to self—to remain employed. But if the employer permits or requires actions that the employee considers immoral, an ethical dilemma is created, forcing the worker to choose among two or more unsatisfactory alternatives.

There are no easy resolutions to ethical dilemmas, but we all must be guided by conscience. Obviously, this can involve some difficult decisions. By determining your purpose, analyzing your audience, and considering the moral dimensions of the situation, you will achieve the correct tone for any communication. As we have seen, this is crucial for dealing with potentially resistive readers (especially those above you in the workplace hierarchy) and when rectifying errors for which you are accountable. In all instances, however, a courteous, positive, reader-centred, and ethical approach gets the best results.

Exercises

Exercise 1.1

Revise each of the following three communications to achieve a tone more appropriate to the purpose and audience.

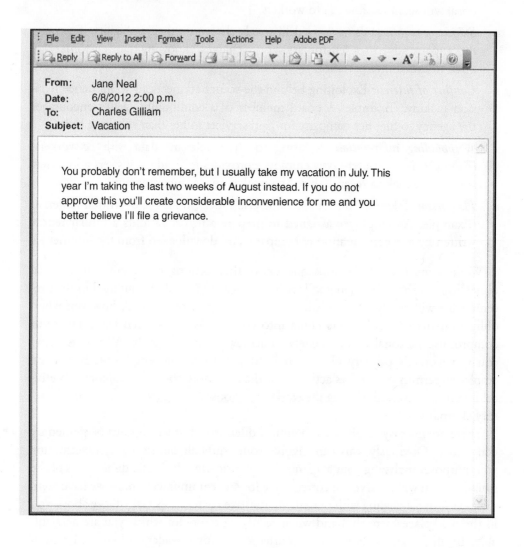

File   Edit   View   Insert   Format   Tools   Actions   Help   Adobe PDF

Reply   Reply to All   Forward

From: Jane Neal
Date: 6/8/2012 2:00 p.m.
To: Charles Gilliam
Subject: Vacation

You probably don't remember, but I usually take my vacation in July. This year I'm taking the last two weeks of August instead. If you do not approve this you'll create considerable inconvenience for me and you better believe I'll file a grievance.

Exercise 1.1 (Continued)

MINISTRY OF COMMUNITY AND
SOCIAL SERVICES

MEMO

DATE: March 17, 2013

TO: All Caseworkers

FROM: Cheryl Alston, Case Supervisor CA

SUBJECT: Goofing Off

A lot of you seem to think that this is a country club and are spending
entirely too much time in the break room! As you well know, you're
entitled to one 15-minute break in the morning and another in the
afternoon. The rest of the time you're supposed to be AT YOUR DESK
unless signed out for fieldwork.

Exercise 1.1 (Continued)

Clear Creek Community College

MEMORANDUM

DATE: May 4, 2011

TO: All Employees

FROM: Charles Rigney, Chief of Security CR

SUBJECT: Burglarized Vehicles

Recently, there's been a rash of burglaries in the faculty/staff parking lot. Items such as CD players, cellular phones, and even a personal computer have been reported missing from vehicles.

After investigating, however, we've learned that several of these vehicles had been left unlocked. Don't be stupid! Always lock your car or else be prepared to get ripped off. My staff can't be everywhere at once, and if you set yourself up to be victimized, it's not our fault.

Exercise 1.2

Revise each of the following three letters to achieve a tone more appropriate to the purpose and audience.

Bancroft's in the Mall

West Edmonton Mall—Edmonton, Alberta T5T 4J2

February 18, 2012

Ms. Barbara Wilson
365 Albert St.
Edmonton, AB   T5A 3M2

Dear Ms. Wilson:

Your Bancroft's charge account is $650.55 overdue. We must receive a payment immediately.

If we do not receive a minimum payment of $50 within three days, we will refer your account to a collection agency and your credit rating will be permanently compromised.

Send a payment at once!

Sincerely,

Michael Modoski

Michael Modoski
Credit Department

Exercise 1.2 (Continued)

Southeast Insurance Company

Southeast Industrial Park   Saskatoon, SK S7L 6A4
Telephone: (306) 555-0123   FAX: (306) 555-3210

November 5, 2012

Mr. Francis Tedeschi
214 Summit Avenue
Saskatoon, SK S7L 0V8

Dear Mr. Tedeschi:

This is to acknowledge receipt of your 10/30/12 claim.

Insured persons entitled to benefits under the Saskatoon
Manufacturing Co. plan effective December 1, 2010, are required to
execute statements of claims for semi-private hospital room expense
benefits only in the manner specifically mandated in your certificate
holder's handbook.

Your claim has been quite improperly executed, as you have
neglected to procure the Physician's Statement of Services Rendered.
The information contained therein is prerequisite to any consideration
of your claim.

Enclosed is the necessary form. See that it's filled out and returned to
us without delay, or your claim cannot be processed.

Yours truly,

Ann Jurkiewicz

Ann Jurkiewicz
Claims Adjustor

Enclosure

Exercise 1.2 (Continued)

DEPARTMENT OF HEALTH AND COMMUNITY SERVICES

St. John's, NL A0L 1C0
(709) 555-0123

November 10, 2011

Easton Savings Bank
36 Bank Street
St. John's, NL A0L 2B6

Re: Charles Mangan (Social Insurance Number # 000-000-000)

To Whom It May Concern:

The above individual has applied for additional medical benefits. This department requires that a 30-month banking history accompany all such applications. You must send us the necessary information immediately.

Provide a listing of each month's average balance for the period of March 1, 2010, to November 1, 2010, along with verification of all closed or transferred accounts during that period.

This directive is mandated by the provincial government. All banking organizations must furnish such information to authorized representatives of the Department of Health and Community Services to verify eligibility for any form of public assistance.

Sincerely,

Mary Louise Martin

Mary Louise Martin
Caseworker

Exercise 1.3

Revise each of the following three emails to eliminate inappropriate tone and/or content.

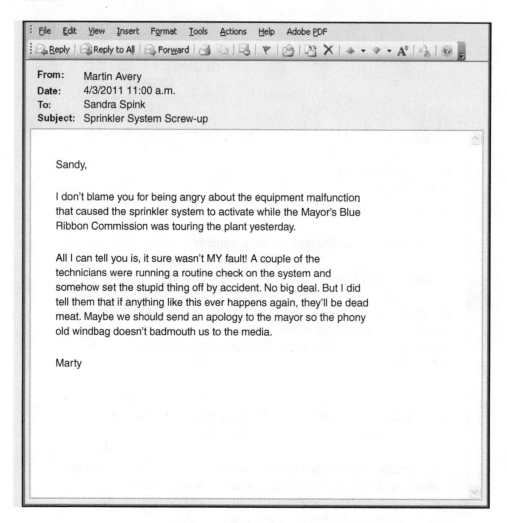

File   Edit   View   Insert   Format   Tools   Actions   Help   Adobe PDF

Reply | Reply to All | Forward

From: Martin Avery
Date: 4/3/2011 11:00 a.m.
To: Sandra Spink
Subject: Sprinkler System Screw-up

Sandy,

I don't blame you for being angry about the equipment malfunction that caused the sprinkler system to activate while the Mayor's Blue Ribbon Commission was touring the plant yesterday.

All I can tell you is, it sure wasn't MY fault! A couple of the technicians were running a routine check on the system and somehow set the stupid thing off by accident. No big deal. But I did tell them that if anything like this ever happens again, they'll be dead meat. Maybe we should send an apology to the mayor so the phony old windbag doesn't badmouth us to the media.

Marty

Exercise 1.3 (Continued)

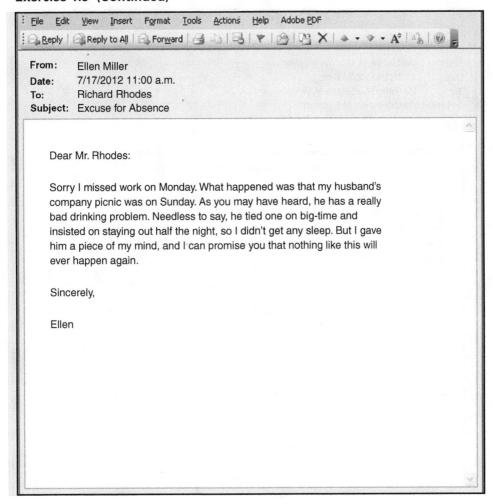

File   Edit   View   Insert   Format   Tools   Actions   Help   Adobe PDF

Reply | Reply to All | Forward

From: Ellen Miller
Date: 7/17/2012 11:00 a.m.
To: Richard Rhodes
Subject: Excuse for Absence

Dear Mr. Rhodes:

Sorry I missed work on Monday. What happened was that my husband's company picnic was on Sunday. As you may have heard, he has a really bad drinking problem. Needless to say, he tied one on big-time and insisted on staying out half the night, so I didn't get any sleep. But I gave him a piece of my mind, and I can promise you that nothing like this will ever happen again.

Sincerely,

Ellen

Exercise 1.3 (Continued)

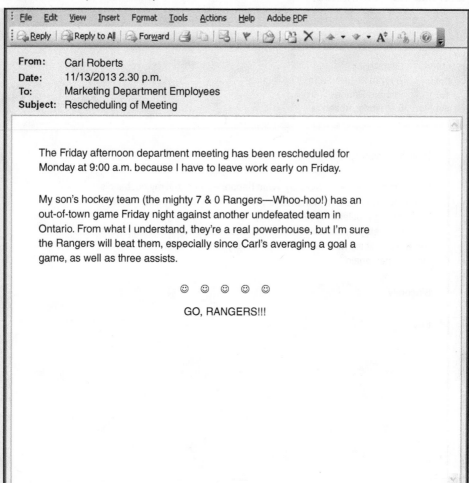

File   Edit   View   Insert   Format   Tools   Actions   Help   Adobe PDF

Reply | Reply to All | Forward

From: Carl Roberts
Date: 11/13/2013 2.30 p.m.
To: Marketing Department Employees
Subject: Rescheduling of Meeting

The Friday afternoon department meeting has been rescheduled for Monday at 9:00 a.m. because I have to leave work early on Friday.

My son's hockey team (the mighty 7 & 0 Rangers—Whoo-hoo!) has an out-of-town game Friday night against another undefeated team in Ontario. From what I understand, they're a real powerhouse, but I'm sure the Rangers will beat them, especially since Carl's averaging a goal a game, as well as three assists.

☺   ☺   ☺   ☺   ☺

GO, RANGERS!!!

Exercise 1.4
Revise each of the following three letters to eliminate wording that might create legal liability.

Fin & Feather Pet Supplies

133 Court Street, Vancouver, BC V5P 2X4

January 15, 2012

Mr. Robert Ryan
352 Stegman Street
Vancouver, BC V7X 1S2

Dear Mr. Ryan:

We have received your letter of January 3, and we regret that the heating unit we sold you malfunctioned, killing your tropical fish worth $1500.

Because the unit was purchased more than three years ago, however, our storewide warranty is no longer in effect, and we are therefore unable to accept any responsibility for your loss. Nevertheless, we are enclosing a Fin & Feather discount coupon good for $20 toward the purchase of a replacement unit or another product of your choice.

We look forward to serving you in the future!

Sincerely,

Sandra Kouvel

Sandra Kouvel
Store Manager

Enclosure

Exercise 1.4 (Continued)

Appliance World

521 Scott Street, Flin Flon, MB R8A 2C4

February 20, 2011

Ms. Christine Nguyen
230 Fairview Street
Flin Flon, MB R8A 3D2

Dear Ms. Nguyen:

Thank you for your recent letter about the faulty toaster oven you purchased at Appliance World. We are glad to hear that the fire it caused resulted in only minor damages to your apartment.

If you bring the unit in, we'll gladly exchange it for a more reliable one. Customer satisfaction is our #1 priority!

We are happy to assist you with all your appliance needs.

Yours truly,

Peter Keane

Peter Keane
Store Manager

Exercise 1.4 (Continued)

High Roller
Bikes & Boards

516 Bridge Street Phoenix, AZ 85001 U.S.A.

August 17, 2012

Mr. Patrick Casey
202 Front Street
Toronto, ON M5W 1E6 Canada

Dear Mr. Casey:

We are sorry that the bicycle rim we sold you burst during normal use, causing personal injury resulting in lingering lower back pain.

Certainly we will replace the rim free of charge if you simply bring your bicycle into our shop any weekday during the hours of 9:00 a.m. to 5:00 p.m. If you are unable to do that, just send us your old rim and we'll ship a new one to you.

Thank you for purchasing your bicycle supplies at High Roller! Next time you're in Phoenix, please drop in and see us again!

Sincerely,

Monica Lamb

Monica Lamb
Store Manager

mycanadiantechcommlab

Visit www.mycanadiantechcommlab.ca for everything you need to help you succeed in the job you've always wanted! Tools and resources include the following:

- Composing Space and Writer's Toolkit
- Document Makeovers
- Grammar Exercises—and much more!

CHAPTER

2

Electronic
Communication

LEARNING OBJECTIVE

When you complete this chapter, you'll be able to use basic format and organization patterns to write effective email messages, blog postings, and instant messages (IM).

OF ALL THE FORMS OF WRITTEN COMMUNICATION used in the workplace, memos (which will be discussed in Chapter 3) and email are certainly among the most common. Any large corporation, agency, or other organization generates thousands of such documents daily. Even in a small setting, they are fundamental to office procedure. In addition, many companies are embracing Web 2.0 technology and using social networking programs, such as Twitter, which are allowing them to interact with a wider range of potential customers. Rapidly changing technology is also allowing companies to create in-house communication tools, such as instant messaging (IM) programs. In addition to the above, some companies also provide employees with PDAs or BlackBerrys so that employees can communicate quickly and easily with the office and clients. Focusing on both format and content, this chapter explains how to handle electronic communication.

EMAIL

An email is essentially just an electronic memo. Indeed, email has nearly replaced the memo altogether, especially in situations where speed of delivery is important, confidentiality is not required, and the message is brief.

By now almost everyone is familiar with how to use email. Typically, a worker logs on to the system by typing his or her user name and a secure password that prevents unauthorized access. To read new email stored in the inbox, the worker clicks the mouse to access each message. Depending on one's preferences, messages can then be deleted, saved for future reference, printed, answered, or forwarded—or a combination of these options. To respond to a message, the writer clicks on the appropriate prompt (in Microsoft Outlook, it's Reply) and inserts the new message above the existing one. To create an entirely new email, the writer clicks on the appropriate prompt (in Microsoft Outlook, it's New), causing a blank template to appear on the screen, ready to be completed. When the writer finishes the message, a click of the mouse sends it to as many other users as the writer wishes—one or everyone—depending on how the To line has been addressed. The new email is also stored in the writer's electronic Sent file and can be kept there indefinitely for future reference. Figure 2.1 is a typical email memo, similar to those you saw in Chapter 1.

Email is typically written in a direct format, which means that messages are clear and concise. Unnecessary information is left out, as this can clutter the message and cause confusion. Email messages also typically address one subject only. This helps the reader maintain focus on the main issue being discussed in the body of your email. Figure 2.2 shows how confusing an email is when it has more than one topic.

James, the receiver of this message, is asked to do a number of things. The first is to download and print a new policy document, which he is supposed to bring to the next meeting. It is not until later in the message that he is asked to direct any questions to the sender before the meeting. This information is placed after the

Figure 2.1 Email

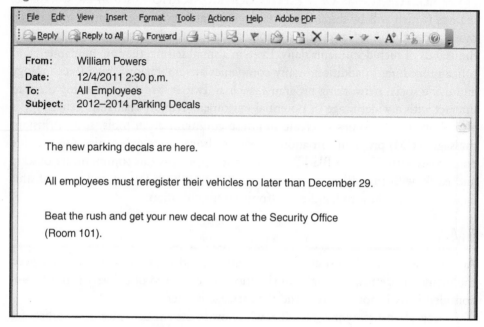

questions about the end-of-the-year party. This type of email message will, at best, get a response to only one of the action items requested. In order to avoid this type of dilemma, the writer, Kaz, needs to send out two separate messages: one that deals only with the new company policy, and one that deals only with the questions about the upcoming event.

There are good reasons email has been so widely adopted since becoming generally available in the 1990s. On the most obvious level, email is incomparably faster than traditional correspondence. In the past, communicating by memo or letter involved at least five distinct steps:

1. Drafting
2. Typing (usually by a secretary)
3. Proofreading and initialling by the writer
4. Photocopying for the writer's file
5. Routing to the intended reader

Depending on office workload and clerical staffing levels, this process could be very time consuming. With email, however, all five steps are compressed into one, thereby permitting speedy communication. Additionally, email allows for rapid-fire

Figure 2.2 Ineffective Email Message

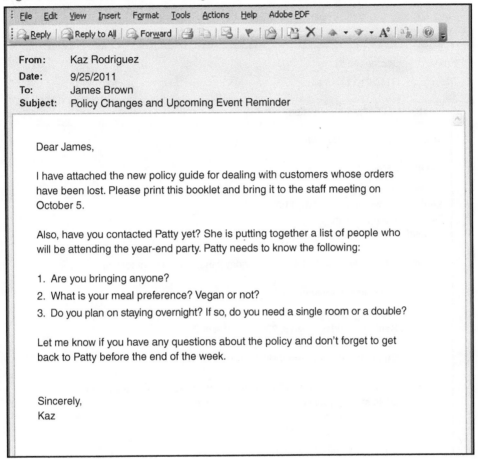

File   Edit   View   Insert   Format   Tools   Actions   Help   Adobe PDF

Reply | Reply to All | Forward |

From: Kaz Rodriguez
Date: 9/25/2011
To: James Brown
Subject: Policy Changes and Upcoming Event Reminder

Dear James,

I have attached the new policy guide for dealing with customers whose orders have been lost. Please print this booklet and bring it to the staff meeting on October 5.

Also, have you contacted Patty yet? She is putting together a list of people who will be attending the year-end party. Patty needs to know the following:

1. Are you bringing anyone?
2. What is your meal preference? Vegan or not?
3. Do you plan on staying overnight? If so, do you need a single room or a double?

Let me know if you have any questions about the policy and don't forget to get back to Patty before the end of the week.

Sincerely,
Kaz

exchanges, and the most recent transmittal can reproduce a complete record of all that has gone before, as shown in Figure 2.3.

Unfortunately, email can also create some problems. One major drawback is that the very ease with which email can be generated encourages overuse. In the past, a writer would not bother to send a memo without good reason; too much time and effort were involved to do otherwise. Now, though, much needless correspondence is produced. The situation represented in Figure 2.3, for example, could probably have been handled more efficiently with one phone call. Many of yesterday's writers would wait before acting on an email or passing it along to others until they had received complete information on a given topic and had organized and considered that information. But today it's not uncommon for many emails to be written on

Figure 2.3 Email Correspondence

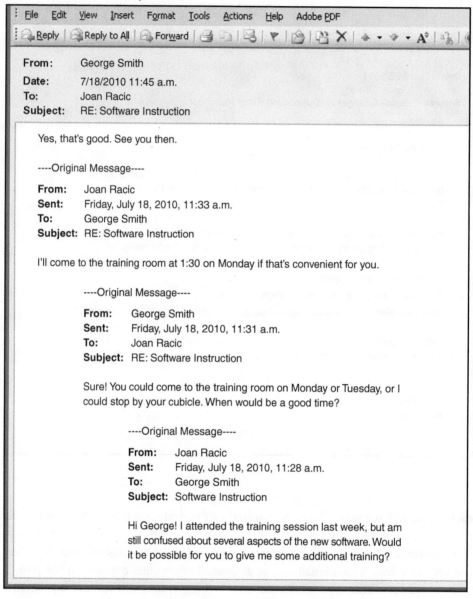

the same subject, doling out the information piecemeal, sometimes within a very short time span. The resulting fragmentation wastes the energies of writer and reader alike and increases the possibility of confusion, often because of premature response. One way to minimize this danger is to scan your entire menu of incoming messages, taking special note of multiple mailings from the same source before responding to any.

Similarly, emails about sensitive issues are often dashed off "in the heat of battle," without sufficient reflection. In the past, most writers had some time to reconsider a situation before reacting. There was usually the option of revising or simply discarding a memo if, upon proofreading, it came to seem a bit too harsh or otherwise inappropriate. The inherent rapidity of email, however, all but eliminates any such opportunity for second thoughts. In addition, hasty composition causes a great many keyboarding miscues, omissions, and other fundamental blunders. These must then be corrected in subsequent messages, creating an inefficient proliferation of "email about email." Indeed, hurried writing combined with the absence of a secretarial filter has given rise to a great deal of embarrassingly bad prose in the workplace. You risk ridicule and loss of credibility unless you closely proofread every email before sending it. Make sure that the information is necessary and correct and that all pertinent details have been included.

Be particularly careful to avoid typos, misspellings, faulty capitalization, sloppy punctuation, and basic grammatical errors. Virtually all email systems include spell-checkers; although not foolproof, they help minimize typos and misspellings. Similarly, grammar checkers can detect basic sentence problems. It is important to remember, though, that most spell-checkers adhere to either American English or British English. Canadian English follows neither completely, so be aware of words

Checking your document or having another check it before sending helps save embarrassment later.

that require special consideration when you have the spell-checker set up. For instance, if you are using an American English spell-checker, besides the usual problem of needing the letter u in words such as honour, certain words, such as jewellery, double some consonants in Canadian English. To help you determine whether a word is spelled correctly, use a good, recent Canadian English dictionary. Finally, asking a colleague to read over your document carefully can help because often a fresh pair of eyes can catch errors you might have missed because you are too familiar with the message.

Because of the ease of use and speed with which email can be sent, more writers are taking shortcuts that are inappropriate in many work situations. Using "text-speak" (the shortened versions of words frequently used while sending text messages) is not accepted in many organizations. The reasons for this are numerous. The most common complaint is that it is not understood by everyone. Age, language, and culture can all affect clear understanding by the receiver of the message. Not everyone, for example, will understand a message signed off with *TTYL*. Text-speak also rapidly changes meaning, so your audience may misunderstand what you meant. Therefore, you should avoid text-speak. Email senders also need to follow grammar rules. Capital letters must be used appropriately, and punctuation is important. As discussed in Chapter 1, make sure you compose for the audience and do not take shortcuts that may affect the reader's understanding of your message.

When you're creating an email, depending on the characteristics of the system you're using, the To line may include only the receiver's name (or email address), omitting the receiver's title and/or department. This is because an email message is electronically transmitted (rather than being physically delivered) to the intended reader, appearing on that person's screen shortly after you send it. Likewise, your name (or email address) is automatically activated as soon as you log on to the system, thereby eliminating the need for you to type it on each document you create.

Although the To and From lines on an email eliminate the need for a letter-style salutation ("Dear Ms. Bernstein") or complimentary close ("Yours truly"), most writers do use these features when sending email to make their messages seem less abrupt and impersonal. The relative formality or informality of these greetings and sign-offs depends on the relationship between writer and reader. In any case, if your own email name and address do not fully reveal your identity, you must include a complimentary close to inform your readers who you are. Most email systems enable you to create a signature file for this purpose. Figures 2.4 and 2.5 provide examples.

Understand also that email is not private. Recent court decisions—some involving high-profile government scandals—have confirmed the employer's right to monitor or inspect workers' email (and internet activity). Indeed, it's not uncommon for workers to be fired for impropriety in this regard. A good rule of thumb is, "Don't

Figure 2.4   Informal Email

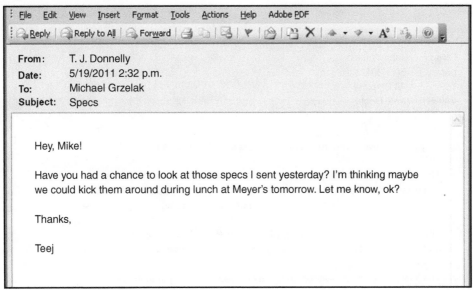

say it in an email unless you'd have no problem with it appearing on the front page of your company newsletter." In some situations a given message may be entirely appropriate but may contain highly sensitive information. In such cases the best choice may be a paper memo personally delivered in a sealed envelope.

As mentioned in Chapter 1, the company email network is no place for personal messages or an excessively conversational style. Many employers provide a separate email "bulletin board" on which workers can post and access announcements about garage or vehicle sales, car-pooling, unwanted theatre and sports tickets, and the like. Such matters are appropriate only as bulletin board content.

Now that nearly all organizations are online, email is no longer just an intramural communications medium; indeed, it's beginning to rival the business letter as the major form of correspondence across company boundaries. When you're sending email to readers at other locations, tone takes on even greater importance than usual. Because the writer and the reader probably do not know each other personally, a higher level of courteous formality is in order. Additionally, the subject matter is often more involved than that of in-house correspondence, so email sent outside the workplace is commonly longer and more fully developed than messages intended for co-workers. And outside email nearly always includes a letter-style salutation and complimentary close unless the writer and the reader have established an ongoing professional relationship.

Figure 2.5   Formal Email with Signature File

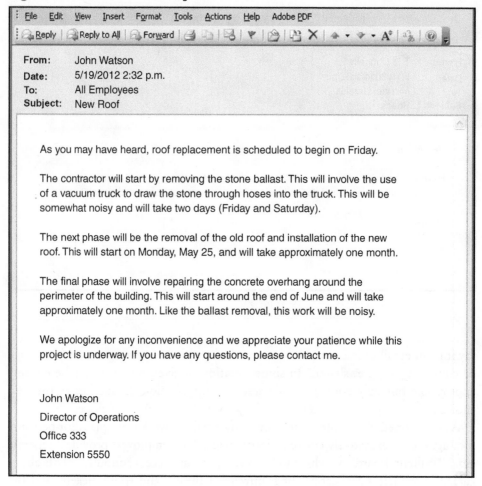

File   Edit   View   Insert   Format   Tools   Actions   Help   Adobe PDF

Reply | Reply to All | Forward

From:	John Watson
Date:	5/19/2012 2:32 p.m.
To:	All Employees
Subject:	New Roof

As you may have heard, roof replacement is scheduled to begin on Friday.

The contractor will start by removing the stone ballast. This will involve the use of a vacuum truck to draw the stone through hoses into the truck. This will be somewhat noisy and will take two days (Friday and Saturday).

The next phase will be the removal of the old roof and installation of the new roof. This will start on Monday, May 25, and will take approximately one month.

The final phase will involve repairing the concrete overhang around the perimeter of the building. This will start around the end of June and will take approximately one month. Like the ballast removal, this work will be noisy.

We apologize for any inconvenience and we appreciate your patience while this project is underway. If you have any questions, please contact me.

John Watson

Director of Operations

Office 333

Extension 5550

Tech Tips

Despite its seemingly informal, spontaneous nature, email is no less official and permanent than a memo printed on paper. It's important, therefore, to use this medium thoughtfully, efficiently, and responsibly. These guidelines will help:

■ New computer viruses crop up constantly. Although most workplaces use spam filters to weed out junk mail and potentially troublesome material, some dangerous clutter does find its way through. Guard against it by never opening attachments from unknown or suspicious sources; simply delete.

■ Resist the temptation to forward chain letters, silly jokes, political rants, pornographic images, and the like. They not only waste people's time, but in certain circumstances can also be hazardous to your professional health.

■ Never forward legitimate email to other readers without the original writer's knowledge and permission. The message may have been intended for you alone.

■ If you do forward an email, delete the original sender's contact information.

■ Create new email only when necessary, sending only to the person(s) needing it; resist the urge to mass-mail. Similarly, when responding to a mass-mailing, do not click Reply All unless there's a valid reason to do so; reply only to the sender.

■ Remember that email is only partially able to convey tone of voice. For this reason, voice mail or actual conversation is often preferable, allowing your reasoning and feelings to be understood more accurately. This is especially true in complicated or delicate situations, particularly those involving negative messages—the denial of a request, for example.

■ If no response is required from your reader, say so. In a related vein, you should not feel obliged to reply to every routine message you receive. If a reply is necessary, however, you should answer promptly—within a day or two at most.

■ Some readers routinely ignore attachments, so don't create one if you can build the information into the body of the email, where it's more likely to be read. Because very large attachments can clog readers' accounts, it may be better to send hard copy of such material.

■ If you're using an attachment, provide a one- or two-sentence summary in the body of the email to prompt the reader to open it.

■ When you're engaged in a lengthy back-and-forth, the discussion often evolves. In such cases, it's wise to continuously revise the Subject line to reflect that fact.

■ Never attempt to communicate when angry. Observe the standard rules of email etiquette. Avoid "flaming" (openly hostile or abusive comments, whether directed at the reader or at a third party). The fact that you're communicating electronically does not exempt you from accepted norms of workplace courtesy.

■ If you need someone else to be aware of your communication but that person is not involved directly, use the Cc function. Cc stands for "computer copy." At times, you may want another person to be aware of the communication, but you do not want other recipients to know who else is receiving the email. In this case, use the Bcc function. Bcc stands for "blind computer copy." The receiver of the Bcc message is the only one (besides the sender) who is aware that he or she is a receiver.

NOTE: For more information on email etiquette (sometimes called "netiquette"), you can consult these websites:

■ www.101emailetiquettetips.com
■ www.emailreplies.com
■ www.albion.com/netiquette

OTHER FORMS OF ELECTRONIC COMMUNICATION

In the following section, other forms of electronic communication will be discussed. However, it is quite possible that by the time you read this, the technology will have advanced and its uses will have become more sophisticated. The basic rules governing the writing contained within each category will, no doubt, remain the same.

Blogs

Weblogs, or blogs, as they are now known, are becoming another helpful tool that tech-savvy companies are using to interact with clients, employees, and the general public. For example, Microsoft has a community page devoted to blogs that employees write on a variety of topics, including, but not limited to, new technology being developed at Microsoft. You can find this at www.microsoft.com/communities/blogs/PortalHome.mspx.

Like email, blogs should be well written and focused on the audience. If readers do not see the blog's relevance to themselves, they will not read it. As well, blogs should be relatively short so that the audience can read through them quickly. Lists often help readers see the important points at a glance, which may encourage them to read the post more thoroughly. Few people read a blog word-for-word, however, so make sure that your writing is clear and that you leave out anything unnecessary. The writing style should be informal and almost conversational. This does not mean, though, that you can ignore proper spelling and grammar rules. Blogs also require titles, which are much like subject lines. The titles should be clear and concise and should summarize the blog's main idea.

Blogs should be updated frequently. There is no magic number for the number of posts you need to make, but they should be frequent enough that readers will continue accessing your blog. Once you find a rhythm that seems to work for you, stick to that. The worst thing you can do is update the blog infrequently. Finally, to ensure readers know there is new content, add an RSS feed. (RSS stands for "Really Simple Syndication.") Readers will be able to click on the RSS icon and subscribe to your blog updates.

Wikis

The word *wiki* is Hawaiian for "fast." Wikis are becoming a quick and easy way for people to collaborate on projects, even when colleagues are separated by long distances. Some companies are using wikis so that customers can interact with company employees to provide valuable feedback quickly or to make suggestions in the research and development stage. The advantage of a wiki is that people who are granted access can add, modify, and create content. Wikis also allow you to set levels of access, so some may be able to help with content while others are able to provide feedback only in forums or on discussion boards.

One of the most famous wikis is Wikipedia. Anyone can add content to this wiki, and it is constantly being updated. One drawback to wiki use, however, is that misinformation can be posted and mistakes can be overlooked unless there are vigilant editors who check the posts regularly. This is one of the reasons why so many instructors at the college and university level discourage students from using Wikipedia as an information source for school projects. While most of the information is accurate and up-to-date, there may be errors, and unless you are an expert, you won't know what is or isn't correct.

If you use a wiki, make sure you write clearly and concisely. As with blogs, people tend to skim the content rapidly, looking for information they can use quickly. Your writing should also be error free—check your facts and numbers, and make sure you proofread before posting so that you catch any grammar errors or typos. Nothing can make people distrust your authority faster than a mistake that could have been easily avoided.

Social Networking Sites

In addition to blogs and wikis, companies (and even colleges and universities) are using social networking sites to interact with both existing and potential clients. People creating company sites will usually include the company brand or logo so that it is easy for people to recognize the organization. MySpace and Facebook are, at the time of writing, the most popular sites used for social networking. These sites allow you to upload links and post photos and information to your potential market segment. Twitter is becoming more popular, but has a 140-character limitation for each posting, so it is more restrictive than many of the other networking sites. For professionals who are interested in networking for their careers, LinkedIn is yet another site. On this site, employers can also search for potential new employees; as a result, first impressions are important, which means following the rules mentioned in the section about email and also creating content for a specific audience, as discussed in Chapter 1.

If you are creating a profile on a social networking site for your company, you need to ensure you are using materials that the company has authorized. For example, unless you have permission to use the company logo, you could be facing copyright issues. You also want to make sure you are correctly portraying the company image. Again, audience awareness is extremely important, as is tone. If you are unsure, check with colleagues and also look at other companies on the networking sites and see what they have done well, or what they have done poorly.

A major drawback of these types of sites is the lack of privacy. Once you are part of these networks, anyone can see you unless you set very specific privacy settings. Also, these types of sites encourage people to dash off a posting to let others know what is happening in their lives or in the company. Because of the swiftness and ease of these postings, many people forget to check for typos and grammar errors before they post. Once a mistake is on a posting, though, it can be very embarrassing for all involved. While you may be able to go back and delete the post, there is no guarantee that someone has not already seen the mistake and shared it with his or her network before a correction is made.

Finally, if you are going to be using social networking sites at work, remember that you are using the company computer and internet access and that anything you do can be seen by anyone in the company. Therefore, do not use company time for personal correspondence. Nothing is private, and people have been fired for the content they have accessed or the messages they have sent while at work.

The following article highlights some of the dangers of misusing social networking sites.

Fired on Facebook: Don't Rip Boss When He's Your "Friend"; Woman Let Go after Rant: "I Guess You Forgot about Adding Me on Here?"

In tech terms, it's called a cascading failure.

A woman in Britain being called "Lindsay" made a big one this week, and it cost her her job.

First, she came home after a hard day and, rather than complaining to the cat, decided to do it on the web.

Lindsay opened up her Facebook account and posted a fairly vulgar description of her boss.

"OMG, I HATE MY JOB!" Lindsay wrote. "My boss is a total pervvy wanker always making me do s– stuff." Mistake No. 2.

Mistake No. 3. was forgetting that her boss was one of her Facebook friends, and thus had access to all of her posted comments.

Mistake No. 4 was firing this broadside two weeks before the end of a six-month trial period.

Five hours after Lindsay posted her lament, her boss replied.

"I guess you forgot about adding me on here?" his post began.

Then he proceeded to rip her straight back.

"That 's– stuff' is called your 'job,' you know, what I pay you to do? But the fact that you seem able to f– up the simplest of tasks might contribute to how you feel about it."

Angry boss then points out that Lindsay is a couple of weeks shy of the end of her trial period and delivers the coup de grace.

"Don't bother coming in tomorrow. I'll pop your P45 (pink slip) in the post, and you can come in whenever you like to pick up any stuff you've left here. And, yes, I'm serious."

The Schadenfreude moment appears to be genuine. A screen capture of the exchange—with names blacked out—has been circulating the web for several days.

"It is pretty hysterical," said labour lawyer Mary Beth Currie. "Well, not for her."

According to Currie, the sort of treatment Lindsay received at her boss's hands could also happen in Canada.

"Yes, a termination would be possible," Currie said. "People have to realize that they can't disparage their employer after working hours like this."

It is now normal practice in this country to include a paragraph addressing what can and can't be done on social networking sites into the section of employee agreements covering Internet policy.

"This is not unusual," said Peter Biro, a partner at WeirFoulds LLP. "You're going to see kajillions of cases like this out there."

This is the latest in a series of headline-grabbing stories of irked employees typing and living to regret it.

From a Swiss insurance worker chopped for Facebooking while home ill, to a Brit public relations drone axed for complaining about being "bored" in her work, people are learning the hard way that bad moods are temporary, but the Internet is forever.

Nor would it be the first time someone's been cut via a social networking site. B.C. aesthetician Crystal Bell made headlines in January after she was fired over Facebook, though not for anything she had written online.

In Lindsay's case, the lesson is clear. Choose your (Facebook) friends wisely.

(Source: Kelly, Cathal. *Toronto Star*. 15 Aug. 2009. Web. 21 Aug. 2009. Reprinted with permission—Torstar Syndication Services.)

PDAs and BlackBerrys

Cell phones, personal digital assistants (PDAs), and BlackBerrys have become common tools for professionals. Not only do these devices have calendars, to-do lists, and phones, but they also allow users to send email and text messages, or in the case of BlackBerrys, PINs. Being able to send email or text messages while away from the office is clearly advantageous for many professionals. However, because the number of devices has increased, so, too, has the amount of information that is being sent and received. As with the email recommendations earlier in the chapter, users should ensure that only messages that are important are sent. Otherwise, people become overwhelmed and either start ignoring the devices, or they become like addicts, never straying far from their smart phones. Also, when texting, make sure short forms of words, such as *c u*, are acceptable within the company, and ensure that the receiver can understand exactly what you mean; otherwise, additional messages will have to be sent for clarification.

As with all other forms of electronic communication, the guidelines below should be followed when using portable devices:

- Keep messages clear and concise.
- Respond promptly to incoming messages, but do not interrupt a conversation or a meeting to take a call or send a message unless permission has been granted previously.
- Maintain relevance. Respond only to the topic under discussion; if a new issue comes up, create a new email or text message for that.
- Use text-speak only if you are sure your audience understands and approves of it.
- Before sending, check messages for typos and grammar errors.

Because technology is changing rapidly, companies often find that rules or protocols governing use of it are adapted regularly. In addition, new technology also changes the way business is being done. The iPhone, for example, has introduced a new level of technology that, just six years ago, was unheard of. In fact, new apps are being created by businesses daily. New technology is also modifying the way businesses are being run. The traditional "bricks and mortar" model, for example, is changing, with people working from the comfort of home or elsewhere. Because new technology is rapidly changing the world we work in, the guidelines above are general, so always check your company's specific rules before using technology to communicate with colleagues, customers, or potential clients.

To sum up, electronic communication is no different from any other form of workplace communication in requiring close attention to audience, purpose, and tone—not to mention ethical considerations. Just as you would after composing a conventional memo on paper, assess your electronic communication by consulting the checklist as shown below.

✓ **Checklist**   Evaluating Electronic Messages

A good electronic message

___ Follows standard format;

___ Is organized into paragraphs (one is often enough) covering the subject fully in an orderly way;

___ Includes no inappropriate content;

___ Uses clear, simple language;

___ Maintains an appropriate tone, neither too formal nor too conversational;

___ Contains no typos or mechanical errors in spelling, capitalization, punctuation, or grammar.

Email

___ Includes certain features:

▢ Date line (appears automatically in email);

▢ To line, which includes the name and email address of the receiver;

▢ From line, which includes the name and email address (appears automatically in email) of the sender;

▢ Subject line, which is a clear, accurate, but brief statement of what the message is about.

Exercises

Exercise 2.1

You're the assistant to the personnel manager of a metals fabrication plant. Monday is Labour Day, and most of the 300 employees will be given a paid holiday. The company is under pressure, however, to meet a deadline. Therefore, a skeleton force of 40—all in the production department—will be needed to work on the holiday. Those who volunteer will have the option of being paid overtime at the standard time-and-a-half rate or receiving two vacation days. If fewer than 40 employees volunteer, others will be assigned to work on the basis of seniority, with the most recently hired employees chosen first. The personnel manager has asked you to alert affected employees. Write an email.

Exercise 2.2

You're an administrative assistant at the regional office of a provincial agency. Normal working hours for civil service employees in your province are 8:30 a.m. to 4:30 p.m., with a lunch break from 12:00 to 12:30 p.m. During the summer, however, the hours are 8:30 a.m. to 4:00 p.m., with lunch unchanged. Summer hours are in effect from July 1 to September 2. It is now mid-June, and the busy office supervisor has asked you to remind employees of the summer schedule. Write an email.

Exercise 2.3

You work in the lumberyard of a building supplies company. Every year on the July 1 weekend, the town sponsors the Canada Day Run, a 10K road race. This year, for the first time, local businesses have been invited to enter five-member teams to compete for the Corporate Cup. The team with the best combined time takes the trophy. There will be no prize money involved but much good publicity for the winners. Because you recently ran Nunavut Midnight Sun Marathon, the company president wants you to recruit and organize a team. It's now April 21. You'd better get started. Write a blog to post on the company's internal system.

Exercise 2.4

You're the security chief at a manufacturing company that makes small metal hand tools. The plant employs roughly 100 people. Management has told you that many tools have disappeared. According to company records, the plant produces approximately 50 000 per day, but far fewer are actually being shipped out. After double-checking the figures to ensure their accuracy, you have concluded that pilferage is the only possible explanation. A metal detector positioned at the employee exit near the time clock would catch anyone trying to smuggle tools out of the factory. Because the purchase cost of a metal detector is prohibitive, you have decided to rent one. Anyone caught stealing will immediately be fired, and a note to that effect will become part of the individual's personnel file. You don't want to create an atmosphere of hostility, but you do need to inform the employees about these developments. Write a memo to be posted on the main bulletin board, and send an email as well.

Exercise 2.5

You're a caseworker at a new municipal agency that assists troubled youths by placing them in group homes run by the agency. There are five boys or girls per home, supervised by specially trained counsellors. You find this job rewarding, although it involves more paperwork than you'd prefer. Yesterday, for example, the agency psychiatrist recommended a medication change for a boy named Eli Bradley, who resides at Group Home #6. The boy has been diagnosed as hyperactive and has been receiving a daily dosage of 30 mg of Ritalin (one 10-mg tablet in the morning, one at noon, and one at bedtime). The doctor has decided to increase the dosage to 35 mg daily by changing the 10-mg morning tablet to 15 mg. You have no reason to question the doctor's judgment, but you must inform the boy's counsellors. Send an email.

Exercise 2.6

You have just been hired to work at a new restaurant that is opening right before Thanksgiving. Because your boss knows that you are taking this writing course, she has asked you to compose Twitter postings in order to create excitement about the restaurant. The location is quite close to your campus, and the restaurant's focus is on home cooking at affordable prices. Fair-trade coffee is also on the menu. Breakfast will be available all day and the restaurant will be open 24 hours a day, which will be great for many students who want a late-night snack or coffee. Create a series of seven Twitter posts that will be used by the company. Remember that each post may contain only 140 characters.

Exercise 2.7

Proofread and rewrite the following email, correcting all errors.

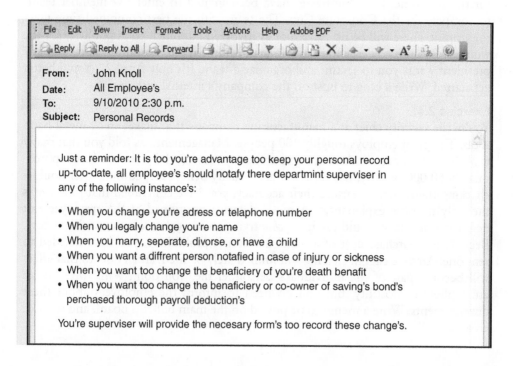

File   Edit   View   Insert   Format   Tools   Actions   Help   Adobe PDF

Reply | Reply to All | Forward

From: John Knoll
Date: All Employee's
To: 9/10/2010 2:30 p.m.
Subject: Personal Records

Just a reminder: It is too you're advantage too keep your personal record up-too-date, all employee's should notafy there departmint superviser in any of the following instance's:

- When you change you're adress or telaphone number
- When you legaly change you're name
- When you marry, seperate, divorse, or have a child
- When you want a diffrent person notafied in case of injury or sickness
- When you want too change the benaficiery of you're death benafit
- When you want too change the benaficiery or co-owner of saving's bond's perchased thorough payroll deduction's

You're superviser will provide the necesary form's too record these change's.

Exercise 2.8

Go online and examine company blogs. Evaluate at least three using what you have learned in this chapter. What makes them good? Bad? Uninteresting? Create one for your place of business or school.

Exercise 2.9

Think of a situation in which effective communication did not occur when you used electronic communication. Using what you have learned in this chapter, analyze what went wrong. How would you change your communiqué so that it would be properly received? In the future, what would you do differently?

PEARSON
mycanadiantechcommlab

Visit www.mycanadiantechcommlab.ca for everything you need to help you succeed in the job you've always wanted! Tools and resources include the following:

- Composing Space and Writer's Toolkit
- Document Makeovers
- Grammar Exercises—and much more!

CHAPTER

3

Memos and Business Letters

LEARNING OBJECTIVE

When you complete this chapter, you'll be able to use basic format and organization patterns to write effective memos and business letters.

OF ALL THE FORMS OF WRITTEN COMMUNICATION used in the workplace, memos and email are certainly among the most common. Any large corporation, agency, or other organization generates thousands of such documents daily. Even in a small setting, they are fundamental to office procedure. Focusing on both format and content, the first part of this chapter explains how to handle memos. Business letters, while equally important, are not used as often as memos and email. However, format and content are just as relevant for letters, which the second half of the chapter discusses.

Memos can be sent to specific individuals or posted in a common area for all to see.

MEMOS

While the memo may be written to one person or to a group, traditionally, it is a vehicle for internal or intramural communication–a message from someone at Company X to someone else at Company X.

The writer and reader of a memo may be well acquainted. They may even have had lunch together. Indeed, the contents of the memo may already be known to all parties involved in the exchange. Although the usual purpose of a memo is to inform, often its function is to create a written record of a request or other message previously communicated in person, over the phone, or through the grapevine.

Accordingly, a memo is usually quite direct in approach. It should come to the point quickly and not ramble on. A common error is to obscure the central issue and confuse the reader with irrelevant details. A good memo focuses sharply, zooming in on what the reader needs to know. Depending on the subject, a memo should make its point in three or four short paragraphs: a concise introduction, a middle paragraph or two conveying the details, and perhaps a brief conclusion. If the message is quite simple, however, you should get to the point quickly. Some memos are as short as one paragraph, or even one sentence. Like so many other features of workplace communications, memo length is determined by purpose and audience.

Format

A memo has essentially one basic format. Although minor variations do exist, practically all memos share certain standard format features:

- The word *Memo, Memorandum,* or some equivalent term at or near the top of the page.

- The To line, enabling the memo to be addressed, and the From line, enabling it to be signed. When creating a memo, always use the recipient's full name, title, and/or department. This not only ensures that the memo will reach its intended destination but also creates a more complete record for anyone reviewing the file later. For the same reason, use your own full name, title, and/or department in the From line.

- The Date line.

- The Subject line, identifying the topic. Like a newspaper headline, but even more concise, the Subject line orients and prepares the reader for what is to follow. To write a good subject line, answer this question: "In no more than three words, what is this memo really about?"

- Of course, the message or content of the memo. As explained earlier, three or four paragraphs should be sufficient.

The memo in Figure 3.1 embodies all these features and provides an opportunity to explore further the principle of *tone* introduced in Chapter 1.

The personnel manager has picked her words carefully to avoid sounding bossy. She says "You *may want* to send him a . . . card," not "You *should* send him a . . . card," even though that's what she really means. As discussed in Chapter 1, a tactful writer can soften a recommendation, a request, or even a command simply by phrasing it in a diplomatic way. In this situation, an employee's decision whether to send a card is strictly a matter of personal choice, so the memo's gentle tone is particularly appropriate. But the same strategy can also be used when conveying important directives you definitely expect the reader to follow.

For the sake of convenience, most word-processing programs include at least one preformatted memo form, called a template. The template automatically generates formatted headings and inserts the date. The writer simply fills in the blanks. Microsoft Word, the most widely used software program, provides several memo templates, one of which is reproduced in Figure 3.2.

Figure 3.1 Basic Memo Format

CITY MANUFACTURING
MEMORANDUM

DATE: May 9, 2012

TO: All Employees

FROM: Susan Lemley, Manager   SL,
            Personnel Department

SUBJECT: James Mahan

As many of you already know, James Mahan of the Maintenance
Department was admitted to Memorial Hospital over the weekend
and is scheduled to undergo surgery on Tuesday.

Although Jim will not be receiving visitors or phone calls for a while,
you may want to send him a Get Well card to boost his spirits. He's
in Room 325.

We'll keep you posted on Jim's progress.

BUSINESS LETTERS

Unlike memos, business letters are typically used for *external* communication, a
message from someone at Company X to someone elsewhere—a customer or client,
perhaps, or a counterpart at Company Y. As mentioned in Chapter 2, however,
email is now often used in situations that in the past would have required letters,
and this trend is increasing. Nevertheless, countless letters are still written every day
for an enormous variety of reasons. Some of the more typical purposes of a letter
are to do the following:

- Purchase a product or service (order)
- Request payment (collection)
- Voice a complaint (claim)
- Ask for information (inquiry)

Figure 3.2 Microsoft Word's Professional Memo Template

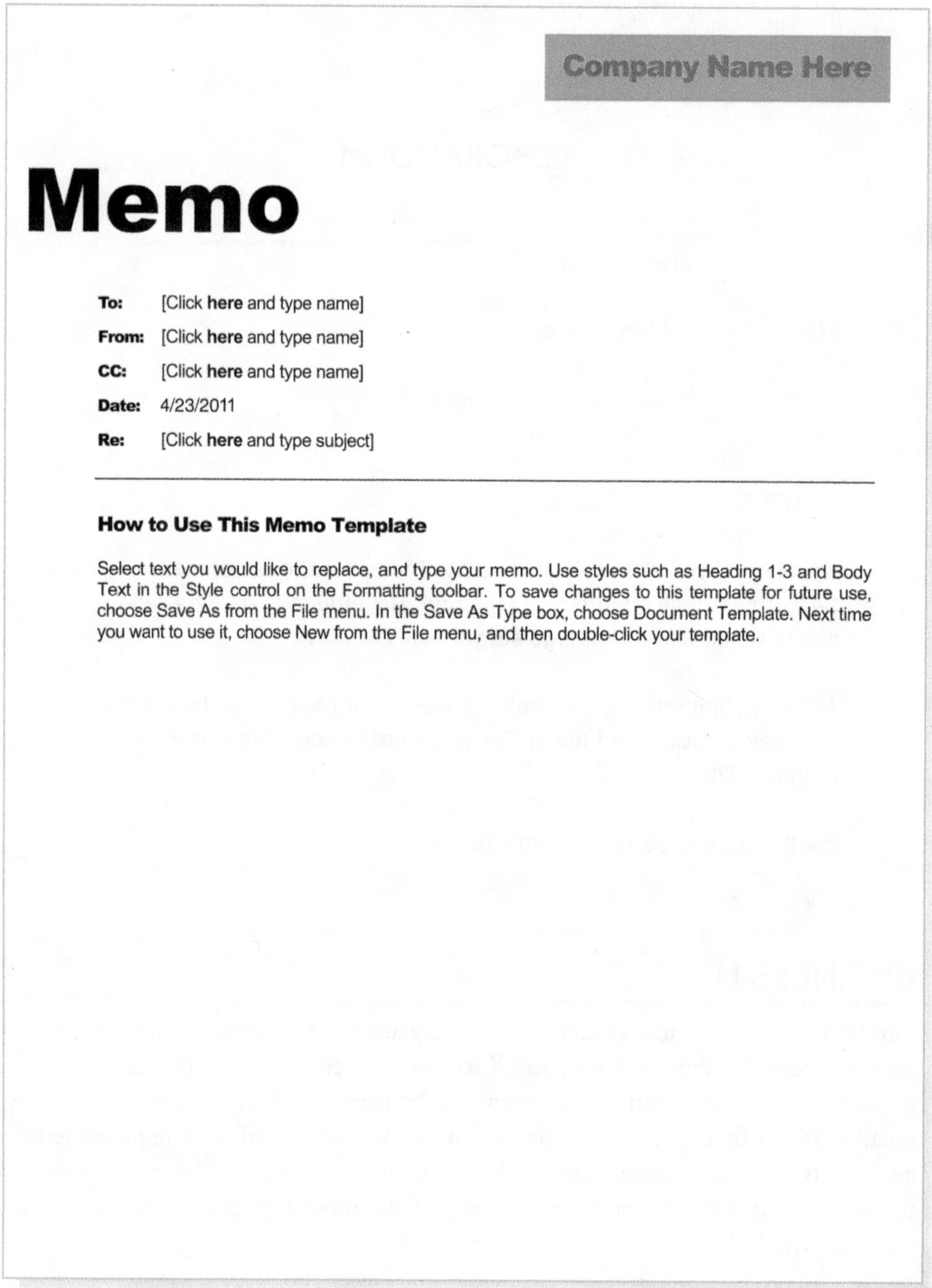

Company Name Here

Memo

To: [Click **here** and type name]

From: [Click **here** and type name]

CC: [Click **here** and type name]

Date: 4/23/2011

Re: [Click **here** and type subject]

How to Use This Memo Template

Select text you would like to replace, and type your memo. Use styles such as Heading 1-3 and Body Text in the Style control on the Formatting toolbar. To save changes to this template for future use, choose Save As from the File menu. In the Save As Type box, choose Document Template. Next time you want to use it, choose New from the File menu, and then double-click your template.

✓ Checklist   Evaluating a Memo   ✓•

A good memo

___ Follows standard format;

___ Includes certain features:

☐ Date line

☐ To line, which includes the name and often the title and/or department of the receiver

☐ From line, which includes the name and often the title and/or department of the sender; on a paper memo, the From line must be initialled by the writer before the memo is sent

☐ Subject line, which is a clear, accurate, but brief statement of what the memo is about

___ Is organized into paragraphs covering the subject fully in an orderly way;

___ Includes no inappropriate content;

___ Uses clear, simple language;

___ Maintains an appropriate tone, neither too formal nor too conversational;

___ Contains no typos or mechanical errors in spelling, capitalization, punctuation, or grammar.

- Sell a product or service (sales)
- Respond to a complaint (adjustment)
- Thank someone (acknowledgment)

Figures 3.3 through 3.10 provide examples of letters serving these needs.

Format

Regardless of purpose, a letter can be formatted in various ways. The three most common formats are the modified block style, the modified block style with indented paragraphs, and the full block style. As with memos, Microsoft Word provides a template for letters, which is shown in Figure 3.11.

Modified Block Style

As shown in Figures 3.3 through 3.5, the date, the complimentary close, and the sender's identification begin at the centre of the page. If the sender's address is not preprinted on company letterhead (as it is in each of the examples), it should begin at the centre of the page, above the date. All other lines (including the first line of each paragraph) are flush with the left margin.

Figure 3.3 Order Letter in Modified Block Style

Southton High School

62 Academy Street, Gander, NL A1V 1A4
Telephone (709) 555-1234 · Fax (709) 555-4321

July 10, 2011

Value-Plus Office Supplies
462 Decatur Street
St. John's, NL A1A 2G8

Dear Value-Plus:

It's time once again for Southton High to order a shipment of custom-printed, spiral-bound notebooks for use by our students.

You may charge the following order to our account (#2468).

Catalog #	Quantity	Description	Unit Cost	Total
471	300	100 pages	$1.00	$300
472	200	250 pages	2.00	400
473	100	350 pages	3.00	300
			Subtotal	$1,000
			Tax (15%)	150
			Shipping	30
			Total	$1,180

Please provide blue covers with the gold SHS logo (which you have on file) and ship as promptly as possible.

Sincerely,

Karl Bradbury

Karl Bradbury, Vice-principal

Figure 3.4 Collection Letter in Modified Block Style

West Edmonton Mall
#5119–8882 — 170 Street   Edmonton, AB   T5T 4J2

June 16, 2010

Mr. William Britton
55-A Jackson Road
Edmonton, AB T5A 0A2

Dear Mr. Britton:

We appreciate your continued patronage of Greene's. We note, however, that your charge account is now $565.31 overdue, and that we
have not received your monthly payment since April.

If you have recently sent in your payment, please ignore this friendly
reminder. If not, we would appreciate a minimum remittance of
$50.00 at your earliest convenience.

If you have any questions about your account, please call me at
555-0123, Ext. 123.

Sincerely,

Heather Sutcliffe

Heather Sutcliffe
Credit Services Department

Figure 3.5 Corporate Claim Letter in Modified Block Style

Jane's Homestyle Restaurants, Inc.

Jane's Homestyle Restaurants, Inc.
755 Vanalman Avenue Victoria, BC V8Z 3B8 (250) 555-9876

October 29, 2011

Mr. Joseph Chen, Director
Sales & Service Department
Ace Technologies Corporation
154 Stoneyvale Lane
Victoria, BC V8N V8Z

Dear Mr. Chen:

I purchased the Ace Cash Register System 3000 for my three restaurants in December 2010 and have experienced continuous problems with the video monitors since then.

As recently as September of this year, another of the monitors had to be sent in for repairs. Yesterday afternoon that same unit failed again. This occurrence is not uncommon, as you can see by the nine repair invoices I have enclosed for your reference.

Given the many problems we have had with these monitors, I am requesting that you replace them, free of charge. Please call me about this as soon as possible.

Sincerely,

Jane Pelham

Jane Pelham, Owner

Enclosures

Modified Block Style with Indented Paragraphs

As shown in Figures 3.6 and 3.7, the date, the complimentary close, and the sender's identification begin at the centre of the page. Again, if the sender's address is not preprinted on company letterhead, it should begin at the centre of the page, above the date. The first line of each paragraph is indented five spaces. All other lines are flush with the left margin.

Full Block Style

As shown in Figures 3.8 through 3.11 and in Figures 3.14 and 3.15, every line (including the first line of each paragraph) is flush with the left margin.

The three formats share several features: all are single-spaced throughout (except between the separate elements, where double-spacing is used), are centred on the page, and are framed by margins of 1 to $1^1/_2$ inches. All three formats are in common use, with the modified block style with indented paragraphs considered the most traditional format (and rather old-fashioned). Full block style, on the other hand, is the most contemporary and is rapidly becoming the norm. Regardless of its format, however, every letter includes certain essential components that are set forth on the page in the following sequence:

1. Writer's address (often preprinted on letterhead) at the top of the page (do not include the writer's name in this section)

2. Date (like email, letters sent by fax are automatically imprinted with the exact time of transmission as well)

3. Inside address (the full name, title, and address of the receiver)

4. Salutation, followed by a colon (avoid gender-biased salutations such as "Dear Sir" or "Gentlemen")

5. Body of the letter, using the three-part approach outlined later in this chapter

6. Complimentary close ("Sincerely" is best), followed by a comma

7. Writer's signature

8. Writer's name and title beneath the signature

9. Enclosure line, if necessary, to indicate item(s) accompanying the letter

Along with these standard components, all business letters—irrespective of format—also embrace the same three-part organization:

1. A brief introductory paragraph establishing context (by referring to previous correspondence, perhaps, or by orienting the reader in some other way) and stating the letter's purpose concisely

2. A middle section (as many paragraphs as needed) conveying the content of the message by providing all necessary details in the most logical sequence

3. A brief concluding paragraph politely requesting action, thanking the reader, or providing any additional information pertinent to the situation

Figure 3.6 Inquiry Letter in Modified Block Style with Indented Paragraphs

P.O. Box 123
Montreal, QC H7M 4B6
Telephone (450) 555-1234 • Fax (450) 555-4321

February 24, 2012

Chief Joseph Kealy
Montreal Police Department
911 Brunswick Blvd
Montreal, QC H3G 1M8

Dear Chief Kealy:

    It is our understanding that a Montreal resident, Mr. Alex Booth, is the subject of an investigation by your department. In keeping with the provisions of Canada's Access to Information Act, I am requesting information about Mr. Booth's arrest.

    This information is needed to provide our readership with accurate news coverage of the events leading to Mr. Booth's current situation. *The Weekly News* prides itself on fair, accurate, and objective reporting, and we are counting on your assistance as we seek to uphold that tradition.

    Because the police blotter is by law a matter of public record, we will appreciate your full co-operation.

Sincerely,

Nancy Muller

Nancy Muller, Reporter

Figure 3.7 Sales Letter in Modified Block Style with Indented Paragraphs

Fashion First

254 Westrose Blvd, Mississauga, ON L4X 2T4   •   telephone (905) 555-1234

March 3, 2010

Ms. Sarah Levy
643 Glenwood Avenue
Mississauga, ON L4X 2B5

Dear Ms. Levy:

As a preferred customer and holder of our special Gold Card, you won't want to miss our annual Savings Spectacular.

All the fine clothing pictured in the enclosed brochure has been marked down a full 25 percent! To take advantage of these incredible bargains, you need only complete the order form on the back cover of the brochure. Or, if you prefer, you may simply telephone your order. Our operators are standing by.

Purchases totaling $300 or more are entitled to another 10 percent off! But you must act quickly! The sale—open to Gold Card customers exclusively—ends on March 10. Order now!

Sincerely,

Jorgé Figueroa

Jorgé Figueroa, Manager
Customer Services Department

Enclosure

Figure 3.8 Consumer Claim Letter in Full Block Style

65 Jarvis Street
Whitehorse, YT Y1A 5B3
June 30, 2011

Consumer Relations Department
Superior Foods, Inc.
130 Maple Grove Road
Kitchener, ON N2G 4M5

Dear Superior Foods:

Superior microwave dinners are excellent products that I have
purchased regularly for many years. Recently, however, I had an
unsettling experience with one of these meals.

While enjoying a serving of Pasta Alfredo, I discovered in the food
what appeared to be a thick splinter of wood. I'm sure this is an iso-
lated incident, but I thought your quality control department would
want to know about it.

I've enclosed the splinter, taped to the product wrapper, along with
the sales receipt for the dinner. May I please be reimbursed $4.98 for
the cost?

Sincerely,

George Eaglefeather

George Eaglefeather

Enclosures

Figure 3.9 Adjustment Letter in Full Block Style

Superior Foods, Inc.

130 Maple Grove Road, Kitchener, ON N2G 4M5 • (519) 555-1234

July 7, 2011

Mr. George Eaglefeather
65 Jarvis Street
Whitehorse, YT Y1A 5B3

Dear Mr. Eaglefeather:

Thank you for purchasing our product and for taking the time to contact us about it. We apologize for the unsatisfactory condition of your Pasta Alfredo dinner.

Quality is of paramount importance to all of us at Superior Foods, and great care is taken in the preparation and packaging of all our products. Our quality assurance staff has been notified of the problem you reported. Although Superior Foods does not issue cash refunds, we have enclosed three coupons redeemable at your grocery for complementary Superior dinners of your choice.

We appreciate this opportunity to be of service, and we hope you will continue to enjoy our products.

Sincerely,

John Roth

John Roth
Customer Services Department

Enclosures (3)

Figure 3.10   Acknowledgment Letter in Full Block Style

VALUE-PLUS OFFICE SUPPLIES

462 Decatur Street • St. John's, NL A1A 2G8 • (204) 555-3003

March 19, 2011

Ms. Helen Reynard, Owner
Reynard's Auto Palace
1125 Portage Ave
Winnipeg, MB R2M 2Y1

Dear Ms. Reynard:

For the past 10 years, Value-Plus Office Supplies has purchased all
our delivery vans from your dealership, and we have relied on your
service department for routine maintenance and necessary repairs.
During that time I have been repeatedly impressed by the professionalism of your employees, especially Jarel Carter, who staffs the service desk.

Both in person and on the telephone, Jarel has always been exceptionally knowledgeable, helpful, and courteous and is always willing
to go the extra mile to ensure customer satisfaction. Just last week,
for example, he interrupted his lunch break to get me some information about a part that has been on back order.

If you can continue to attract employees of Jarel's calibre, you shouldn't
have any difficulty remaining the area's #1 dealership. Be sure to
keep him in mind the next time you're considering merit raises!

Sincerely,

Gary Richie

Gary Richie, Owner

Figure 3.11   Microsoft Word's Professional Letter Template in Full Block Style

Company Name Here

[Click **here** and type return address]

April 3, 2007

[Click **here** and type recipient's address]

Dear Sir or Madam:

Type your letter here. For more details on modifying this letter template, double-click ⊠. To return to this letter, use the Window menu.

Sincerely,

[Click **here** and type your name]
[Click **here** and type job title]

Table 3.1 provides guidance in applying this three-part approach in each of the basic letter-writing situations.

Tech Tips

Letters and other documents are often sent by a facsimile (fax) machine— basically, a scanner with a modem that converts documents into digital data that are then transmitted over telephone lines to the receiver's fax machine, which prints out hard copy. Like email, this technology has the obvious advantage of speed; a letter that might take one or two weeks to arrive by conventional mail can be received instantaneously by fax.

But whenever you fax anything, you must fax a cover memo along with it. In this memo you should include any additional information that might be necessary to orient the reader and indicate how many pages (including the cover memo itself) you have included in the transmission so that the reader will know if there's anything that was sent but not received. You should also include your fax number, telephone number, and email address so the reader has the option of replying. Here's an example:

DONROC, INC.

36 College St., Toronto, ON M5G 1K9

FAX

DATE:	November 14, 2010 (3:15 p.m.)
TO:	John Lapinski, Main Office Comptroller, Fax: (416) 123-4567
FROM:	George Smith, Branch Office Manager, Fax: (416) 891-0111 Telephone: (416) 555-2595, email: gsrls@sarge.com
SUBJECT:	Cosgrove Letter
PAGES:	2

Here's Michael Cosgrove's letter of November 10. Let's discuss this at Thursday's meeting.

As with memos and letters, Microsoft Word provides three fax templates, one of which is shown in Figure 3.12.

Although the fax-machine-to-fax-machine scenario is the most common, computer software now permits interface between fax machines and computers. Another option, of course, is to send the cover memo as an email, with the accompanying document scanned in as an attachment. With so many workplace computers equipped with scanners, fax machines may eventually be rendered obsolete, especially because computer printers produce better hard copy. At least for now, though, the fax machine remains a useful device.

Table 3.1   Letter Content Guidelines

Letter Type	Introduction	Middle Paragraphs	Conclusion
Order (Fig. 3.3)	Establish that this is indeed an order letter, and state what you want to purchase.	Provide all relevant details about your order (product numbers, prices, quantities, method of payment, etc.). A table is often the best format for presenting this information.	Thank the reader in advance for filling the order. If you must have the product or service by a certain date, specify it. Make sure you've provided all the information the reader will need to ship the order (address, billing address, method of delivery).
Collection (Fig. 3.4)	Open with a polite but firm reminder that the reader's payment is overdue. (In a second or third collection letter, the tone of the introduction can be more urgent.)	If you have not already done so in the introduction, provide all the relevant details about how much is owed, when it was due, and when it must be paid to avoid penalty, but acknowledge the possibility of error at your end.	Repeat the payment request and encourage the reader to contact you with any concerns or to discuss payment options. Make sure you've provided all the information the reader will need to respond (address, phone number, email address). It's a good idea to include a stamped, self-addressed envelope.
Claim (Figs. 3.5, 3.8)	Provide some background information, but come quickly to the point, identifying the problem.	Politely provide all relevant details about what has gone wrong and what you want the reader to do about it. If appropriate, provide copies of bills, receipts, contracts, etc.	Thank the reader in advance for correcting the problem and make sure you've provided all the information the reader will need to contact you (address, phone number, email address).
Inquiry (Fig. 3.6)	Briefly explain the reason for your inquiry, and clearly identify what you are inquiring about.	Provide all relevant details about your inquiry. Concretely specify what you want to know, why the reader should	Thank the reader in advance for complying with your request. If you must have a reply by a certain date,

(continued on next page)

Table 3.1   (Continued)

Letter Type	Introduction	Middle Paragraphs	Conclusion
		provide this information, and what you'll use it for. If you have more than one question, create a bulleted list.	specify it. Make sure you've provided all the information the reader will need to reply (address, phone number, email address). It's a good idea to provide a stamped, self-addressed envelope.
Sales (Fig. 3.7)	Get the reader's attention, perhaps by asking a question, describing a situation, presenting an interesting fact, or using a quotation (the same strategies explained in Chapter 11 for opening a speech), and state what you're selling.	Provide all relevant details about the product or service you're selling and create an incentive by explaining to the reader the advantages of purchasing.	Thank the reader in advance for becoming a customer and make sure you've provided all the information the reader will need to place an order (price list or catalogue, order form, address, website, phone number, email address).
Adjustment (Fig. 3.9)	Thank the reader for bringing the problem to your attention, and, if the complaint is justified, apologize.	If the complaint is justified, explain what you'll do to fix the problem. If not, tactfully explain why you must deny the claim.	Thank the reader again for writing to you and provide reassurances that everything will be satisfactory in the future.
Acknowledgment (Figs. 3.10, 3.14, 3.15)	Briefly explain why you are writing the acknowledgment and identify the person, group, or situation you're commending.	Provide all relevant details about why the person, group, or situation deserves commendation.	Conclusions vary greatly depending on the nature of the situation. Commonly, you'll thank the reader for considering the remarks and invite a reply. In such cases, make sure you've provided all the information the reader will need to contact you (address, phone number, email address).

Figure 3.12   Microsoft Word's Professional Fax Template

[Click **here** and type return address and phone and fax numbers]

Company Name Here

To:	[Click **here** and type name]	**From:**	[Click **here** and type name]
Fax:	[Click **here** and type fax number]	**Pages:**	[Click **here** and type # of pages]
Phone:	[Click **here** and type phone number]	**Date:**	1/21/2005
Re:	[Click **here** and type subject of fax]	**CC:**	[Click **here** and type name]

☐ **Urgent**   ☐ **For Review**   ☐ **Please Comment**   ☐ **Please Reply**   ☐ **Please Recycle**

● **Comments:** Select this text and delete it or replace it with your own. To save changes to this template for future use, choose Save As from the File menu. In the Save As Type box, choose Document Template. Next time you want to use it, choose New from the File menu, and then double-click your template.

Figure 3.13   Standard Abbreviations

Term	Abbreviation	Term	Abbreviation
Alberta	AB	Road	RD
British Columbia	BC	Highway	HWY
Manitoba	MB	Circle	CIR
New Brunswick	NB	Square	SQ
Newfoundland and Labrador	NL	Court	CT
Nova Scotia	NS	Lane	LN
Northwest Territories	NT	Street	ST
Nunavut	NU	North	N
Ontario	ON	West	W
Prince Edward Island	PE	Southwest	SW
Quebec	QC	East	E
Saskatchewan	SK	Northeast	NE
Yukon	YT	Northwest	NW
Avenue	AVE	South	S
Expressway	EXPY	Southeast	SE
Parkway	PKWY	Room	RM
Boulevard	BLVD	Suite	STE
Freeway	FWY	Apartment	APT

Source: Canada Post. "Addressing Guidelines: Symbols and Abbreviations Recognized by Canada Post." *Canadapost.ca.* Web. 7 October 2010. Adapted with the permission of Canada Post.

Figure 3.13 lists standard abbreviations used in letter writing. A fairly recent development in letter writing is the open punctuation system, in which the colon after the salutation and the comma after the complimentary close are omitted. Figure 3.14 illustrates this variation, which is gaining widespread acceptance. A more radical change is the trend toward a fully abbreviated, "no punctuation, all capitals" approach to the inside address, as shown in Figure 3.15. This derives from Canada Post's recommendation that envelopes be so addressed to facilitate computerized scanning and sorting. Because the inside address has traditionally matched the address on the envelope, such a feature may well become standard, at least for letters sent by conventional mail rather than by electronic means. Indeed, many companies using "window" envelopes have already adopted this style.

As mentioned earlier, more and more companies are communicating with each other through email and other forms of electronic messaging rather than by business letter. The letter is still preferred, however, for more formal exchanges, especially those in which speed of delivery is not a major factor. In situations involving individual customers and clients (some of whom may still rely on conventional mail), the business letter is also the best choice. At least for the immediate future, therefore, the letter will continue to be a major form of workplace correspondence,

Figure 3.14 Acknowledgment Letter in Full Block Style with Open Punctuation

VALUE-PLUS OFFICE SUPPLIES

462 Decatur Street • St. John's, NL A1A 2G8 • (204) 555-3003

March 19, 2011

Ms. Helen Reynard, Owner
Reynard's Auto Palace
1125 Portage Avenue
Winnipeg, MB R2M 2Y1

Dear Ms. Reynard

For the past 10 years, Value-Plus Office Supplies has purchased all our delivery vans from your dealership, and we have relied on your service department for routine maintenance and necessary repairs. During that time I have been repeatedly impressed by the professionalism of your employees, especially Jarel Carter, who staffs the service desk.

Both in person and on the telephone, Jarel has always been exception-ally knowledgeable, helpful, and courteous and is always willing to go the extra mile to ensure customer satisfaction. Just last week, for example, he interrupted his lunch break to get me some information about a part that has been on back order.

If you can continue to attract employees of Jarel's calibre, you shouldn't have any difficulty remaining the area's #1 dealership. Be sure to keep him in mind the next time you're considering merit raises!

Sincerely

Gary Richie

Gary Richie, Owner

Figure 3.15   Acknowledgment Letter in Full Block Style with Capitalized Inside Address

VALUE-PLUS OFFICE SUPPLIES

462 Decatur Street • St. John's, NL A1A 2G8 • (204) 555-3003

March 19, 2011

MS. HELEN REYNARD
REYNARD'S AUTO PALACE
1125 PORTAGE AVE
WINNIPEG MB R2M 2Y1

Dear Ms. Reynard:

For the past 10 years, Value-Plus Office Supplies has purchased all our
delivery vans from your dealership, and we have relied on your service
department for routine maintenance and necessary repairs. During
that time I have been repeatedly impressed by the professionalism of
your employees, especially Jarel Carter, who staffs the service desk.

Both in person and on the telephone, Jarel has always been exception-
ally knowledgeable, helpful, and courteous and is always willing to go
the extra mile to ensure customer satisfaction. Just last week, for
example, he interrupted his lunch break to get me some information
about a part that has been on back order.

If you can continue to attract employees of Jarel's calibre, you shouldn't
have any difficulty remaining the area's #1 dealership. Be sure to keep
him in mind the next time you're considering merit raises!

Sincerely,

Gary Richie

Gary Richie, Owner

although its role will almost certainly undergo further redefinition as various forms of electronic communication become increasingly widespread.

Like all successful communication, a good letter must employ an appropriate tone. Obviously, a letter is a more formal kind of communication than an in-house memo or email because it's received by people outside the company. Accordingly, a letter should uphold the image of the sender's company or organization by reflecting a high degree of professionalism. However, although a letter's style should be polished, the language should be natural and easy to understand. The key to achieving a readable style—in a letter or in anything else you write—is to understand that writing should not sound pompous or official. Rather, it should sound much like ordinary speech—polished up just a bit. Whatever you do, avoid stilted, old-fashioned business clichés. Strive instead for direct, conversational phrasing. One way to achieve this is to use active rather than passive verbs. Instead of saying, for example, "Your report has been received," it's better to say "We have received your report." Here's a list of overly bureaucratic constructions, paired with "plain English" alternatives:

Cliché	Alternative
As per your request	As you requested
Attached please find	Here is
At this point in time	Now
In lieu of	Instead of
In the event that	If
Please be advised that X	X
Pursuant to our agreement	As we agreed
Until such time as	Until
We are in receipt of	We have received
We regret to advise you that X	Regrettably, X

If you have a clear understanding of your letter's purpose and have analyzed your audience, you should experience little difficulty achieving the appropriate tone for the situation. In addition, if you have written your letter following one of the three standard formats described earlier, and if you have used clear, accessible, and mechanically correct language, your correspondence will likely accomplish its objectives. As noted earlier, you must scrupulously avoid typos and mechanical errors in memos and emails. This is equally important when you compose letters intended for outside readers, who will take their business elsewhere if they perceive you as careless or incompetent. Always proofread carefully, making every effort to ensure that your work is error-free, and consult the following checklist.

✔ Checklist   Evaluating a Letter

A good letter

___ Follows a standard letter format (full block is best);

___ Includes certain features:

☐ Sender's complete address

☐ Date

☐ Receiver's full name and complete address

☐ Salutation, followed by a colon

☐ Complimentary close ("Sincerely" is best), followed by a comma

☐ Sender's signature and full name

☐ Enclosure notation, if necessary

___ Is organized into paragraphs, covering the subject fully in an orderly way:

☐ First paragraph establishes context and states the purpose

☐ Middle paragraphs provide all necessary details

☐ Last paragraph politely achieves closure

___ Includes no inappropriate content;

___ Uses clear, simple language;

___ Maintains an appropriate tone, neither too formal nor too conversational;

___ Contains no typos or mechanical errors in spelling, capitalization, punctuation, or grammar.

Technology continues to change rapidly. For instance, fax machines were high tech in the 1980s and 90s and businesses relied on them to communicate quickly with other businesses or between offices. Today, because of advances in computer technology that you read about earlier in the chapter, many offices are equipped with printers that also act as scanners, copiers, and fax machines. Stand-alone fax machines are becoming more uncommon in offices. Because of the technological changes that are occurring, the information in this chapter is accurate for today, but by the time you are out in the workforce, some forms of communication mentioned here may be obsolete. It is important to remember, though, that attention to audience and purpose are always key when communicating, no matter what the medium.

Exercises

Exercise 3.1

You're an office worker at a large paper products company that has just installed an upgraded computer system. Many employees are having difficulty with the new software. The manufacturer's representatives will be on-site all next week to provide training. Because you are studying computer technology, you've been asked to serve as liaison. You must inform your co-workers about the training, which will be delivered in Conference Room 3 from Monday through Thursday in eight half-day sessions (9:00 a.m. to 12:00 p.m. and 1:00 to 4:00 p.m.), organized alphabetically by workers' last names, as follows: A–B, C–E, F–I, J–M, N–P, Q–SL, SM–T, and U–Z. Workers unable to attend must sign up for one of two makeup sessions that will be held on Friday. You must ensure that everyone understands all these requirements. Write a memo to be posted on all bulletin boards.

Exercise 3.2

You're the manager of the employee cafeteria at a printing company. For many years the cafeteria has provided excellent service, offering breakfast from 7:00 to 8:30 a.m., and lunch from 11:00 a.m. to 2:00 p.m. It also serves as a break room, selling coffee, soft drinks, and snacks all day. But the cafeteria is badly in need of modernization. Work is scheduled to begin next Wednesday. Naturally, the cafeteria will have to be closed while renovations are in progress. Employees will still be able to have lunch and breaks, however, because temporary facilities are being set up in Room 101 of Building B, a now-vacant area formerly used for storage. The temporary cafeteria will provide all the usual services except breakfast. Obviously, employees need to know about the situation. Write a memo.

Exercise 3.3

You're the production manager for a computer parts manufacturer. Last month four machines had excessive downtime. As a result, the company's production of Part #Z43 has dropped. Two of your best customers have complained about late shipments of Part #Z43. One customer has cancelled a standing order and is now buying the part from your principal competitor. For the past two months, the company's production of Part #Y01 has also been declining. To discuss the situation, all production supervisors will meet in Conference Room G, in the west wing of the main building, at 10:00 a.m. next Monday. Each supervisor should bring to the meeting up-to-date figures on costs, equipment, personnel, and so on. You must inform the production supervisors about the meeting. Write a memo.

Exercise 3.4

For 10 days, save all the business letters you receive. Even though the bulk of them will be junk mail, make a list identifying the *purpose* of each letter. Prepare a brief oral presentation explaining which letter is the best and which is the worst, and why. (It may be helpful to create overhead transparencies or to distribute photocopies to the class, assuming the letters do not contain confidential information.)

Exercise 3.5

A consumer product that you especially like is suddenly no longer available in retail stores in your area. Write the manufacturer an inquiry letter requesting information about the product and how to place an order.

Exercise 3.6

Proceeding as if you've received the information requested in Exercise 3.5, write a letter ordering the product.

Exercise 3.7

Pretend you've received the product ordered in Exercise 3.6, but it's somehow unsatisfactory. Write the manufacturer a claim letter expressing dissatisfaction and requesting an exchange or a refund.

Exercise 3.8

Team up with a classmate, exchange the claim letters you each wrote in response to Exercise 3.7, and write adjustment letters to each other.

Exercise 3.9

Write a claim letter expressing dissatisfaction with some product or service that you have actually been disappointed with in the recent past. After the letter has been returned to you with your instructor's corrections, you should actually mail your claim letter and see if you receive a reply or perhaps even some form of compensation.

Exercise 3.10

Write an acknowledgment letter to the editor of either your campus newspaper or a regional daily, expressing your approval of some meaningful contribution made by a local person or organization.

Exercise 3.11
Proofread and rewrite the following memo, correcting all errors.

Memorial Hospital

MEMORANDUM

DATE: September 8, 2012

TO: All Employes

FROM: Roger Sammon, Clerk,
Medical Recrods Department

SUBJECT: Patricia Klosek

As many of you allready know. Patricia Klosik from the Medical records Depratment is retiring next month. After more then thirty years of faithfull service to Memorial hospital.

A party is being planed in her honor. It will be at seven oclock on friday October 17 at big Joes Resturant tickets are $35 per person whitch includes a buffay diner and a donation toward a gift.

If you plan to atend please let me no by the end of this week try to get you're check to me by Oct 10

Exercise 3.12

The writer of this next form letter appears to have no knowledge of standard styles of letter layout. Rewrite the letter, adjusting and correcting irregularities.

Centerton High School

100 School Street Centerton, Manitoba   R3A 0J5

January 14, 2011

Dear Classmate,

Remember when the Centerton football team beat City Vocational 7–6 for the County Championship in '99? Or when the Math Club went all the way to the finals in province-wide competition? Or when Mr. Fisk lost his eyeglasses and accidentally went into the women's lavatory at the highway rest area during the class trip? It's hard to believe, but this spring will mark the 10th anniversary of our graduation from good old Centerton High! To celebrate this landmark, a Class of '01 committee—myself included—is working on a special reunion event starting at 6:00 p.m. on Saturday, May 10, at the Legion on Main Street. Husbands, wives, and "dates" are of course welcome in addition to the grads. Cost is $70 per person, which includes buffet dinner, cash bar, reunion T-shirt and a DJ playing all our favourite songs from the good old days. Mr. Fisk and many of our other teachers—some now retired—are also being invited to attend (free of charge). Please try to make it—the reunion won't be the same without you. You can complete the enclosed preregistration form indicating your intention to attend and your T-shirt size. We'd also like payment (or at least a $30/person deposit) at this time. Hope to see you at the reunion!

Yours truly, *Jane Hermanski (Class of '01),* CHS Guidance Counselor

Exercise 3.13
The writer of the next letter has adopted a highly artificial and self-important style. Rewrite the letter to convey the message in "plain English."

MINISTRY OF COMMUNITY AND SOCIAL SERVICES

Queen's Park, Toronto, ON M5G 4C2

November 9, 2012

Ms. Sally Cramdon
359 Roberts Road
Toronto, ON M3C 7F3

Dear Ms. Cramdon:

We are in receipt of your pay stubs and your letter of 5 November 2012 and have ascertained a determination re: your application for social assistance.

Enclosed please find photocopy of social assistance guideline sheet prepared by this office on above date, counterindicating eligibility at this point in time. Per provincial eligibility stipulations, it is our judgment that your level of fiscal solvency exceeds permissible criteria for a household the size of your own (four persons).

In the subsequent event that your remuneration should decrease, and remain at the decreased level for a period of thirty (30) calendar days or more, please do not hesitate to petition this office for a reassessment of your eligibility status at that juncture.

Very truly yours,

William Hanlon

William Hanlon
Casework Aide

Exercise 3.14

The writer of the following letter has committed a great many fundamental blunders, typos, and mechanical errors. Rewrite the letter, fixing all problems.

20/20 Optical Supply, Inc.

North Side Plaza Fredericton, NB E3C 5G7

August 11, 2011

Service Manger
Fredericton Plumbing
23 Reynolds street
Fredericton, Nb E3A-7D3

Dear Fredericton Plumbing;

Last week your worker's installed a new 50-gallon hot water heater in the basement of are North Side Plazza retail store, now the heater is leaking all over the floor.

Every time I call your phone number I get a recording thet say's you will return my call but you never do. As this has been going on for more than a weak I must ensist that you either call imediatley or send a service person.

I'm getting tried of moping up water!!!

Please see to this at your very earlyest convience!

Your's truely

Robert Creech

Robert Creech
Store Manger

Summaries

LEARNING OBJECTIVE

When you complete this chapter, you'll be able to write clear, concise, and complete summaries that convey the content and emphasis of the original sources.

IN THE BROADEST SENSE, *ALL* WRITING is a form of summary. Whenever we put words on paper or computer screen, we condense ideas and information to make them coherent to the reader. Ordinarily, however, the term *summary* refers to a brief statement of the essential content of something heard, seen, or read. For any kind of summary, the writer reduces a body of material to its bare essentials. Creating a summary is, therefore, an exercise in *compression,* requiring logical organization, clear and concrete terminology, and sensitivity to the reader's needs. By that definition, a summary is the same as any other kind of workplace communication. Summary writing, however, demands an especially keen sense of not only what to include but also of what to *leave out.* The goal is to highlight the key points and not burden the reader with unnecessary details. In the workplace context, the most common summary application is in the abstracts and executive summaries that accompany long reports. This chapter explores the main principles governing the writing of summaries, a valuable skill in many work settings.

TYPES OF SUMMARIES: DESCRIPTIVE, INFORMATIVE, AND EVALUATIVE

In general, summaries can be classified into three categories: descriptive, informative, and evaluative.

A **descriptive summary** states what the original document is about but does not convey any of the document's specific information. It is much like a table of contents in paragraph form. Its main purpose is to help a reader determine whether the document summarized is of any potential use in a given situation. For example, a pamphlet providing descriptive summaries of government publications on workplace safety may be quite helpful to a personnel director wishing to educate employees about a particular job-related hazard. Similarly, a purchasing agent might consult descriptive summaries to determine the potential relevance of outside studies on needed equipment or supplies. A descriptive summary might look something like this:

> This report discusses a series of tests conducted on industrial-strength coil springs at the TopTech Laboratories in Brampton, Ontario, in January 2010. Three kinds of springs were evaluated for flexibility, durability, and heat resistance to determine their relative suitability for several specific manufacturing applications at Northton Industries.

After reading this summary, someone seeking to become better informed about the broad topic of coil springs might decide to read the report.

An **informative summary,** on the other hand, goes considerably further and presents the document's content, although in greatly compressed form. A good informative summary that includes the document's conclusions and recommendations (if any) can actually enable a busy reader to *skip* the original altogether. Here is an informative version of the previous descriptive summary:

> This report discusses a series of tests conducted on industrial-strength coil springs at the TopTech Laboratories in Brampton, Ontario, in January 2010. Three kinds of springs—all manufactured by the Mathers Spring Co. of Cambridge, Ontario—were tested: serial numbers 423, 424, and 425. The springs were evaluated for flexibility, durability, and heat resistance to determine their relative suitability for several specific manufacturing applications at Northton Industries. In 15 tests using a Flexor Meter, #423 was found to be the most flexible, followed by #425 and #424, respectively. In 15 tests using a Duro Meter, #425 proved the most durable, followed by #423 and #424, respectively. In 15 tests using a Thermal Chamber, #423 was the most heat resistant, followed by #424 and #425, respectively. Although #423 compiled the best overall performance rating, #425 is the preferred choice because the applications in question require considerable durability and involve relatively few high-temperature operations.

The **evaluative summary** is even more fully developed and includes the writer's personal assessment of the original document. The following is an evaluative version of the same summary. Notice that the writer inserts subjective value judgments throughout.

> This rather poorly written and finally unreliable report discusses a series of flawed experiments conducted on industrial-strength coil springs at the TopTech Laboratories in Brampton, Ontario, in January 2010. Three kinds of springs—all manufactured by the Mathers Spring Co. of Cambridge, Ontario—were tested: serial numbers 423, 424, and 425. The springs were evaluated for flexibility, durability, and heat resistance to determine their relative suitability for several specific manufacturing applications at Northton Industries. In 15 tests using the notoriously unreliable Flexor Meter, #423 was rated the most flexible, followed by #425 and #424, respectively. In 15 tests using the equally outdated Duro Meter, #425 scored highest, followed by #423 and #424, respectively. In 15 tests using a state-of-the-art Thermal Chamber, #423 was found to be the most heat resistant, followed by #424 and #425, respectively. Although #423 compiled the best overall performance rating, the report recommends #425 on the grounds that the specific applications in question require considerable durability and involve relatively few high-temperature operations. However, these conclusions are questionable at best. TopTech Laboratories has since shut down after revelations of improper procedures. Two of the three test sequences involved obsolete instruments, and #425 proved markedly inferior to #423 and #424 in the only test sequence that can be considered reliable.

Of the three categories, the informative summary is by far the most common. As in a *Reader's Digest* condensed version of a longer original article, the purpose of an informative summary is to convey the main ideas of the original in shorter form. To make an informative summary concrete and to-the-point rather than vague and rambling, be sure to include hard data—such as names, dates, and statistics—as well as the original document's conclusions and recommendations, if any. Sometimes including a good, well-focused quotation from the original can also be very helpful to the reader. Avoid lengthy examples and sidetracks, however, because a summary must always be *brief*—usually no more than a quarter of the original document's length.

❃   In addition, a summary should retain the *emphasis* of the original. For example, a relatively minor point in the source should not take on disproportionate significance in the summary (and perhaps should be omitted altogether). However, crucial information in the original should be equally prominent in the summary, and all information in the summary should spring directly from something in the source. Unless the summary's purpose is to evaluate, no new or additional information should appear, nor should personal opinion or comments be included.

For clarity, all workplace writing should be worded in the simplest possible terms. This is especially important in a summary, which is meant to stand alone. If the reader must go back to the original to understand, the summary is a failure. Therefore, the summary should be coherently organized and written in complete sentences with unmistakably clear meaning. As with other types of work-related documents, active verbs are best. They are especially helpful in a summary because they enable you to express ideas in fewer words than passive constructions do.

Depending on its nature, a summary that accompanies a long report is called an abstract or executive summary. If the summary is intended simply to provide a general overview of the report, it appears near the beginning of the report and is called an abstract (for an example of an abstract, see Figure 10.3). If the summary is intended to assist management in making decisions without having to read the report it precedes, it is called an executive summary.

Summarizing Print Sources

To summarize information that already exists in a written document, follow these simple steps:

1. Read the entire document straight through to get a general sense of its content. Pay particular attention to the introduction and the conclusion.

2. Watch for context clues (title, subheadings, visuals, boldface print, etc.) to ensure that you have an accurate understanding of the document.

3. Go back and underline or highlight the most important sentences in each paragraph. Write down all those sentences.

4. Now edit the sentences you selected, compressing, combining, and streamlining. When producing a summary of something you've written yourself, it's permissable to *abridge* the material, retaining some of the original wording. This is strictly prohibited, however, when summarizing someone else's work. Instead, you must rephrase the content in your own words. Otherwise, you're guilty of *plagiarism*–a serious offense for which you can incur severe penalties. This issue is discussed at greater length in Chapter 10.

5. Reread your summary to check that it flows smoothly. Insert transitions—such as *therefore*, *however*, and *nevertheless*—where necessary to eliminate any abrupt jump from one idea to another.

6. Include concrete facts, such as names, dates, statistics, conclusions, and recommendations. This is especially important in a summary, which is typically written as one long paragraph incorporating many ideas.

7. Correct all typos and mechanical errors in spelling, capitalization, punctuation, and grammar.

Figures 4.1 through 4.7 depict the major steps in the creation of an effective summary from an existing text, in this case a newspaper article about Canadian inventors and their inventions. Figures 4.8 and 4.9 show an example of how that summary might be submitted as an assignment in memo report format.

Summarizing Nonprint Sources

To summarize a speech, briefing, broadcast, or other oral presentation for which no transcript exists, you must rely on your own notes. Therefore, you should develop some sort of personal system of shortcuts, incorporating abbreviations, symbols, and other notations, to enable you to take notes quickly without missing anything important. Figure 4.10 lists 20 such shortcuts. You will likely develop others of your own. This strategy is no help, however, if you have to think about it. To serve its purpose, your shortcuts have to become instinctive. Furthermore, you must be able to translate your shortcuts back into regular English as you review your notes. Like anything, this process becomes easier with practice.

Any words, even those spoken, can be summarized for workplace purposes.

Figure 4.1 Article with Most Important Sentences Underlined, Page 1

A BRIEF HISTORY OF CANADIAN INVENTION

*What Have We Humble Canadians Invented That
Is of Any Real Significance in Today's World?*

The answer, of course, is that <u>we have invented a great deal</u>. There is an element of truth to the popular image of Canadians as "hewers of wood and drawers of water"—<u>our nation and our economy have truly been built around the strength of our natural resources. But we are also a nation of inventors</u>.

Entire books have been written about Canadian inventions. <u>Well over one million patents have been registered in Canada</u>. In fact, <u>the one millionth Canadian patent was delivered in 1976, to James Guillet, a Toronto chemistry professor, and Dr. Harvey Troth, a British researcher, for their discovery of a new plastic that turns to dust when continually exposed to sunlight.</u>

Where else to start but <u>the telephone</u>—an invention that happens to be claimed by both Canada and the United States.

Pick up an American encyclopaedia and you're likely to find a reference to <u>Alexander Graham Bell</u>, the "American" inventor. But Bell was actually <u>born in Scotland, emigrated to Canada</u> as a young man to escape a tuberculosis epidemic, and <u>did much of his most creative work in Brantford, Ontario, where he invented the telephone in 1876.</u>

<u>Another telecommunications blockbuster is radio.</u> In his book *Inventing Canada: One Hundred Years of Innovation*, Ottawa inventor and author Roy Mayer writes that <u>Canadian Reginald Fessenden, and not Guglielmo Marconi, was the real "Father of Radio."</u> While Marconi sent a wireless telegraph signal one-way across the Atlantic in 1895, <u>Fessenden was the first to achieve two-way voice transmission by radio.</u> He also made the <u>first public broadcast of music and voice on Christmas Eve in 1906.</u> When he died in 1932, Reginald Fessenden had 500 patents to his name.

Some Canadian inventions stand as living proof of the adage that "necessity is the mother of invention." The <u>snowmobile</u>, another of Canada's best-known inventions, also falls into this category. It is also an example of a <u>discovery that led to the creation of a Canadian-owned international manufacturing conglomerate—the Bombardier company.</u>

It was another 23 years before Bombardier perfected a machine designed to carry a single traveller. <u>The machine was called the Ski-Dog, but a typographical error in the literature changed the name to Ski-Doo.</u> Although numerous manufacturers have entered the business with dozens of models over the past 50 years, to many people the term <u>"ski-doo" continues to be synonymous with snowmobile.</u>

Some other Canadian inventions in the field of transportation are also in use around the world. <u>In 1854, Samuel McKeen of Nova Scotia designed an early version of the odometer,</u> a contraption that was <u>attached to the side of a carriage</u> to strike off the miles with the turning of the wheels.

<u>Canadian technology is now playing a crucial role in</u> a new travel frontier—<u>space</u>. The <u>Canadarm was developed by an industry team</u> in Canada, <u>initially under the direction of the National Research Council and under the Canadian Space Agency.</u>

Another legendary Canadian inventor was <u>Thomas Ahearn of Ottawa.</u> He <u>brought the first electric street cars to this city in the early 1890s</u>

Figure 4.2   Article with Most Important Sentences Underlined, Page 2

and went on to patent numerous other inventions, including the electric oven, an electric heater and sound machinery.

Canadians are also credited with inventing the bush plane and, later, the first true short take-off and landing aircraft—the famous deHavilland Beaver.

Abraham Gesner of Halifax was also a leading Canadian inventor in the last century. He developed kerosene oil in the mid-1800s and set up a plant to manufacture it on Long Island. In no time, kerosene was the standard lighting fuel in North American homes.

Canadian researchers and inventors have made significant contributions to the field of medicine. Sir Frederick Banting and Charles Best were key players in a research team that in 1921 made one of the major medical discoveries of this century—insulin—a lifesaving therapy for thousands upon thousands [of] sufferers of diabetes.

Canadians are probably less aware that one of their countrymen invented the first heart pacemaker. John Hopps was born in Winnipeg, trained as an electrical engineer at the University of Manitoba and joined the National Research Council in 1941, at 21 years of age. In 1949 he was seconded from the NRC to the University of Toronto to conduct research on hypothermia. While using radio-frequency heating to restore body temperature, he made an unexpected discovery: if a heart stopped beating due to cooling, it could be started again by artificial stimulation using mechanical or electric means. In 1950, Hopps returned to the NRC and built the first pacemaker—a device that initially was far too large to be implanted in humans. Over the next few years the technology was dramatically reduced in size and improved operationally, and the first pacemaker was implanted in a human body in 1958. Twenty-seven years later, Dr. Hopps himself was fitted with a pacemaker to regulate his heartbeat.

Sometimes an invention can be tied directly to a catastrophic event. After the Titanic sank in 1912, Reginald Fessenden, who as mentioned earlier invented radio and television, developed radio sonar to prevent similar accidents in the future.

Not surprisingly, one of the most catastrophic events of this century—the Second World War—triggered a huge wave of government and industry spending on research and innovation. Many of the technologies developed specifically to support the war effort were later extended to the civilian world and are now part of our every day lives.

For example, Canadian research before and during the war years helped significantly in such technological breakthroughs as radar and air navigation. In 1940, Wilbur Franks and several of his colleagues at the University of Toronto invented the world's first anti-gravity suit, which allowed pilots to carry out high-speed manoeuvres without losing consciousness.

The paint roller was invented by Norman Breakey of Toronto in 1940. It hasn't saved lives or opened new frontiers of travel or communication—but what would life be like without it?

The list of Canadian inventions goes on and on. Three Canadians—Grahame Ferguson, Roman Kroiter and Robert Kerr—invented the IMAX motion pictures for the Canadian pavilion at Expo 1970.

Canadians are also credited with inventing canola oil, the walkie talkie, 3-D vision technology, the electronic flight simulator, the geostationary communications satellite, and pablum, to name but a few.

Henry Woodward of Toronto along with Matthew Evans patented the light bulb in 1875. Unfortunately, the two entrepreneurs could not raise the financing to commercialize their invention. An enterprising American by the name of Thomas Edison, who had been working on the same idea, bought the rights to their patent. Capital

Figure 4.3 Article with Most Important Sentences Underlined, Page 3

was not a problem for Edison: he had the backing of a syndicate of industrial interests with $50,000 to invest—a sizeable sum at the time. Edison successfully demonstrated the light bulb in 1879 and, as they say, the rest is history.

In the 1970s, scientists Nestor Burtnyk and Marcelli Wein developed key frame animation (the algorithm for computer animation), which eliminates the need for the artist to draw each and every frame. An animator simply designates a beginning and end point in movement, and computerized logic fills in the intermediate steps. This technology revolutionized the animation industry worldwide and earned the inventors an Academy Award in 1997. It also led to the development of a multi-million dollar Canadian animation industry. By the mid-1980s, three of the world's five major computer animation companies were Canadian. But today, the three companies—Alias, SoftImage and Vertigo—although still located in Canada, are American-owned.

Around the same time, another Nova Scotian, John Patch, was testing the marine propeller, which amazed people for its ability to literally leave other boats in its wake.

The path the inventor or innovator has to walk is not easy. Not everyone or even every company is willing to go through what is called here "the dark night of the innovator."

If the past 100 years have seen us move forward in leaps and bounds, imagine what the 21st century offers. So, who is to know when that next great Canadian invention will hit the streets, or where it will come from? One thing we do know for certain is that scientific and technological knowledge will drive the global economy in the new century, and that means Canadians need to continue to invest in ideas.

(From Carty, A.J. "A Brief History of Canadian Invention: What Have We Humble Canadians Invented that Is of Any Real Significance in Today's World?" Excerpted from a speech by Dr. A.J. Carty, then president of the National Research Council at the annual meeting of Canadian Science Writers in Ottawa on 28 May 1999 and reprinted in *The Hamilton Spectator,* 28 February 2007: IN13. Print. Courtesy of Dr. A. J. Carty.)

Figure 4.4   Compilation of Article's Most Important Sentences, Page 1

. . .

. . . we have invented a great deal.

. . . our nation and our economy have truly been built around the strength of our natural resources. But we are also a nation of inventors.

Well over one million patents have been registered in Canada.

. . . the one millionth Canadian patent was delivered in 1976, to James Guillet, a Toronto chemistry professor, and Dr. Harvey Troth, a British researcher, for their discovery of a new plastic that turns to dust when continually exposed to sunlight.

. . . . the telephone

. . . Alexander Graham Bell . . . born in Scotland, emigrated to Canada . . . did much of his most creative work in Brantford, Ontario, where he invented the telephone in 1876.

Another telecommunications blockbuster is radio.

. . . Canadian Reginald Fessenden . . . was the real "Father of Radio." . . . Fessenden was the first to achieve two-way voice transmission by radio. . . . first public broadcast of music and voice on Christmas Eve in 1906.

. . . snowmobile . . . discovery that led to the creation of a Canadian-owned international manufacturing conglomerate—the Bombardier company.

The machine was called the Ski- Dog, but a typographical error in the literature changed the name to Ski-Doo. . . . "ski-doo" continues to be synonymous with snowmobile.

In 1854, Samuel McKeen of Nova Scotia designed an early version of the odometer . . . attached to the side of a carriage . . .

Canadian technology is now playing a crucial role in . . . space. The Canadarm was developed by an industry team . . . initially under the direction of the National Research Council and under the Canadian Space Agency.

. . . Thomas Ahearn of Ottawa . . . the first electric street cars to this city in the early 1890s and went on to patent numerous other inventions, including the electric oven, an electric heater and sound machinery.

. . . Canadians . . . credited with inventing the bush plane . . . and the first true short take-off and landing aircraft . . . deHavilland Beaver.

Abraham Gesner of Halifax . . . developed kerosene oil in the mid-1800s. . . . kerosene was the standard lighting fuel in North American homes.

. . . significant contributions to the field of medicine. Sir Frederick Banting and Charles Best . . . key players in a research team . . . 1921 . . . —insulin—a life-saving therapy . . . sufferers of diabetes.

Figure 4.5   Compilation of Article's Most Important Sentences, Page 2

. . . one of their countrymen invented the first heart pacemaker. John Hopps was born in Winnipeg . . . the University of Toronto to conduct research on hypothermia . . . using radio-frequency heating to restore body temperature, he made an unexpected discovery: if a heart stopped beating due to cooling, it could be started again by artificial stimulation. . . . In 1950, Hopps . . . built the first pacemaker . . . the first pacemaker was implanted in a human body in 1958. Twenty-seven years later, Dr. Hopps himself was fitted with a pacemaker to regulate his heartbeat.

After the Titanic sank in 1912, Reginald Fessenden . . . developed radio sonar to prevent similar accidents in the future.

. . . the Second World War . . . many of the technologies developed specifically to support the war effort were later extended to the civilian world and are now part of our every day lives.

. . . helped . . . such technological breakthroughs as radar and air navigation. In 1940, Wilbur Franks and several of his colleagues at the University of Toronto invented the world's first anti-gravity suit . . . allowed pilots to carry out high-speed manoeuvres without losing consciousness.

. . . paint roller . . . invented by Norman Breakey of Toronto in 1940.

. . . list . . . goes on and on. Grahame Ferguson, Roman Kroiter and Robert Kerr invented the IMAX motion pictures . . . 1970.

. . . inventing canola oil, the walkie talkie, 3-D vision technology, the electronic flight simulator, the geostationary communications satellite, and pablum . . .

Henry Woodward of Toronto . . . Matthew Evans patented the light bulb in 1875. . . Thomas Edison . . . bought the rights to their patent.

. . . 1970s, scientists Nestor Burtnyk and Marcelli Wein developed key frame animation . . . eliminates the need for the artist to draw each and every frame. An animator simply designates a beginning and end point in movement, and computerized logic fills in the intermediate steps. This technology revolution-ized the animation industry worldwide . . . earned the inventors an Academy Award in 1997 . . . also led to the development of a multi-million dollar Canadian animation industry.

. . . same time . . . Nova Scotian, John Patch, was testing the marine propeller . . . ability to literally leave other boats in its wake.

If the past 100 years have seen us move forward in leaps and bounds, im-agine what the 21st century offers . . . scientific and technological knowledge will drive the global economy in the new century, and that means Canadians need to continue to invest in ideas.

Figure 4.6   Article's Most Important Sentences, Edited and Revised, Page 1

Canada has many natural resources, which contribute to the growth of the country, but Canadians also invent many things.

In 1976, the one millionth patent was given to James Guillet of Toronto and his British partner, Dr. Harvey Troth. The patent was issued for a disintegrating plastic.

The first Canadian patent was granted for the invention of the telephone, which was invented by Alexander Graham Bell. Bell, born in Scotland, immigrated to Brantford, Ontario, where he did much of his work.

Two-way radio transmission was also a Canadian invention. In 1906, on Christmas Eve, Reginald Fessenden, the "Father of Radio," broadcast both music and words publicly for the first time.

Bombardier invented the snowmobile. It was originally called the Ski-Dog, but, because of a typing error, people now know the Bombardier machine as the Ski-Doo. This is also the name used by many people when they refer to snowmobiles.

Nova Scotian Samuel McKeen invented the odometer in 1854. It was attached to the wheels of carriages to measure distance travelled.

Canadian inventions are also in space. The National Research Council, along with the Canadian Space Agency, led the team that created the Canadarm.

In the 1890s, Ottawa had the first electric street cars. The inventor, Thomas Ahearn, also obtained patents for various other items, such as the electric stove and an electric heater.

The deHavilland Beaver and the bush plane are also Canadian inventions.

Kerosene oil, which was used across North America for lights, was created by Haligonian Abraham Gesner. He developed this fuel in the 1800s.

In 1921, Sir Frederick Banting and Charles Best, along with researchers, discovered insulin, which is used for patients with diabetes.

While studying hypothermia at the University of Toronto, John Hopps found that hearts could be restarted and thus, he created the first pacemaker in 1950. In 1958, the first pacemaker was used on a human. Even Dr. Hopps received a pacemaker more than 20 years later.

Reginald Fessenden, the "Father of Radio" mentioned above, was responsible for the invention of radio sonar. He began work after the Titanic sank so that accidents like that would not happen again.

Because of World War II, Canadians invented new technology, such as radar and air navigation, that was used primarily for the war. However, after the

Figure 4.7 Article's Most Important Sentences, Edited and Revised, Page 2

war ended, much of that technology became part of non-military life. Even an anti-gravity suit was created by a team of researchers, including Wilbur Franks. They developed this suit for pilots in 1940 so that high-speed manoeuvres could be performed and the pilots would remain conscious.

Norman Breakey is responsible for the paint roller. He developed this in Toronto in 1940.

In 1970, Grahame Ferguson, Roman Kroiter and Robert Kerr unveiled the first IMAX motion pictures. The Canadian pavilion at Expo was the spot for this first.

The list of inventions continues with " . . . canola oil, the walkie talkie, 3-D vision technology, the electronic flight simulator, the geostationary communications satellite, and pablum."

Even though many people associate the light bulb with Thomas Edison, he was the one who bought the patent. Torontonians Henry Woodward and Matthew Evans, in 1875, were the actual inventors.

Canadian scientists Nestor Burtnyk and Marcelli Wein won the Academy Award for their invention, key frame animation, which they created in the 1970s. The technology allows the computer to fill in the animation between the beginning and end points, which are created by the animator. Hand drawing was no longer needed for each frame, and this led to Canada's entry into the animation industry.

In the 1970s, a very fast marine propeller was developed by John Patch of Nova Scotia.

Technology is expected to dominate economies around the world. Canadians have invented much that has driven the world in the past and Canada must keep doing this.

Figure 4.8 Summary (Memo Report Format), Page 1

George Brown College

MEMORANDUM

DATE: March 24, 2011

TO: Dr. Mary Ann Evans, Professor,
            Communications Department

FROM: George Eliot

SUBJECT: Summary of Article about Canadian Inventors and
            Inventions

The article "A Brief History of Canadian Invention: What Have We
Humble Canadians Invented That Is of Any Real Significance in Today's
World?" from *The Spectator*, retrieved August 26, 2009, discusses
the importance of Canadians in the world of inventing. ("A Brief History"
IN13.)

Canadians have obtained over 1 000 000 patents. For developing a disintegrating plastic, James Guillet of Toronto and his partner were given
the one-millionth in 1976. One hundred years before this, the first
Canadian patent was granted in 1876 to Alexander Graham Bell for the
invention of the telephone. Bell, while born in Scotland, invented the
telephone in Brantford, Ontario. In addition to the telephone, two-way
radio transmission is a Canadian invention. In 1906, Reginald Fessenden,
known as the "Father of Radio," broadcast publicly for the first time.

Transportation has also been influenced by Canadians. Bombardier
invented the "Ski-Doo." Nova Scotian Samuel McKeen invented the
odometer in 1854, which was attached to carriage wheels. The
Canadarm was invented to be used in space. In the 1890s, Ottawa had
the first electric street car, thanks to prolific inventor Thomas Ahearn,
who was also responsible for other items, such as the electric stove and
an electric heater. Bush planes and the deHavilland Beaver plane are
also attributed to Canadians.

Other Canadian inventions have improved lifestyles. Kerosene oil, which
was used across North America for lighting, was created by Haligonian

Figure 4.9   Summary (Memo Report Format), Page 2

Abraham Gesner. He created this fuel in the 1800s. Banting, Best, and other researchers discovered insulin in 1921. Today, insulin is regularly used to regulate diabetes. After studying hypothermia at the University of Toronto, John Hopps created the first pacemaker in 1950. In 1958, Hopps received his own pacemaker. The "Father of Radio," Reginald Fessenden, invented radio sonar after the Titanic sank. He was motivated by the wish to prevent similar accidents in the future.

Canadians have contributed to military life as well as civilian life. Radar, air navigation, and anti-gravity suits were invented by Canadians around World War II. After the war, this technology began to be used by civilians. The electronic flight simulator and the geostationary communications satellite are attributed to Canadians, too.

Other inventions may not have helped national security but are useful nonetheless. In 1940, Norman Breakley invented the paint roller. In 1970, the first IMAX motion picture played at Expo 1970. Grahame Ferguson, Roman Kroiter, and Robert Kerr are responsible for this invention. Canadians also invented canola oil, pablum, the walkie-talkie, and 3-D technology.

Many people believe that Thomas Edison invented the light bulb, but he only bought the patent from Torontonians Henry Woodward and Matthew Evans. The Academy Awards recognized Canadian scientists Nestor Burtnyk and Marcelli Wein for their invention of key frame animation, which allowed animators to use the computer to complete animation. All that was required for this technology was the input of beginning and end points, and the computer completed the rest. Key frame animation led to Canada's entry into the animation industry. And finally, in the 1970s, a very fast marine propeller was developed by John Patch of Nova Scotia.

Technology is expected to dominate economies around the world in the current century. Canadians have invented much that has driven the world in the past and Canada must continue encouraging inventive minds.

Figure 4.10 Note-Taking Shortcuts

Notation	Meaning	Explanation
=	Is	Symbol instead of word
#	Number	Symbol instead of word
&	And	Symbol instead of word
∴	Therefore	Symbol instead of word
2	To, too, two	Numeral instead of word
4	For, four	Numeral instead of word
B	Be, bee	Letter instead of word
C	See, sea	Letter instead of word
U	You	Letter instead of word
Y	Why	Letter instead of word
R	Are	Letter instead of word
R̸	Are not	Slash to express negation
w.	With	Abbreviation
w̸.	Without	Slash to express negation
bcs	Because	Elimination of vowels
2B	To be	Blend of numeral and letter
B4	Before	Blend of letter and numeral
rathan	Rather than	Blend of two words
rite	Right	Phonetic spelling
turn handle	Turn the handle	Elimination of obvious

To facilitate summarizing from nonprint sources, you can use a hand-held micro-cassette recorder or download the material to your computer via digital recorder. This will allow you to listen more attentively afterward, at your own pace, under more conducive conditions. But this is a good strategy only if there's no rush or if an exact quotation is crucial. And even if recording, it's still important to take good notes–both to maximize understanding through attentive listening and to guard against mechanical failure. Of course, your notes should always highlight the most important points so that you can review them later. But searching for those sections on the tape or in audio files can be very time-consuming unless your notes provide orientation. Helpfully, the better cassette recorders are equipped with a counter similar to an automobile's mileage odometer. You can save yourself a lot of frustration by including counter numbers in your notes. If your notes indicate, for example, that Point A was discussed when the counter was at 075, Point B was discussed at 190, and Point C at 250, locating the desired sections of the tape will now be much easier. You can achieve an even higher level of efficiency by using a digital recorder. Even the least expensive ones are available with DSS Player Pro software, which helps you manage and locate recorded files. Higher-end models enable you to navigate through the menu to assign contact points and then easily find and make selections. Some even use voice activation to access specific texts.

✓ Checklist   Evaluating a Summary

A good summary

____ is no more than 25 percent as long as the original;

____ accurately reports the main points of the original;

____ includes no minor or unnecessary details;

____ includes nothing extraneous to the original;

____ preserves the proportion and emphasis of the original;

____ is well organized, providing transitions to smooth the jumps between ideas;

____ maintains an objective tone;

____ uses clear, simple language;

____ contains no typos or mechanical errors in spelling, capitalization, punctuation, or grammar.

Exercises

Exercise 4.1

Here are three summaries of the same article, Joseph Hall's "Butterfly Antennae Like GPS, Study Finds" in the *Toronto Star* (see next page). Identify each of the three summaries as descriptive, informative, or evaluative.

Summary A

Researcher Dr. Steven Reppert has published a new study that shows the monarch butterflies use their antennae to help them find their way. Previously, researchers believed that the butterflies used part of their brain for migration purposes and that the antennae were used only for smell. However, after finding information recorded 50 years ago by Canadian butterfly observer Fred Urquhart, Reppert duplicated Urquhart's findings, showing that monarchs with damaged antennae did not seem to be able to navigate properly.

Butterfly Antennae Like GPS, Study Finds
A "Huge Surprise" to Monarch Researchers

September 25, 2009

Joseph Hall, Health Reporter

Researchers showed the existence of photosensitive cells in monarch butterflies' antennae, which were long thought to provide them with their sense of smell alone. These cells appear to act like a GPS as the monarchs make their fall migration.

Researchers showed the existence of photosensitive cells in monarch butterflies' antennae, which were long thought to provide them with their sense of smell alone. These cells appear to act like a GPS as the monarchs make their fall migration.

Monarch butterflies reach out for the sun with their antennae to navigate their miraculous, pinpoint migrations to and from Mexico, a new study has discovered.

"It was a huge surprise," says Dr. Steven Reppert, a University of Massachusetts neurobiologist and senior study author, of the finding.

"We thought we had it nailed," he says of the previous theory—that the butterfly's brain provided its sense of direction.

The study appears today in the journal *Science*.

In it, researchers showed the existence of photosensitive cells in the insects' antennae, which were long thought to provide them with their sense of smell alone.

These cells, Reppert says, appear to act like a GPS as the monarchs make their fall migration.

Reppert happened on observations made 50 years ago by Canadian butterfly observer Fred Urquhart, who noted that the insects seem to lose their sense of direction when their antennae are removed.

"We thought, well, we'll try this and see, and lo and behold it's true." Scientists clipped the antennae from a number of butterflies, or painted others with black enamel, tethered them and placed them in an outdoor flight simulator.

These butterflies would still fly in a straight line, but in all kinds of different directions, Reppert says.

(From Hall, Joseph. "Butterfly Antennae Like GPS, Study Finds." *Toronto Star.* 25 September 2009. Web. October 2009. Reprinted with permission—Torstar Syndication Services.)

Summary B

This brief article discusses new research based on observations made 50 years ago by a Canadian butterfly observer. The article is too short to really be able to evaluate whether the current research is valid or not. The researcher, Dr. Steven Reppert, believed that monarch butterflies used a sensory mechanism in their brain in order to help them navigate. However, his new study, which appears in the journal *Science*, claims to prove that monarchs use their antennae for this purpose. Previously, researchers dismissed the antennae as assisting only with the sense of smell for the butterflies. When Dr. Reppert found 50-year-old observations recorded by Fred Urquhart, he decided to try manipulating the butterflies' antennae to see if the monarchs could really fly in the proper direction. While he was able to prove, in a scientific experiment, that Urquhart's observations were valid, the article does not mention whether further studies will be conducted to ensure that this study's results are accurate and not merely an anomaly.

Summary C

This article discusses the findings of a new study that demonstrate how monarch butterflies use cells in their antennae as direction finders. It further discusses the previous theories about monarch migration and how the discovery of observations made by a Canadian 50 years earlier have influenced new findings. The current study explains what happens when the monarch butterflies no longer have use of their antennae.

Exercise 4.2

Write a 100-word descriptive summary of a recent article from a reputable periodical or website in your field of study or employment. Submit the article along with the summary.

Exercise 4.3

Write a 250-word informative summary of the same article mentioned in Exercise 4.2. Submit the article along with the summary.

Exercise 4.4

Write a 300-word evaluative summary of the same article mentioned in Exercises 4.2 and 4.3. Submit the article along with the summary.

Exercise 4.5

Write a 200-word informative summary of the plot of a recent episode of your favourite television show.

Exercise 4.6

Write a 250-word informative abstract of a term paper you have completed in the past for another course. Submit the term paper along with the abstract.

Exercise 4.7

Write an informative summary of an article from a popular periodical (for example, *Maclean's, Canadian Geographic,* or *Walrus*). Make the summary no more than 20 percent as long as the article, and submit the article along with the summary.

Exercise 4.8

Summarize a lecture given by the instructor of one of your other classes. Limit the summary to roughly 500 words.

Exercise 4.9

Write a 75-word informative summary of an article from your local newspaper. Select an article that is at least 300 words in length. Submit the article along with your summary.

Exercise 4.10

Write a 50-word descriptive abstract of the sample report in Chapter 10 (pages 249–262).

mycanadiantechcommlab

Visit www.mycanadiantechcommlab.ca for everything you need to help you succeed in the job you've always wanted! Tools and resources include the following:

- Composing Space and Writer's Toolkit
- Document Makeovers
- Grammar Exercises—and much more!

Effective Visuals:

TABLES, GRAPHS, CHARTS, AND ILLUSTRATIONS

LEARNING OBJECTIVE

When you complete this chapter, you'll be able to enhance your written and oral reports with effective visual elements, such as tables, graphs, charts, and pictures.

PEOPLE OFTEN COMMUNICATE WITHOUT the benefit of written or spoken language–through gestures and facial expressions, for example, and of course by means of diagrams, pictures, and signs. Consider the familiar displays shown here:

Workplace communications make extensive use of visual aids along with text. Proposals, manuals, instructions, and reports of all kinds contain numerous illustrations to capture and hold people's attention and help convey information. To function successfully in today's increasingly sophisticated workplace, an employee must be well acquainted with these visual elements. This chapter begins with a brief overview of basic principles governing the use of visuals. It then explores the four main categories of visuals–tables, graphs, charts, and illustrations–and explains the principal features and applications of each.

PRINCIPLES OF EFFECTIVE VISUALS

Until the 1980s, inserting visuals of any kind into a document was a fairly cumbersome process. Blank space would have to be provided so that tables, graphs, and charts could be created by hand and pasted in. Then the result would be photocopied to create the finished page. Unless trained in illustration, people responsible for creating documents that required actual drawings faced a particularly challenging task. Therefore, most would purchase clip art files–collections of prepackaged illustrations suitable for a broad range of situations.

With the widespread adoption of word-processing programs, however, it was suddenly much easier to create and insert tables, graphs, and charts "on the fly," just by activating those programs' graphics capabilities. With today's software packages you can assemble data on a spreadsheet, for example, and then display it in whatever format is most suitable. For drawings and photographs, you can choose from the vast array of electronic clip art now readily available. Computer technology produces highly polished results while encouraging a great deal of experimentation with various design features. Like computerized text, graphics stored electronically have the added advantage of easy revision if your data change.

Ironically, the one potential drawback of computer-generated graphics derives from the same versatility that makes these programs so exciting to work with.

Inexperienced users can become carried away with the many options at their disposal, creating cluttered, overly elaborate visuals that confuse rather than illustrate. As with writing and page design, simpler is better. Always bear in mind that visuals should never be introduced simply for their own sake, to "decorate" a document. Theoretically, every visual should be able to stand alone, but its true purpose is to clarify the text it accompanies.

Like good writing, effective visuals are simple, clear, and easy to understand. It's also very important to choose the most appropriate *type* of visual for the task at hand. When using any kind of visual aid, however, you must observe the following fundamental rules:

- Number and title every visual in your document sequentially, with outside sources clearly identified. If the document contains only one visual, you can omit the number. Titling a visual is much like writing a subject line for a memo or email. The title should be brief, accurate, and informative. To write a good title, answer this question: in just a few words, what does this visual depict? The number, title, and source usually appear *beneath* rather than above the visual. (Tables, however, are an exception to this rule; they are often numbered and labelled *above*.)

- Any information that you provide in a visual, you must first discuss in the text. The text should refer the reader to the visual (for example, "See Figure 5"), and the visual should be positioned logically, as soon as possible *after* the reference.

- Present all visuals in an appealing manner. Each visual should be surrounded by ample white space, not crowded by the text or squeezed in between other visuals.

- Clearly label all elements of the visual and provide a "key" whenever necessary to show scale, direction, and the like. Labels must be easy to read, with their terms matching those used in the text; you cannot call something "x" in the text and label it "y" in the visual if you expect the reader to find it easily.

- When visuals accompany instructions, the point of view in the visuals must be the same as that of the reader performing the illustrated procedure. For example, an overhead view might be confusing if the reader will be approaching the task head-on.

- A visual should never omit, distort, or otherwise manipulate information to deceive or mislead the reader. Because the purpose of a visual is to reinforce the meaning of your text, any visual you include is subject to the same ethical standards of honesty and accuracy that your text must meet.

- Avoid spelling mistakes, poor grammar, inconsistent formatting, or other blunders in the labels, key, title, or other text accompanying a visual. Nothing undermines the credibility of a visual faster than a careless error.

Advertisers and marketers often use words and visuals together effectively.

TABLES

The purpose of tables is to portray statistical and other information for easy comparison. Tables consist of horizontal rows and vertical columns in which the data are presented. The top row, which holds the column headings, is called the boxhead; the leftmost column, which holds the row headings, is called the stub. This arrangement permits ready access to information that would be exceptionally difficult to sort out if it were presented only as text. A convenient example is the league standings that appear on the sports pages of most newspapers, enabling fans to determine at a glance the ranking, won/lost records, and other information pertaining to team performance.

Figure 5.1 Table Showing 2009 Regular Season Standings of American League East Baseball Teams

Team	Won	Lost	Percentage	Games Behind
New York	103	59	.636	
Boston	95	67	.586	8
Tampa Bay	84	78	.519	19
Toronto	75	87	.463	28
Baltimore	64	98	.395	39

Source: Major League Baseball. "Standings." *MLB.com*, 4 October 2009. Web. October 2009.
Major League Baseball trademarks and copyright are used with permission of Major League Baseball Properties, Inc., and MLB Advanced Media, L. P. All rights reserved.

Consider, for instance, the following paragraph, which is so full of statistical detail that it is impossible to retain it all.

> In 2009, New York led Boston in the American League East, with a record of 103 wins and 59 losses, for a .636 percentage. Boston was 8 wins behind, with 95 wins and 67 losses, for a .586 percentage. Tampa Bay was third, 19 games behind New York, with 84 wins and 78 losses, for a .519 percentage. Next was Toronto, 28 games behind, with 75 wins and 87 losses, for a .463 percentage. Baltimore was last, 39 games behind, with 64 wins and 98 losses, for a .395 percentage.

Certainly, this would be far better presented in table format, as in Figure 5.1.

Sometimes a table includes subdivisions within categories. In such cases you can use various design options to avoid confusion. In Figure 5.2, on the following two pages, for example, the main categories of specialty are written in capital letters and are in bold font. These are then separated by a horizontal line. In addition, subcategories are indented.

GRAPHS

Graphs are used to display statistical trends, changes, and comparisons. There are essentially two kinds: line graphs and bar graphs.

Line Graphs

The primary purpose of line graphs is to portray change over time. A line graph is created by plotting points along horizontal and vertical axes (the x-axis and y-axis, respectively), and then joining the points by means of straight lines. The horizontal axis identifies the categories of information that are being compared (the fixed, or independent, variables—usually, chronological intervals), whereas

Figure 5.2   Table Showing Number of Physicians by Province/Territory and Specialty, Canada, 2010

Specialty	CANADA	NL	PEI	NS	NB	QC	ON	MB	SK	AB	BC	TERR
FAMILY PHYSICIANS	*36,024*	*756*	*161*	*1,296*	*990*	*8,694*	*12,133*	*1,305*	*1,158*	*3,946*	*5,479*	*106*
General Practice[1]	**17,040**	496	91	691	507	4,458	4,663	748	802	1,757	2,787	40
Family Medicine	**18,984**	260	70	605	483	4,236	7,470	557	356	2,189	2,692	66
MEDICAL SPECIALISTS	**24,482**	*303*	*59*	*787*	*371*	*6,194*	*9,546*	*846*	*472*	*2,563*	*3,327*	*14*
Clinical Specialists	**22,891**	*281*	*55*	*737*	*343*	*5,772*	*8,999*	*792*	*433*	*2,399*	*3,066*	*14*
Anaesthesia	**2,843**	37	6	107	55	631	1066	104	82	311	443	1
Community Medicine	434	2	0	5	5	186	128	17	6	31	54	0
Critical Care Medicine	**78**	0	0	1	0	14	34	8	2	10	9	0
Dermatology	**546**	9	1	15	11	188	188	12	5	49	68	0
Diagnostic Radiology	**2,248**	38	5	87	59	535	848	64	61	249	302	0
Emergency Medicine	**613**	2	1	17	3	122	236	18	2	99	113	0
Internal Medicine	**7,506**	*86*	*17*	*234*	*103*	*2,026*	*2,992*	*237*	*146*	*804*	*856*	*5*
General Internal Medicine	**2,642**	31	12	83	30	552	1,168	104	66	272	321	3
Cardiology	**1,108**	11	1	38	18	376	415	21	23	107	98	0
Clinical Immunology/Allergy	150	1	0	4	0	56	54	8	1	10	16	0
Endocrinology/Metabolism	406	7	0	10	4	141	157	8	4	36	39	0
Gastroenterology	575	8	1	20	9	178	206	12	4	78	58	1
Geriatric Medicine	220	1	0	10	5	56	84	7	1	17	39	0
Haematology	333	6	1	9	4	80	152	11	7	24	38	1
Infectious Diseases	217	0	0	11	4	22	91	14	7	43	25	0
Medical Oncology	401	6	1	12	3	130	140	8	1	47	53	0
Nephrology	517	8	0	16	12	152	181	24	12	59	53	0
Respiratory Medicine	601	3	1	7	7	200	214	11	15	75	68	0
Rheumatology	336	4	0	14	7	83	130	9	5	36	48	0
Medical Genetics	74	1	0	3	0	21	22	5	1	12	9	0
Neurology	814	8	2	24	9	238	280	22	14	99	118	0
Nuclear Medicine	246	3	0	6	3	92	77	10	5	22	28	0

(continued on next page)

Figure 5.2   (Continued)

Specialty	CANADA	NL	PEI	NS	NB	QC	ON	MB	SK	AB	BC	TERR
Occupational Medicine	53	0	0	1	0	5	26	1	1	11	8	0
Paediatrics	2,321	38	9	77	28	550	920	107	40	276	271	5
Physical Medicine/Rehabilitation	391	1	1	13	11	70	163	16	9	39	68	0
Psychiatry	4,302	50	12	138	48	1,006	1,835	160	53	338	659	3
Radiation Oncology	422	6	1	9	8	88	184	11	6	49	60	0
Laboratory Specialists	*1,591*	*22*	*4*	*50*	*28*	*422*	*547*	*54*	*39*	*164*	*261*	*0*
Anatomical Pathology	833	14	2	32	21	191	328	36	21	91	97	0
General/Clinical Pathology	285	4	2	8	3	2	112	7	9	46	92	0
Haematologic Pathology	70	0	0	4	0	7	23	3	3	7	23	0
Medical Biochemistry	89	0	0	2	1	51	17	0	2	1	15	0
Medical Microbiology	278	3	0	2	3	169	51	6	3	13	28	0
Neuropathology	36	1	0	2	0	2	16	2	1	6	6	0
SURGICAL SPECIALISTS	*8,737*	*112*	*30*	*302*	*212*	*2,249*	*3,286*	*287*	*198*	*791*	*1,256*	*14*
Cardiovascular/Thoracic Surgery	332	5	0	14	8	73	130	10	9	29	54	0
General Surgery	1,995	29	7	76	42	536	735	73	49	178	264	6
Neurosurgery	281	3	0	9	10	76	92	8	7	37	39	0
Obstetrics/Gynecology	1,799	24	8	65	40	408	738	58	48	176	230	4
Ophthalmology	1,137	13	6	47	25	306	396	32	23	98	190	1
Otolaryngology	669	10	2	25	16	205	242	22	7	46	92	2
Orthopaedic Surgery	1,367	17	4	35	35	344	506	48	28	133	216	1
Plastic Surgery	531	4	1	11	17	134	200	15	14	48	87	0
Urology	626	7	2	20	19	167	247	21	13	46	84	0
ALL SPECIALISTS	*33,219*	*415*	*89*	*1,089*	*583*	*8,443*	*12,832*	*1,133*	*670*	*3,354*	*4,583*	*28*
MEDICAL SCIENTISTS	24	0	0	1	0	7	10	1	0	1	4	0
ALL PHYSICIANS	**69,267**	**1,171**	**250**	**2,386**	**1,573**	**17,144**	**24,975**	**2,439**	**1,828**	**7,301**	**10,066**	**134**

Note: Excludes residents and physicians over age 80; includes non-clinicians licensed to practice
[1]Includes non-certified specialists

Source: Canadian Medical Association. "Number of Physicians by Province/Territory and Specialty, Canada, 2010." *CMA Master File*, January 2010. Web. July 2010. Courtesy of the Canadian Medical Association.

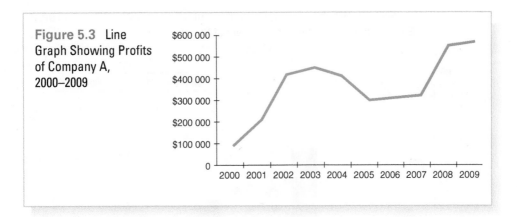

Figure 5.3 Line Graph Showing Profits of Company A, 2000–2009

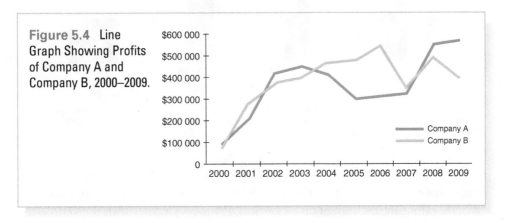

Figure 5.4 Line Graph Showing Profits of Company A and Company B, 2000–2009.

the vertical axis identifies the incremental values that are being compared (the dependent variables). Figure 5.3 is a graph of a company's annual profits during a 10-year period.

Additional lines can be added for purposes of comparison, but each line must appear different to avoid confusion. For example, one line can be solid and another broken, or lines can be drawn in contrasting colors, as in Figure 5.4, which compares the annual profits of two competing companies during a 10-year period. Notice the key, which indicates that the blue line represents Company A and the orange line represents Company B.

Bar Graphs

Another useful tool for comparing data is the bar graph. Like line graphs, bar graphs consist of horizontal and vertical axes that depict the dependent and

Figure 5.5   Vertical Bar Graph Showing Percentage of Graduates Who Pursued Further Education after Graduation, by Level of Study

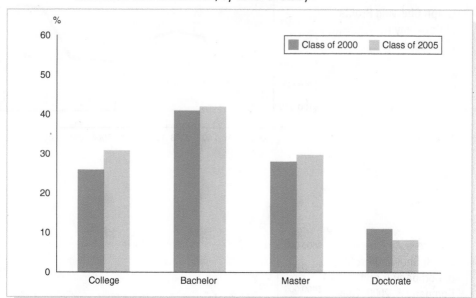

Source: Statistics Canada, "Percentage of Graduates Who Pursued Further Education after Graduation by Level of Study." *Graduating in Canada: Profile, Labour Market Outcomes and Student Debt of the Class of 2005.* 22 April 2009. Web. 25 October 2009.

independent variables. But which axis depicts which variable is determined by whether the bars are horizontal or vertical. If the bars are vertical, the vertical axis identifies the dependent variables, and the horizontal axis identifies the independent variables. Figure 5.5, for example, is a vertical bar graph that portrays the proportion of graduates working, unemployed, and out of the labour force, by level of study.

If the bars are horizontal, the arrangement is reversed, with the horizontal axis showing the dependent variables and the vertical axis showing the independent variables. A horizontal bar graph is useful for accommodating many bars and offers the added advantage of permitting the independent variables to be labelled horizontally if those labels are relatively lengthy. This feature is helpful, for example, in Figure 5.6.

To create comparisons within categories of information in a bar graph, each bar can be presented alongside an accompanying bar or two, but the additional bar(s) must be coloured or shaded differently to avoid confusion. Figure 5.7 is illustrative. Notice the key, provided to show which shade represents which block of hours.

Figure 5.6   Horizontal Bar Graph Showing Federal R&D Spending

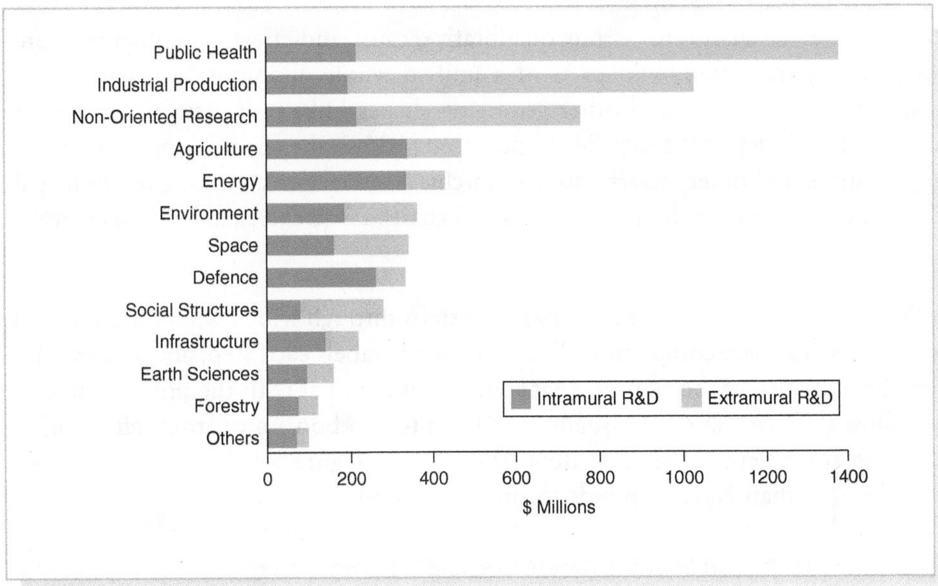

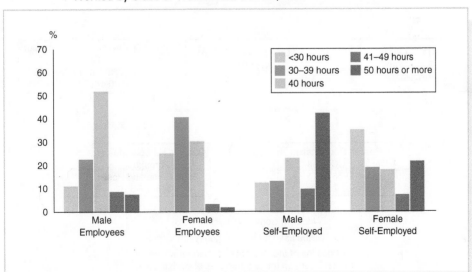

Source: Statistics Canada, "Federal R&D Spending by Socio-Economic Objective, 2006." *Science Statistics, 32*(7), November 2008. Web. 25 October 2009.

Figure 5.7   Vertical Bar Graph Showing Percentage Distribution of Usual Weekly Hours Worked by Class of Worker and Gender, 2007

Source: Statistics Canada, "Percentage Distribution of Usual Weekly Hours Worked by Class of Worker and Gender." Based on *Labour Force Survey*, April 2008. Web. 25 October 2009. Reproduced with the permission of the Minister of Public Works and Government Services Canada, 2010.

CHARTS

The purpose of a chart is to portray quantitative, cause-and-effect, and other relationships among the component parts of a unified whole. Comprising squares, rectangles, triangles, circles, and other geometric shapes linked by plain or arrowhead lines, charts can depict the steps in a production process, the chain of command in an organization, and other sequential or hierarchical interactions. Among the principal kinds of charts are flow charts, organizational charts, circle charts, and Gantt charts.

Flow Charts

A flow chart is typically used to portray the steps through which work (or a process) must "flow" to reach completion. The chart clearly labels each step, and arrows indicate the sequence of the steps so that someone unfamiliar with the process can easily follow it. Flow charts are usually read from top to bottom or from left to right, although some depict a circular flow. The chart in Figure 5.8, for example, shows how the Canadian Navy responds to emergencies.

Figure 5.8 Flow Chart Showing How to Respond to Emergencies

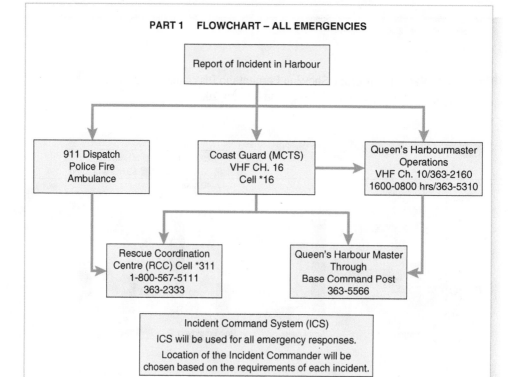

Source: Canadian Navy—MARPAC Forces Pacific Esquimaux Harbour, "Part 1: Flow Chart for All Emergencies," National Defence, n.d. Web. 25 October 2009. Reproduced with the permission of the Minister of Public Works and Government Services, 2010.

Figure 5.9 Organizational Chart Showing Canada's System of Government

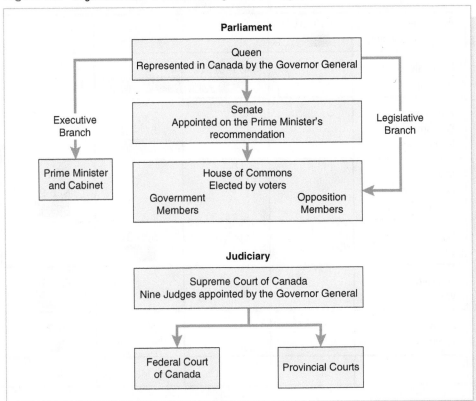

Source: Parliament of Canada. "The Institutions of Our Federal Government: Canada's System of Government" (7th ed.). n.d. Web. 25 October 2009. Reproduced with the permission of the Minister of Public Works and Government Services, 2010.

Organizational Charts

Like flow charts, organizational charts consist of labelled boxes linked by lines or arrows. Organizational charts portray chains of command within businesses, agencies, and other collective bodies, indicating who has authority over whom and suggesting the relationships among various functional areas or components within the organization. Not surprisingly, the most powerful positions are placed at the top, and the least powerful, at the bottom. Those on the same horizontal level are at approximately equal levels of responsibility. Figure 5.9, for example, shows the organization of Canada's system of government.

Gantt Charts

Named after the mechanical engineer Henry Gantt (1861–1919), who invented them, Gantt charts are essentially timeline charts that depict the schedule of necessary activities from start to finish of a project. Often used in proposals (see Chapter 8), they resemble bar graphs. The y-axis identifies the steps in the

Figure 5.10 Gantt Chart Showing Timetable for Company's Expansion

	March	April	May	June
Purchase Adjacent Building	3/1–31 ▇			
Renovate Building		4/1–5/31 ▇▇▇▇		
Purchase Equipment & Furnishings			5/1–31 ▇	
Install Equipment & Furnishings				6/1–20 ▇
Hire Additional Workers			5/1–31 ▇	
Train Additional Workers				6/1–20 ▇
Open Expansion				6/21 ▇

project, whereas the x-axis indentifies the chronological milestones. Obviously, some of the horizontal bars representing the various activities may overlap because the multiple phases of projects often do. For this reason, the beginning and end date of each bar should be specified. Figure 5.10 is a Gantt chart showing the timetable for a company's expansion.

Circle Charts

Among the most familiar of all visual devices, circle (or pie) charts are often used to show the percentage distribution of money. As such, they are helpful in analyzing relative costs and profits. Their more general application is simply to depict relationships among parts within statistical wholes. In that broader context, they facilitate such tasks as risk analysis, needs assessment, and resource allocation.

Each segment of a circle chart resembles a slice of pie and constitutes a percentage. For maximum effectiveness, the pie should include at least three but no more than seven slices. (To limit the number of slices without omitting data, several small percentages can be lumped together under the heading of "Other.") As if the pie were a clock face, the biggest slice usually begins at 12 o'clock, with the slices getting

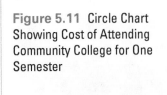

Figure 5.11 Circle Chart Showing Cost of Attending Community College for One Semester

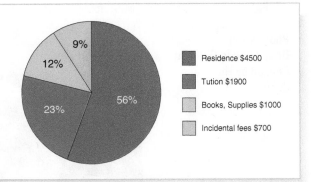

■ Residence $4500

■ Tution $1900

■ Books, Supplies $1000

■ Incidental fees $700

progressively smaller as they continue clockwise around the circle. Each slice is labelled, showing its percentage of the total. (Obviously, the slices must add up to 100 percent.) A key must be provided to identify what each slice represents. Figure 5.11 shows the costs of attending a residential community college for one semester.

ILLUSTRATIONS

Illustrations—be they photographs, drawings, or diagrams—are another highly effective form of visual aid. Each type has certain advantages. As with so many aspects of workplace communications, which type you choose depends on your purpose and on your audience.

Photographs

A photograph is an exact representation; its main virtue, therefore, is strict accuracy. Of course, Adobe Photoshop and other editing programs can be used to alter images. Nevertheless, photos are often required in certain kinds of documents, such as licences, passports, accident reports (especially for insurance purposes), and patent applications. Photos are often used in law enforcement, whether to warn the public of fugitive criminals depicted in "Most Wanted" posters or to document the scene of a crime or accident. Figure 5.12, for example, is a photograph documenting damage caused by a hurricane.

Ideally, photos should be taken by trained professionals. Even an amateur, however, can create reasonably useful photos by observing the following fundamental guidelines:

■ Use a good digital camera.

■ Ensure that the light source, whether natural (the sun) or artificial (floodlamp or other electrically generated light), is behind you; avoid shooting into the light.

■ Stand close enough to your subject to eliminate surroundings, unless they are relevant.

Figure 5.12
Photograph
Documenting Damage
Caused by Hurricane
Juan

- Try to focus on the most significant part of your subject to minimize unwanted detail. (By using Adobe Photoshop, you can crop out unwanted detail and enlarge the remaining image.)

- To provide a sense of scale in photographs of unfamiliar objects, include a familiar object within the picture. In photos of small objects, for example, a coin or paper clip works well. In photos of very large objects, a human figure is helpful.

- Hold the camera absolutely still while taking the picture. If possible, mount the camera on a tripod and use an automatic shutter release.

Drawings

The purpose of most drawings—whether freehand or computer-generated—is to create clear, realistic depictions of objects under discussion. The main advantage is that in a drawing you can easily omit unwanted detail and portray only what is most relevant (see Figure 5.13). In addition, a drawing can clarify information it depicts by simplifying, enlarging, or otherwise emphasizing key features. One obvious example of this is a type of drawing called a floor plan, which—like a map—is much clearer and more informative than an overhead photo (see Figure 5.14).

Other useful applications are the exploded view, which is often used in assembly instructions (see Figure 5.15), and the cross section, or cutaway view, which provides visual access to the interior workings of mechanisms and other objects (see Figure 5.16). Moreover, drawings can be combined with tables, graphs, and charts to create pictographs that enliven otherwise routine documents.

Figure 5.13   Technical Drawing of iPod

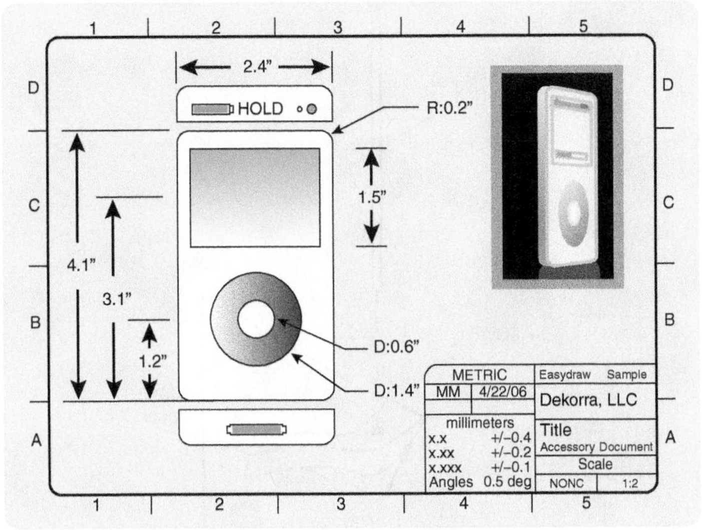

Source: Drawing courtesy of EazyDraw.

Figure 5.14   Floor Plan of Home

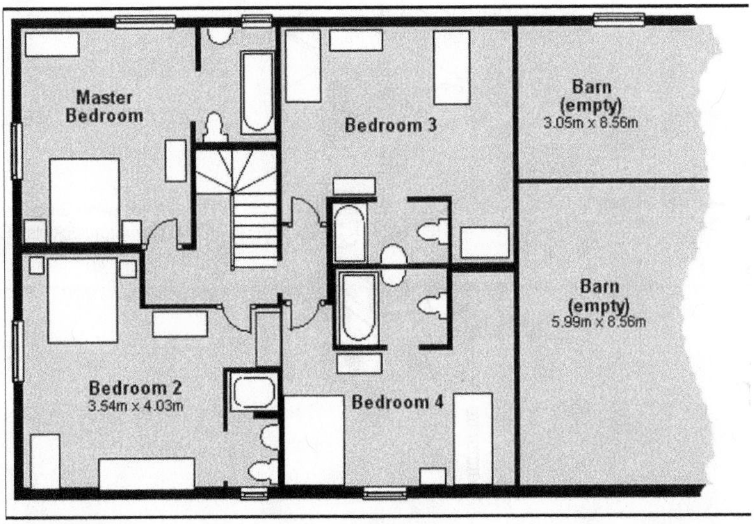

Source: Courtesy of Tina and Arthur Seymour, Gite Les Roches.

Figure 5.15   Exploded View of Kohler Faucet Assembly

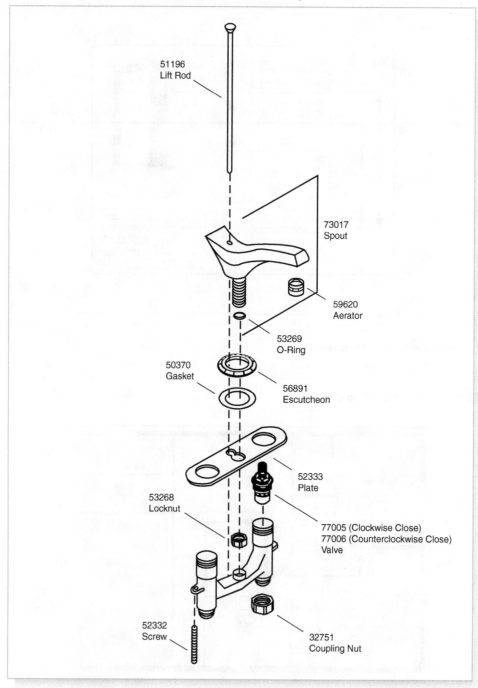

51196
Lift Rod

73017
Spout

59620
Aerator

53269
O-Ring

50370
Gasket

56891
Escutcheon

52333
Plate

53268
Locknut

77005 (Clockwise Close)
77006 (Counterclockwise Close)
Valve

52332
Screw

32751
Coupling Nut

Source: Drawing Courtesy of Kohler Co.

Figure 5.16 Cutaway View Showing Ventilation Requirements for Gas-Fired Boiler

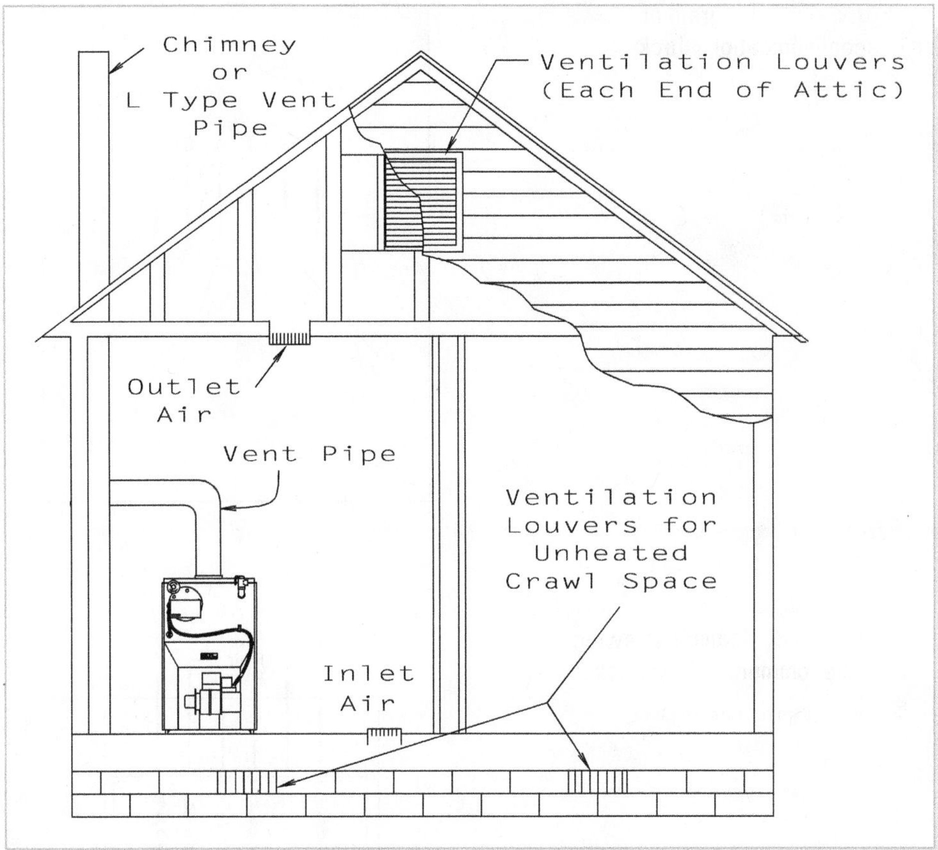

Source: Drawing courtesy of ECR International.

Diagrams

Just as a drawing can be considered a simplified photograph, a diagram can be considered a simplified drawing. Figure 5.17, for example, shows how a telecommunications jack is wired. Even though this is not what the real wiring looks like, anyone conversant with electrical symbols can read the diagram more easily than the realistic—and far more complex—drawing in Figure 5.18. Most diagrams—blueprints, for example, or engineering graphics—require advanced familiarity on the reader's part and are therefore useful only in documents intended for technicians and other specialists.

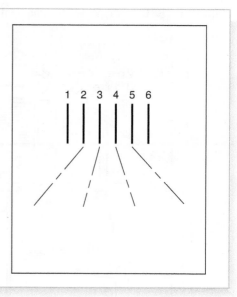

Figure 5.17 Diagram of Telecommunications Jack

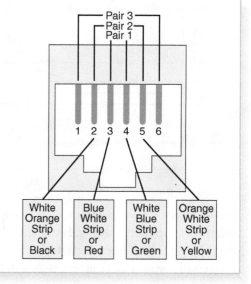

Figure 5.18 Realistic Drawing of a Telecommunications Jack

Source: Diagram courtesy of Omega Electronics, Inc.

Tech Tips

During the 1990s, whole companies sprang into existence for the sole purpose of producing electronic clip-art packages—generic graphics for specific applications. At this point, electronic clip art has almost completely replaced hard-copy drawings, partially because the electronic versions can easily be enhanced, enlarged, reduced, or otherwise modified to suit anyone's needs.

Like traditional clip-art packages, these collections sort the images into categories by topic, thereby simplifying the task of finding what you need. You still cut and paste the images into documents, but now you do it all electronically, much faster and with far less effort.

One especially useful form of clip art is the icon, a simple image with all nonessential detail removed. An icon instantaneously conveys a specific idea visually. The icons for No Smoking, Wheelchair Access, and Restrooms at the beginning of this chapter are good examples. Others would be the toolbar icons that appear on most word-processing screens: to print a document, you simply click on the printer icon; to delete a document, you drag it to the trash-can icon; and so on.

You can purchase clip art separately in disk form or as a component of word-processing software. Disks can include background designs, individual images, stock photographs, and type fonts. Packages intended for use in preparing oral or online presentations commonly feature live-action video, sound effects, and music clips. Purchasing the package entitles you to free use without paying royalty fees.

Electronic clip art is available from mail-order catalogues, local retail stores, and online sources, such as Microsoft Network and Classroom Clipart. Perhaps the most popular link to free electronic clip art, however, is Google Images. Bulletin-board systems greatly expand the range of available images by enabling users to share files.

Like all graphics, however, you should not use clip art excessively. You risk trivializing your work unless you exercise selectivity and restraint. Clip art is a highly useful option, but—as with written text—less is often more.

✓ Checklist   Evaluating a Visual

A good visual

___ is the most appropriate choice—table, graph, chart, or picture—for a particular communication;

___ is numbered and titled, with the source (if any) identified;

___ occupies the best position within the document, immediately after the text it clarifies;

___ does not appear crowded, with enough white space surrounding it to ensure effective page design;

___ includes clear, accurate labels that plainly identify all elements;

___ includes a key if necessary for further clarification;

___ maintains consistency with relevant text in terms of wording, point of view, etc.;

___ upholds strict standards of accuracy;

___ contains no typos or mechanical errors in spelling, capitalization, punctuation, or grammar.

Exercises

Exercise 5.1
Choosing from Column B, identify the most appropriate kind of visual for depicting each item in Column A.

Column A	Column B
Registration procedure at your college	Table
Interest-rate fluctuations in past 10 years	Photograph
Inner workings of a steam boiler	Line graph
Structure of the Ontario Provincial Parliament	Bar graph
Average salaries of six selected occupations	Cutaway view
Uniform numbers, names, ages, hometowns, heights/weights, and playing positions of the members of a college or university rugby team	Diagram
	Flow chart
House for sale	Exploded view
Percentage distribution of your college or university's student body by major	Organizational chart
	Pie chart
Automobile steering mechanism	
Circuitry of an electronic calculator	

Exercise 5.2
Create a table showing the current cost per litre for regular and high octane of three major brands of gasoline. Include self-serve and full-service variables, if applicable.

Exercise 5.3
Create a line graph showing your favourite professional sports team's place in the league standings for the past 10 seasons.

Exercise 5.4
Building on the information in Exercise 5.3, create a graph comparing your favourite professional sports team's place in the league standings for the past 10 seasons to that of one other team.

Exercise 5.5
Create a bar graph showing the total population of the Maritime provinces.

Exercise 5.6
Write a two- or three-page report explaining a process related to your field of study or employment. Include a flow chart depicting that process.

Exercise 5.7

Write a two- or three-page report about a club or other group to which you belong. Include a chart showing its organizational structure.

Exercise 5.8

Create a circle graph showing how you spend your money in a typical month.

Exercise 5.9

Create drawings of any three of the following: a flashlight (cutaway), an electric plug (exploded), the route from your home to your college or university (map), three different kinds of hammer, and the floor plan of a place where you have worked.

Exercise 5.10

Find and photocopy or otherwise reproduce an example of each kind of visual discussed in this chapter. Write a booklet report that incorporates the visuals and evaluates them for clarity and effectiveness.

mycanadiantechcommlab

Visit www.mycanadiantechcommlab.ca for everything you need to help you succeed in the job you've always wanted! Tools and resources include the following:

- Composing Space and Writer's Toolkit
- Document Makeovers
- Grammar Exercises—and much more!

Mechanism and Process/ Procedure Descriptions

LEARNING OBJECTIVE

When you complete this chapter, you'll be able to write clear, accurate mechanism and process/procedure descriptions.

THE SELECTIVE, WELL-ORGANIZED PRESENTATION of significant details accompanied by visuals is an important form of workplace writing called description. An effective description enables a reader to accurately envision (and thereby better understand) an inanimate object, organism, substance, physical site, or activity. Obviously, the description's basic purpose is always to inform, but its specific uses are very broad. Like all workplace communications, the description is governed by its immediate purpose and the needs of the intended reader.

Depending on circumstances, a description may be quite short—like the one- or two-sentence caption accompanying a photograph of a house in a real-estate agency's advertising pamphlet—or fully developed—like the highly detailed description a specialist would consult when preparing to service or repair the air-conditioning system in that same house. Accordingly, a description can stand alone or appear as part of a longer report or other document, such as a proposal, feasibility study, manual, or brochure.

This chapter focuses on the most common workplace applications: descriptions of mechanisms and of processes and procedures.

MECHANISM DESCRIPTION

Mechanism refers to a tool, machine, or other mechanical device—usually with moving parts—designed to perform a specific kind of work. Naturally, your approach to writing a mechanism description (sometimes called a *device* description) will be influenced by your reader's needs. Your reader may need the description to identify, explain, advertise, display, package, ship, purchase, assemble, install, use, or repair the mechanism. It's also possible that your reader's technical understanding is less highly developed than your own. You must therefore gear your description accordingly, taking all the reader's circumstances into account.

Your writing will also be influenced by whether your description is general or specific in nature. As the term suggests, a general description is accurate for every variation of the mechanism, regardless of manufacturer, model, special features, or other variables. A general description of a camera, for example, would apply to all cameras—digitals, disposables, point-and-shoots, Polaroids, 35 mm, and others—by concentrating on the features common to all. A specific description, on the other hand, deals with one particular example of a mechanism—the Minolta Freedom Zoom 125 camera, for instance—and emphasizes its particular and unique features.

Whether general or specific, nearly all mechanism descriptions include the following features:

- Brief introduction defining the mechanism and explaining its purpose
- Precise description of the mechanism's appearance
- List of the mechanism's major parts
- Explanation of how the mechanism works

- One or more visuals that clearly depict the mechanism—photos and drawings, especially exploded and cutaway views, are best in this context (see Chapter 5)
- Conclusion, sometimes incorporating information about the mechanism's history, availability, manufacturer, cost, and so on
- List of outside sources of information, if any

Obviously, the most *descriptive* parts of the description are the second, third, and fourth items on the list, which constitute the bulk of the text and necessitate certain procedures. You must decide, for example, what order of coverage to use in describing the object:

- Top to bottom or bottom to top
- Left to right or right to left
- Inside to outside or outside to inside
- Most important features to least important features, or least important features to most important features

You should use specific, concrete wording—including the correct name of each part—and avoid vague, subjective expressions that may result in misinterpretation. To a reader from a small town, for example, "a tall building" may mean any structure more than two or three stories high. To a reader from Toronto or Vancouver, however, "a tall building" means something quite different. Write exactly what you mean: "a 50-story building" or "a 5-story building." Similarly, don't write "a big long skinny thing"; instead, write "a 43.2 cm carbide spindle." Sometimes a little research is necessary to determine the correct specifications and terms, but this information is certainly available in dictionaries, encyclopedias, owner's and operator's manuals, merchandise catalogues, specialized reference works, online sources such as www.howstuffworks.com, and—for subject matter related to your major field—your textbooks. If you experience difficulty tracking down such information, any reference librarian can assist you.

Using the present tense and predominantly active verbs, explain completely what the mechanism looks like. Mention all significant details: size, weight, shape, texture, and colour. Identify what the mechanism is made of. Using familiar words and expressions, such as *above, behind, to the left of, clockwise, counter-clockwise,* and the like, convey a clear sense of where the various parts are located in relation to each other and how they interact. Evaluative comments can highlight the importance or significance of key details, as in these examples:

> The base of the machine is fitted with heavy-duty casters that, when unlocked, make it easy to move the machine from one location to another despite its great weight.
>
> The machine's simple design provides ready access to the motor, thus facilitating routine servicing and repairs.
>
> The housing's neutral colour (standard on all models) enables it to blend in with the decor of most offices.

Use *analogy* and other forms of comparison to describe parts that are difficult to portray otherwise. Analogy is evident in terms that include capital letters and hyphens, like *A-frame*, *C-clamp*, and *T-square*, and terms that include descriptive words, like *wing nut*, *needle-nose pliers*, and *claw hammer*. A little inventiveness enables you to create fresh, original analogies to help the reader "see" what you're describing. But avoid vague, meaningless comparisons, such as "the design resembles a European flag," which may be essentially accurate but, like the "tall building" example mentioned earlier, can be interpreted in many different ways.

Likewise, avoid analogies that depend on knowledge or understanding the reader may not possess. This is especially relevant now that the workplace is becoming increasingly diverse with respect to employees' national origins. Not everyone, for example, will understand sports analogies, especially those based on lesser-known or exclusively North American games. For example, the statement that a machine housing is "about as high and as wide as a lacrosse goal" would mean very little to a reader unfamiliar with that sport. Instead, use analogies that most people can relate to. Restrict yourself to comparisons involving the universally known and recognized. To evoke the image of a wire surrounded by a layer of insulation, for example, you could liken it to the lead in a wooden pencil.

Ideally, of course, a visual will supplement the text to prevent misunderstanding. In a mechanism description, the most useful visuals are photos and line drawings, especially cutaway and exploded views. As mentioned in Chapter 5, a familiar

---

✓ Checklist Evaluating a Mechanism Description

A good mechanism description

___ opens with a brief introduction that defines the mechanism and explains its function;

___ fully describes the mechanism's component parts and how they interrelate;

___ is clear, accurate, and sufficiently detailed to satisfy the needs of the intended audience;

___ is organized into separate, labelled sections, covering the subject fully in an orderly way;

___ includes helpful comparisons and analogies to clarify difficult concepts;

___ uses the present tense and an objective tone throughout;

___ uses clear, simple language;

___ concludes with a brief summary;

___ includes effective visuals (photographs and line drawings—exploded and/or cutaway views) to clarify the text;

___ contains no typos or mechanical errors in spelling, capitalization, punctuation, or grammar.

object such as a coin, a ruler, or even a human figure can be included in the picture to convey a sense of the mechanism's size if that is not otherwise obvious. In a sense, this strategy is akin to analogy, which seeks to clarify by comparing the unknown to the known.

On the following pages are two mechanism descriptions for your consideration, commonplace examples that demonstrate basic formats, approaches, and strategies that can be adapted to actual workplace applications. Figures 6.1–6.3 constitute a general description of a conventional flush toilet; Figures 6.4–6.6, a specific description of an Ajax Super® ballpoint pen.

Figure 6.1 General Mechanism Description, Page 1

A Conventional Flush Toilet

<u>Introduction</u>

A flush toilet is a mechanical device for the sanitary disposal of bathroom waste matter.

<u>Appearance</u>

Typically made of white porcelain, the toilet consists of two basic components: an oval, water-filled bowl with a hinged plastic seat and cover; and a rectangular water tank positioned directly behind the bowl and fitted with a metal or porcelain flush/trip handle on the upper-left side of its front surface.

The rim of the bowl is approximately 15″ or 38 cm from the floor. The bowl is approximately 15″ or 38 cm across at its widest point. The tank is approximately 20″ or 51 cm wide, 14″ or 36 cm high, and 8″ or 20 cm deep. The tanks of older models held approximately 3.5 gallons or 13 litres of water, while current models hold 1.5 gallons or 5.7 litres.

The seat and cover on newer models are easily removable to facilitate cleaning. The tank lid is also removable, to allow adjustment and repair of the mechanical parts housed inside.

<u>Major Parts</u>

Virtually all the major parts are inside the tank:

- Lift wires
- Guide arm
- Tank ball
- Valve seat
- Float ball
- Float arm
- Ball-cock assembly
- Inlet tube
- Filler tube
- Overflow tube

Figure 6.2 General Mechanism Description, Page 2

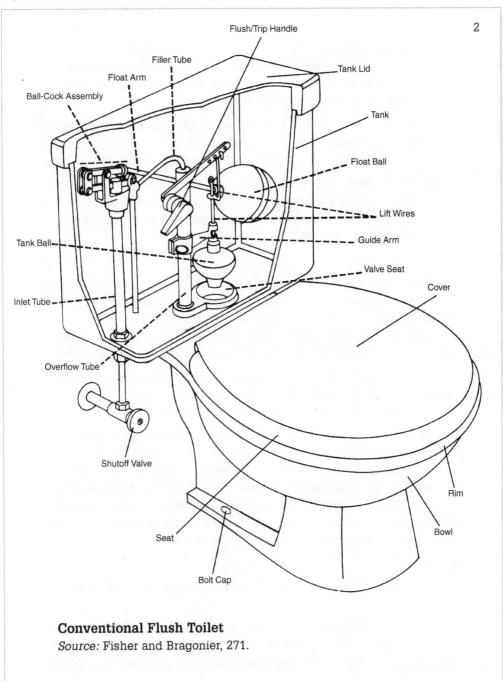

Conventional Flush Toilet
Source: Fisher and Bragonier, 271.

Figure 6.3   General Mechanism Description, Page 3

<u>Operation</u>   3

1. Depressing the flush/trip handle lifts the tank ball from the valve seat, allowing water from the tank to empty into the bowl and carry away waste through a pipe in the floor. When the tank is nearly empty, the ball falls back into the seat and stops the flow.

2. As the water level in the tank falls, so does the float ball. This causes the float arm to open a valve in the ball-cock assembly, letting new water into the inlet tube and allowing both the tank and the bowl to refill through the filler tube.

3. As the water level in the tank rises, so does the float ball. Eventually the float arm closes the valve in the ball-cock assembly, shutting off the water until the next flush. In the event of malfunction, excess water escapes through the overflow tube.

<u>Conclusion</u>

For more than 400 years people have disposed of waste matter efficiently and hygienically by means of the flush toilet. Sir John Harrington, a godson of Queen Elizabeth I of England, invented the flush toilet in 1589. A valve released a flow of water from a cistern tank into a flush pipe. But the valve tended to leak, creating a nearly continuous trickle of water into the bowl.

Chelsea plumber Thomas Crapper's Valveless Water-Waste Preventer, introduced at the Health Exhibition of 1884, solved this problem by incorporating the float-ball principle in use ever since.

Today the leading manufacturers of flush toilets are Kohler and American Standard. A basic model retails for approximately $150, but special features such as brass hardware, elongated bowls, lined tanks, and designer colors can boost the price to $1,000 or more. Low-flow toilets and dual flush are becoming more popular as people become concerned about both the environmental impact of water consumption and the cost of water. These models, however, often start at over $350.00.

<u>Sources</u>

Brain, Marshall. "How Toilets Work." *HowStuffWorks,* n.d. Web. 21 May 2007.

Fisher, David, and Reginald Bragonier, Jr. *What's What: A Visual Glossary of the Physical World*. Maplewood, NJ: Hammond, 1981. Print.

Macaulay, David. *The Way Things Work*. Boston: Houghton Mifflin, 1988. Print.

Reyburn, Wallace. *Flushed with Pride*. London: MacDonald, 1969. Print.

Figure 6.4 Specific Mechanism Description, Page 1

An Ajax Super® Ballpoint Pen

<u>Introduction</u>

A ballpoint pen is a common writing implement used in homes, schools, and offices—indeed, in virtually every setting where writing is done—all over the developed world.

<u>Appearance</u>

Although shorter, the ballpoint pen looks much like a pencil. Some disposable ballpoint pens are of unified construction, but most consist of a tapered barrel and a cap, which—fitted together—give the pen its elongated shape and allow it to be disassembled for the purpose of replacing the tubular ink reservoir inside. Most ballpoint pens have a tension clip mounted on the cap to enable the pen to be secured in the owner's shirt pocket when not in use. (The clip also prevents the pen from rolling off inclined surfaces.) In addition, there is a small push button that protrudes from the top of the cap, where the eraser would be on a pencil. This activates the inner workings, enabling the tiny, socket-mounted, rolling ballpoint writing tip at the end of the reservoir to be extended or retracted.

The visible parts of the pen can be made entirely of metal, although many pens are both metal and plastic (metal cap, clip, and button; plastic barrel). Typically, however, it is made mostly of plastic. Metal surfaces can be shiny or textured. Plastic parts are manufactured in a wide range of colours, and some ballpoint pens are two-tone (one colour for the cap, another for the barrel).

The Ajax Super model described here is exactly 12.7 cm long, with a 0.95 cm diameter at its widest point, where the cap and barrel join. Both cap and barrel are made of bright red styrene plastic. The tension clip and the push button are made of chromed metal.

<u>Major Parts</u>

Exterior parts:
- Push button
- Cap
- Tension clip
- Barrel

Interior parts:
- Plunger mechanism
- Cam recess
- Cam ball
- Ink reservoir
- Spring
- Ball point

Figure 6.5   Specific Mechanism Description, Page 2

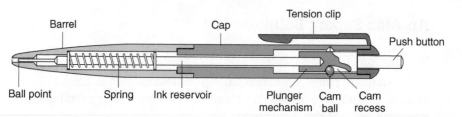

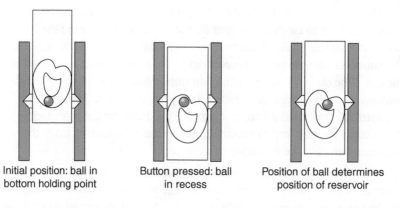

Ajax Super® Ballpoint Pen
Source: How Things Work, 313.

Initial position: ball in   Button pressed: ball   Position of ball determines
bottom holding point   in recess   position of reservoir

Operating Principle
Source: How Things Work, 313.

<u>Operation</u>

1. Depressing the push button causes the interior plunger mechanism to activate, thereby forcing the ink reservoir downward, locking it in place, and causing the ball point to extend through the
   opening at the tapered end of the barrel. Plunger mechanisms vary
   from pen to pen, with some more complicated than others.

Figure 6.6 Specific Mechanism Description, Page 3

3

2. The Ajax Super boasts a rather simple mechanism. When the push button is depressed, a tiny ball rotates in a heart-shaped cam recess in the plunger. After the push button is depressed, the pressure of the spring forces this ball into the topmost holding point within the recess and prevents its return, thus locking the reservoir and the ball point in the extended position.

3. As the ball point rolls across the writing surface, ink is drawn from the reservoir and onto the ball, which then deposits the ink.

4. When the push button is again depressed, the mechanism is disengaged, and the spring causes the cam ball to return to its original holding point within the recess, allowing the reservoir and its ball point to retract into the barrel. The now stationary ball point seals the reservoir, preventing unwanted discharge of ink while the pen is not in use.

Conclusion

The ballpoint pen has evolved greatly since its introduction in the 1940s. Early models were notoriously messy and unreliable, with leakage a constant problem. Indeed, the ballpoint pen was initially banned in many public schools. Since then, however, manufacturers such as Parker, Papermate, Cross, Bic, and others have perfected the device, which is now the most popular handheld writing instrument, having almost completely supplanted the traditional fountain pen. Many varieties of ballpoint pens are available, with prices ranging from less than a dollar for unmechanized, disposable plastic models to literally hundreds or even thousands of dollars for high-prestige, brand-name instruments made of gold or silver.

Sources
Fisher, David, and Reginald Bragonier, Jr. *What's What: A Visual Glossary of the Physical World*. Maplewood, NJ: Hammond, 1981. Print.
How Things Work: The Universal Encyclopedia of Machines. London: Paladin, 1972. Print.
Macaulay, David. *The Way Things Work*. Boston: Houghton Mifflin, 1988. Print.
Russell-Ausley, Melissa. "How Ballpoint Pens Work." *HowStuffWorks*, n.d. Web. 21 May 2007. Print.

Exercises

Exercise 6.1

As discussed in the text and mentioned in the checklist, a mechanism description should open with a brief introduction that defines the mechanism and explains its function. To acquire some practice with this task, write introductions for three of the following metering devices:

- Ammeter
- Barometer
- Odometer
- Psychrometer
- Spectrophotometer

Exercise 6.2

Write a general mechanism description of a common device used in your field of study or employment–for example, a welding torch, compass, or stethoscope.

Exercise 6.3

Write a specific mechanism description of a common kitchen appliance–for example, a toaster, blender, or coffee maker.

Exercise 6.4

Write a specific mechanism description of a piece of sporting equipment–for example, a ski boot, a baseball or softball glove, or a golf club.

Exercise 6.5

Write a general mechanism description of a tool or other piece of equipment commonly used in automobile repair–for example, a creeper, a ratchet wrench, or a bumper jack.

Exercise 6.6

Write a specific mechanism description of a Swiss Army knife.

Exercise 6.7

Write a general mechanism description of a common piece of office equipment–for example, a stapler, a locking file cabinet, or a desk lamp.

Exercise 6.8

Consult some textbooks, periodicals, and websites devoted to your field of study or employment and find 10 examples of the creative use of analogy. Write an email to your instructor discussing your findings.

Exercise 6.9

Consult some textbooks, periodicals, and websites devoted to your field of study or employment and find five examples of effective visuals that successfully clarify the appearance or workings of mechanisms. Write a memo to your instructor in which you discuss your findings. Be sure to include copies of the visuals. Use the examples in this chapter to help you determine the appropriate format and layout of the memo.

Exercise 6.10

As an exercise in precise writing, create a detailed description of the following illustration. When you think your description is as clear as possible, give it to a friend, relative, or co-worker who has not seen the illustration, and ask that person to read the description and reproduce the illustration. If the resulting drawing is not an exact replication of the original, it's probably because your description was not 100 percent clear. Discuss the results with your "artist" to determine exactly what was misleading.

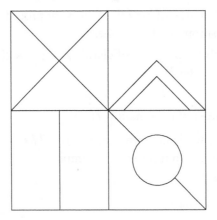

PROCESS/PROCEDURE DESCRIPTION

A process description is similar to a mechanism description. As the term suggests, however, a process description focuses not on an object but on an unvarying series of events producing a predictable outcome. Sometimes referred to as process *analysis*, it enables the reader to understand–but not necessarily to create–a particular process. Indeed, processes are strictly defined as natural phenomena governed by physical laws and are therefore beyond the scope of deliberate human involvement. Photosynthesis is one example of a process, as is continental drift or gene mutation. A more flexible definition of *process* would include human-controlled activities, such as data processing.

A predetermined series of events that occurs under human control is most typically referred to as a procedure. A manufacturing operation such as injection moulding, for example, is a procedure, as is balancing a chequebook or measuring a pulse rate. Therefore, if a process description most commonly answers the question of how and why X *happens,* a procedure description always answers the question of how and why X is *done.* This is a useful distinction.

A procedure description differs sharply from instructions (covered in Chapter 7) because it enables the reader to understand the procedure but not necessarily to perform it. The purpose of a procedure description, like that of a process description, is simply to inform. Indeed, both kinds of descriptions are treated together here because they are so similar. In addition to their common purpose, they are also structured the same. Furthermore, both resemble a mechanism description: both can be presented in a variety of contexts and usually include the following features, which are similar to those of a mechanism description:

- Brief introduction explaining the nature, purpose, and importance of the process or procedure
- Explanation of the natural forces involved and explanations of any materials, tools, and other equipment that might be needed
- Stage-by-stage explanation of how the process or procedure occurs, with all necessary details; transitions are helpful here
- One or more visuals for purposes of clarification; flow charts are often useful in this context (see Chapter 5)
- Brief conclusion
- List of outside sources of information, if any

As in other kinds of workplace writing, use *parallel structure* when phrasing the stage-by-stage explanation. Do not say, for example,

1. Customer drops off the clothing.
2. Clothing is sorted and marked.
3. Clothes you want washed go to washing machines, and clothes to be dry-cleaned go to dry-cleaning machines.

Instead, be consistent by phrasing the description as follows:

1. Clothing is dropped off.
2. Clothing is sorted and marked.
3. Clothing to be washed is sent to washing machines, and clothing to be dry-cleaned is sent to dry-cleaning machines.

The revision is better because the emphasis is now on the same word (*clothing*) in each of the three stages, and the verbs are now all passive. Since the focus in this kind of description is on the process or procedure itself rather than on a human agent, this is one of the few situations in which passive verbs rather than commands or other active constructions are preferable. Indeed, when there is no human agent—as in a sentence like "steam is created as water evaporates"—passive voice is the most natural way to express the idea.

As with mechanism descriptions, the level of detail and technicality in process/procedure descriptions will depend on the needs and background of the audience. If a process description is especially detailed, it may even include sections of mechanism description within it. In any case, the sequential, cause-and-effect, action-and-reaction nature of the information must be conveyed clearly to ensure the reader's understanding. Do not simply say, for example,

1. X happens.
2. Y happens.
3. Z happens.

Instead, use transitions to reveal the relationships among the stages of the process or procedure, like this:

1. X happens.
2. Meanwhile, Y happens.
3. As a result, Z happens.

Just as you might when writing a mechanism description, you can use analogies and familiar comparisons to convey difficult concepts involved in the process or procedure you're describing. Visuals can also be quite helpful. In general, the most appropriate kind of visual to accompany a process/procedure description is the flow chart, which by nature is intended to illustrate activity through a series of stages (see Figure 5.8). Sometimes, though, a more pictorial touch is helpful, as in the process description in Figure 6.8. Conversely, a simple step-by-step narrative can be sufficiently clear by itself, as demonstrated by the procedure description in Figure 6.10.

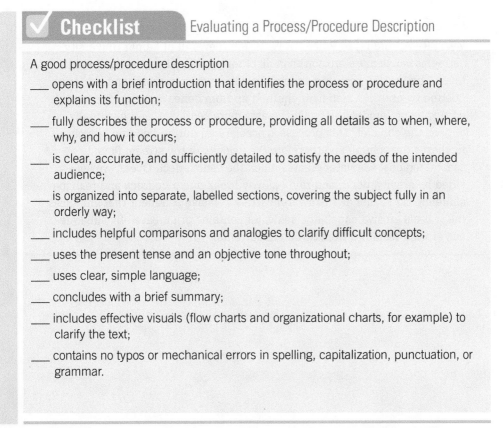

✔ **Checklist**   Evaluating a Process/Procedure Description

A good process/procedure description

____ opens with a brief introduction that identifies the process or procedure and explains its function;

____ fully describes the process or procedure, providing all details as to when, where, why, and how it occurs;

____ is clear, accurate, and sufficiently detailed to satisfy the needs of the intended audience;

____ is organized into separate, labelled sections, covering the subject fully in an orderly way;

____ includes helpful comparisons and analogies to clarify difficult concepts;

____ uses the present tense and an objective tone throughout;

____ uses clear, simple language;

____ concludes with a brief summary;

____ includes effective visuals (flow charts and organizational charts, for example) to clarify the text;

____ contains no typos or mechanical errors in spelling, capitalization, punctuation, or grammar.

Figure 6.7 Process Description, Page 1

Erosion and Sedimentation

<u>Introduction</u>

Broadly defined, erosion and sedimentation constitute the two-step process whereby natural forces carry away soil, rock, and other surface materials and transport them to new locations on the earth's surface.

This process causes a gradual and ongoing reconfiguration of the earth's topography. Over the centuries it has created riverbeds, waterfalls, rapids, and other features.

<u>Natural Forces</u>

The main natural forces involved in erosion and sedimentation are water, ice, and wind.

<u>Process</u>

WATER—According to Professor W. H. Matthews III of Lamar University, "streams cause more erosion than all other geological agents combined" (209). The forceful scouring action of rushing water in rivers and estuaries, abetted by abrasive sediment churned up from beneath the surface and carried along, erodes the banks, creates more sediment, and eventually widens the channel. This process is accelerated during flooding, which increases the volume and therefore the velocity of the stream flow. In coastal regions, seawater creates much the same effect. Ocean waves— aided by gravity, wind, and rain—slowly break down bedrock and reshape shoreline cliffs. Just as freshwater carries abrasive sediment that enhances the water's erosive capability, seawater contains grit created by subaqueous erosion resulting from turbulent currents.

Figure 6.8   Process Description, Page 2

Earth pillars, or hoodoos, are created by wind and rain erosion of the lower layers of soft, sedimentary rock, leaving behind a pillar topped by harder rock.

ICE—As water freezes, it expands with great force, breaking apart rocks whose crevices it occupies. Glaciers, too, have played a major role in erosion. As a glacier moves slowly along, it abrades the earth's surface, partly because of debris quarried from the bedrock by the glacier and embedded in the ice along its base. North America's Great Lakes, in fact, were formed by such glacial activity.

WIND—Wind is a factor primarily in arid, sandy regions where the ground is unprotected by vegetation or other cover. In such areas, whole landscapes of hills and valleys can result, as on the planet Mars and in several locations on Earth.

Figure 6.9   Process Description, Page 3

Conclusion   3

    The process of erosion and sedimentation is positive because in addition to creating some spectacular geophysical phenomena (see illustration) it contributes to the formation of new soil and causes rich deposits on valley floors and at the mouths of rivers. Its harmful effects include the depletion of existing topsoil and fertilizer, and the clogging of drainpipes and reservoirs. Although significant, the process is but one of several related influences on the earth's topography. Others include tectonic activity and surface earth movement (landslides, for example). In recent years, more attention has been paid to the role of human ecology, particularly the consequences of such practices as quarrying, strip mining, and large-scale deforestation.

Sources

"Erosion." *New Encyclopædia Britannica: Micropædia*, 2002. Print.

"Erosion." *Wikipedia*, n.d. Web. 21 May 2007.

Garner, H. F. "Erosion and Sedimentation." *Academic American Encyclopedia*, 1993. Print.

Laflen, John M. "Erosion." *World Book Encyclopedia*, 2000. Print.

Matthews, William H. "Erosion." *Encyclopedia Americana*, 1998. Print.

"Sedimentation." *Wikipedia*, n.d. Web. 21 May 2007.

Figure 6.10 Procedure Description

Problem Resolution at the Conover Corporation

Introduction

The Conover Corporation is committed to maintaining a climate of open, honest communication between employees and their immediate supervisors for the purpose of resolving problems that may undermine morale and thus hinder the achievement of corporate goals. To ensure that problems are resolved promptly and fairly, a procedure has been established, subject to periodic review.

Procedure

1. In the event of a job-related problem, the employee requests a brief conference with the immediate supervisor to agree on a mutually acceptable time, date, and place to meet for discussion.

2. The employee and the supervisor meet. If possible, the supervisor resolves the problem. If additional information, assistance, or time is required, the supervisor arranges a second meeting with the employee, again by mutual agreement.

3. If dissatisfied with the outcome, the employee asks that the matter be referred to the next higher level of supervision. The supervisor tries to arrange this meeting within two working days of the employee's request and summarizes in a memo report the nature of the problem and the initial response given to the employee. Prior to this meeting, copies of the report are given to the employee, the next higher level of supervision, and the Human Resources Department. At the meeting, the employee may explain the problem informally (in conversation, which will result in an oral response) or formally (in the form of a memo report, which will result in a written response).

4. If still dissatisfied, the employee may ask that the matter be referred to the next higher level of management; if necessary, the procedure is repeated until it reaches the point at which a representative of the Human Resources Department joins in the review and the matter is finally resolved.

Conclusion

Employees are encouraged to use this procedure without fear of reprisal or penalty. Records of problem review procedures are not entered into employees' personnel files, nor are they a factor in performance reviews. Such records are maintained in a separate file in the Human Resources Department, for reference only, to ensure consistency in the handling of other such situations.

Exercises

Exercise 6.11

Identify each of the following as either a process or a procedure:

- Alphabetizing and filing
- Corrosion
- Intubation
- Solving a quadratic equation
- Vaporization

Exercise 6.12

As discussed in the text and mentioned in the checklist, a process/procedure description should open with a brief introduction that defines the process or procedure and explains its function. Write such introductions for three of the items in Exercise 6.11.

Exercise 6.13

Write a description of a process related to your field of study or employment—for example, pulmonary arrest, cell regeneration, or food spoilage.

Exercise 6.14

Write a description of a procedure related to your field of study or employment—for example, interviewing, stock rotation, or safety check.

Exercise 6.15

Write a description of a procedure that occurs in the world of sports—for example, the annual Canadian Football League (CFL) draft, the way in which points are awarded in diving competitions, or the way the starting line is organized for marathons.

Exercise 6.16

Write a process description of how cigarette smoking affects the lungs.

Exercise 6.17

Write a process description of how body rot forms on a motor vehicle.

Exercise 6.18

Write a procedure description of how a dealer determines the market value of a collectible—for example, baseball cards, coins, comic books, figurines, or postage stamps.

Exercise 6.19

Write a process description of how spontaneous combustion occurs.

Exercise 6.20

Consult some textbooks, periodicals, and websites devoted to your field of study or employment and find five examples of effective visuals that successfully clarify processes or procedures. Write an e-mail to your instructor in which you discuss your findings. Be sure to include copies of the visuals. Make sure you include the sources you retrieved the visuals from.

PEARSON
mycanadiantechcommlab

Visit www.mycanadiantechcommlab.ca for everything you need to help you succeed in the classroom and in the job you've always wanted! Tools and resources include the following:

- Composing Space and Writer's Toolkit
- Document Makeovers
- Grammar Exercises—and much more!

7

Instructions

LEARNING OBJECTIVE

When you complete this chapter, you'll be able to write clear instructions that will enable the reader to perform a given procedure without unnecessary difficulty or risk.

INSTRUCTIONS SERVE A WIDE VARIETY OF FUNCTIONS. You might write instructions for co-workers to enable them to install, operate, maintain, or repair a piece of equipment, or to follow established policies, such as those explained in employee handbooks. You might also write instructions for customers or clients to enable them to assemble, use, or maintain a product (as in owner's manuals, for example) or to follow mandated guidelines. As in procedure description writing in Chapter 6, the broad purpose of instructions is to inform. The more specific purpose, however, is to enable the reader to *perform* a particular procedure rather than simply to understand it.

Clearly, instructions must be closely geared to the needs of the intended reader. The level of specificity will vary greatly, depending on the procedure's complexity and context and the reader's level of expertise or preparation. Computer documentation intended for a professional programmer, for example, is very different from documentation written for someone with little experience in such matters. Obviously, audience analysis is crucial to writing effective instructions.

INSTRUCTIONS

Just as there are general and specific mechanism descriptions, there are also general and specific instructions. The differences are essentially the same for both types of workplace writing. General instructions explain how to perform a generic procedure—trimming a hedge, for example—and can be adapted to individual situations. Specific instructions explain how to perform a procedure under conditions involving particular equipment, surroundings, or other such variables—operating a 22-inch (55.9 cm) Craftsman Bushwacker electric hedge trimmer, for instance.

Like other kinds of workplace writing, instructions appear in diverse contexts, from brief notes, such as the reminder to "Close cover before striking" that appears on many matchbooks, to lengthy manuals and handbooks. Regardless of context, however, most instruction writing follows a basic format resembling that of a recipe in a cookbook. This format includes the following features:

- Brief introduction explaining the purpose and importance of the procedure

    Note: An estimate of how much time is required to complete the procedure may be included as well as any unusual circumstances that the reader must keep in mind *throughout the procedure*, such as safety considerations.

- Lists of materials, equipment, tools, and skills required, enabling the reader to perform the procedure uninterrupted

- Actual instructions: a numbered, step-by-step, detailed explanation of how to perform the procedure

- In most cases, one or more visuals for clarification

- Brief conclusion

- List of outside sources of information, if any

Although they *look* very easy, instructions are actually among the most difficult kinds of writing to compose. The slightest error or lapse in clarity can badly mislead–or even endanger–the reader. Instructions should always be read in their entirety before the reader attempts the task. Many readers, however, read the instructions a bit at a time, "on the fly," while already performing the procedure. This puts an even greater burden on the writer to achieve standards of absolute precision and clarity.

The best approach is to use short, simple commands that start with verbs and are arranged in a numbered list. This enables the reader to follow the directions without confusion and also fosters consistent, action-focused wording, as in this example:

1. Push the red "On" button.

2. Insert the green plug into the left outlet.

3. Push the blue "Direction" lever to the right.

Notice that instructions are not expressed in "recipe shorthand." Small words such as *a, an,* and *the,* which would be omitted in a recipe, are included in instructions.

Although it's usually best to limit each command to one action, sometimes closely related steps can be combined to prevent the list from becoming unwieldy. Consider the following example:

1. Hold the bottle in your left hand.

2. Twist off the cap with your right hand.

These steps should probably be combined as follows:

1. Holding the bottle in your left hand, twist off the cap with your right hand.

When the procedure is complicated, requiring a long list, a good strategy is to use subdivisions under major headings, like this:

1. Prepare the solution:
   a. Pour two drops of the red liquid into the vial.
   b. Pour one drop of the blue liquid into the vial.
   c. Pour three drops of the green liquid into the vial.
   d. Cap the vial.
   e. Shake the vial vigorously for 10 seconds.

2. Pour the solution into a beaker.

3. Heat the beaker until bubbles form on the surface of the solution.

If two actions must be performed simultaneously, however, present them together. For example, do not write something like this:

Even machines that seem relatively easy to operate have instructions because you can't assume that the user knows all the required steps.

1. Push the blue lever forward.

2. Before releasing the blue lever, push the red button twice.

3. Release the blue lever.

Instead, write this:

1. While holding the blue lever in the forward position, push the red button twice.

2. Release the blue lever.

Figure 7.1 Fault Table

Symptom	Probable Cause	Solution
Starter motor won't work	1. Loose connections 2. Weak battery 3. Worn-out motor	1. Tighten connections 2. Charge battery 3. Replace motor
Starter motor works, but engine won't start	1. Wrong starting procedure 2. Flooded engine 3. No fuel 4. Blown fuse 5. Ignition defect, fuel-line blockage	1. Correct procedure 2. Wait awhile 3. Refuel 4. Replace fuse 5. Contact dealer
Rough idle, stalling	1. Ignition defect, fuel-line blockage	1. Contact dealer

Frequently, the conclusion to a set of instructions takes the form of a troubleshooting section, in which possible causes of difficulty are identified along with remedies. This example is from a bank's instructions on how to balance a cheque book:

> Subtract Line 4 from Line 3. This should be your present register balance. If not, the most common mistakes are either an error in arithmetic or a service charge not listed in your register. If you need further assistance, please bring this statement to your banking office.

Sometimes the troubleshooting guide will be in the form of a three-column "fault table" like the one in Figure 7.1, which appeared in an automobile owner's manual.

Another helpful feature of good instructions is the use of effective visuals. Photographs, line drawings (especially cutaway and exploded views), and flow charts, such as the one in Figure 7.2, can clarify concepts that might otherwise be difficult to understand. As explained in Chapter 5, however, you must choose the right type of visual for each situation, and this is certainly true with respect to writing instructions. Different kinds of instructions are best illustrated by different kinds of visuals. A precise operation involving the manipulation of small parts, for example, may best be rendered by a close-up photograph or line drawing of someone's hands performing the operation. Instructions emphasizing the correct sequence for the steps in a less delicate task, on the other hand, may best be illustrated by a conventional flow chart. There are many free programs on the internet that you can use to create professional-looking flow charts.

Increasingly, instructions designed to accompany products feature visuals alone or with minimal text. The principal reason for this development is that manufacturers wish to target the broadest possible market by accommodating consumers from

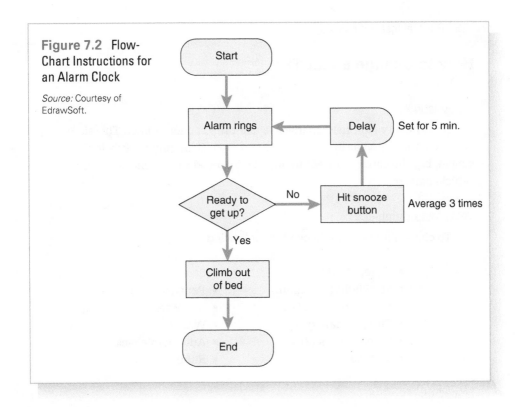

Figure 7.2 Flow-Chart Instructions for an Alarm Clock

Source: Courtesy of EdrawSoft.

various countries and cultures. This trend is likely to grow as we move ever closer to a global economy.

A good way to determine the effectiveness of a set of instructions you have created—whether with text and visuals or with visuals alone—is to field-test the instructions by observing while someone unfamiliar with the procedure attempts to perform it using your directions. For the test to be valid, however, you must resist the temptation to provide verbal assistance if the person expresses uncertainty. This will enable you to detect any unclear sections within the instructions and to determine the cause of the confusion. Another effective test is to ask someone who is familiar with the procedure to critique your instructions. Even better, subject your instructions to both forms of evaluation.

Figures 7.3–7.6 and 7.7 illustrate the two main types of instructions: general and specific. Figures 7.3–7.6 explain how to perform a common procedure: changing a flat tire. Figure 7.7 is the first part of instructions showing how to assemble a specific product: a Weber® barbecue grill. Note that although the Weber instructions rely almost exclusively on visuals, the reader is referred to the hazard alerts explained in the accompanying owner's guide.

Figure 7.3 General Instructions, Page 1

How to Change a Flat Tire

<u>Introduction</u>

Nearly every motorist experiences a flat tire sooner or later. Therefore, you should know what to do in such a situation. Changing a flat is fairly simple, but the correct procedure must be followed to prevent injury or vehicle damage.

<u>Tools and Equipment</u>

To change a tire you will need the following:

- Flares (6–10)
- Flashlight (if at night)
- Spare tire, mounted
- Tire pressure gauge
- Wheel blocks (2)
- Jack handle
- Screwdriver
- Penetrating oil
- Lug wrench
- Wide board
- Automobile jack
- Rubber mallet

<u>Procedure</u>

As soon as you realize you are developing a flat, leave the road and drive your vehicle onto the shoulder. Park as far from the road and on as flat and level a surface as possible. Turn off the engine and activate the hazard warning flashers. Put the transmission in park. (Put a manual transmission in reverse.) Set the parking brake. Ask all passengers to get out of the vehicle and to stand well away from traffic and clear of the vehicle. Raise the hood to warn other motorists and to signal that you may need help. Now you are ready to assess the situation.

WARNING: DO NOT ATTEMPT TO CHANGE A TIRE IF YOUR VEHICLE IS ON AN INCLINE OR SLOPE, OR IF ONCOMING TRAFFIC IS DANGEROUSLY CLOSE TO YOUR VEHICLE. UNDER THESE CONDITIONS, WAIT FOR PROFESSIONAL ASSISTANCE.

1. If conditions are acceptable, open the trunk and set up flares behind and in front of the vehicle to alert other motorists.

Figure 7.4   General Instructions, Page 2

2

2. Remove the spare and other equipment from the trunk.

3. Using the jack handle, pry off the hubcap. If the jack handle is not satisfactory for this, use the screwdriver.

4. Using the lug wrench, loosen (but do not remove) the lug nuts. Nearly all lug nuts are loosened by turning counterclockwise. (If the nuts have left-hand threads and are therefore loosened clockwise, there will be an *L* on the lug bolt.) If the nuts are too tight, apply the penetrating oil, wait a few minutes, and try again.

5. Assemble and position the jack. Because there are several kinds, you must consult your owner's manual for proper assembly and use. If the ground is soft, put the wide board under the jack base to stabilize it.

6. Put the wheel blocks in front of and behind the tire diagonally opposite the one you are changing to minimize the risk of the vehicle rolling off the jack (see Figure 1).

7. Raise the vehicle until the flat tire is just clear of the ground. ALWAYS REMOVE THE JACK HANDLE WHEN NOT IN USE.

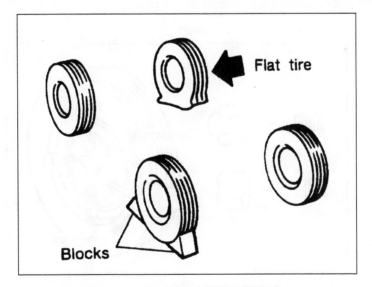

Figure 1   Position of Wheel Blocks

Figure 7.5   General Instructions, Page 3

8. Remove the lug nuts by hand. NEVER USE THE LUG WRENCH WHILE THE VEHICLE IS JACKED UP. If the lug nuts will not come off by hand, lower the car, further loosen them with the wrench, jack the car back up, and then remove them by hand. (Like removing the jack handle, this will minimize the risk of accidentally dislodging the jack—a dangerous error!) Put the lug nuts into the hubcap for safekeeping.

9. Remove the flat.

10. Roll the spare into position and put it on the wheel by aligning the holes in the spare's rim with the lug bolts on the wheel. You may have to jack the vehicle up a bit more to accomplish this because the properly inflated spare will have a larger diameter than the flat tire had.

11. Holding the spare firmly against the wheel with one hand, use your other hand to replace the lug nuts as tightly as possible. Again, DO NOT USE THE WRENCH.

12. Lower the vehicle. Now you may use the wrench to fully tighten the nuts. To ensure that the stress is distributed evenly, tighten the nuts in the proper sequence, as shown in Figure 2.

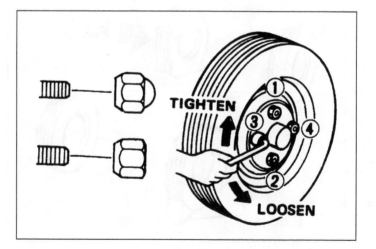

Figure 2   Lug Nut Sequence

Figure 7.6 General Instructions, Page 4

4

13. Replace the hubcap, checking that the tire valve is correctly positioned, protruding through the hole in the hubcap. You may need to tap the hubcap into place with the rubber mallet.

14. Put the flat, jack, and other tools into the trunk.

Conclusion

Most motorists who follow the procedure correctly are able to change a flat tire successfully. The only difficult part of the task is the removal of the lug nuts, which does require some physical strength. As explained earlier, however, penetrating oil will help, as will a long-handled lug wrench, which provides greater leverage. A common practice is to use your foot to push down on the wrench handle.

Sources

Nissan Pulsar NX Owner's Manual. Tokyo, Japan: Nissan Motor Co., Ltd., 1988. Print.

Pettis, A. M. *Monarch Illustrated Guide to Car Care.* New York: Simon & Schuster, 1977. Print.

Reader's Digest Complete Car Care Manual. Pleasantville, NY: Reader's Digest Association, 1981. Print.

Figure 7.7 Specific Instructions

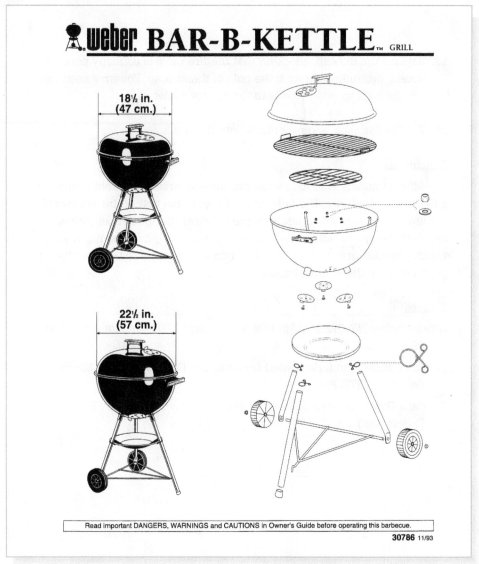

Weber BAR-B-KETTLE™ GRILL

18½ in.
(47 cm.)

22½ in.
(57 cm.)

Read important DANGERS, WARNINGS and CAUTIONS in Owner's Guide before operating this barbecue.

30786 11/93

AVOIDING LIABILITY

Remember that what may seem obvious to you is not necessarily apparent to the reader. Include all information, and provide the reason for each step if the reason is important to enhance performance or prevent error. Sometimes this is best done as a note, as in this example:

■ Note: Lubricate the axle now, because it will be much more difficult to reach after the housing is in place.

Often, as in the preceding example, the reason for doing something a certain way is simply to avoid inconvenience. But if a serious hazard exists, you must alert the reader by using LARGE PRINT, <u>underlining</u>, **boldface**, or some other attention-getter, *before* the danger point is reached. By law, any such alert must identify the hazard, specify the consequences of ignoring it, and explain how to avoid it. There are three levels of hazard alerts:

- *Caution:* Alerts the reader to the risk of equipment failure or damage, as in this example:

    CAUTION: The cutter blades are not designed to cut metal. To prevent damage to the blades, never put tools or other metal objects on the conveyor belt.

- *Warning:* Alerts the reader to the possibility of serious injury, as in this example:

    WARNING: The drill press bit can shred your fingers. To avoid injury, keep your hands far away from the bit.

- *Danger:* Alerts the reader to the probability of serious injury or death, as in this example:

    DANGER: This machine is powered by high-voltage electricity. To avoid death by electrocution, turn the power off before removing the cover plate.

Hazard alerts are commonly accompanied by attention-getting icons like the one in Figure 7.8, which represents the danger of electrical shock. These are often displayed in red for added impact.

Hazard alerts are now more important than ever, not only to avoid malfunction and physical danger, but also to minimize legal liability in case of a mishap. The number of product liability lawsuits has skyrocketed in recent years, with the majority of suits alleging not that the products themselves are defective but that manufacturers have failed to provide sufficient warnings about dangers inherent to their use. As a result, even obvious precautions must be spelled out in very explicit terms. Coffee cups at Tim Hortons, for example, now include a warning that the beverage is hot. This is in response to McDonald's losing $2.7 million in a lawsuit brought by a customer who had been scalded by a spill. Another recent example is the superhero costume that actually carried the following message on its packaging:

FOR PLAY ONLY: Mask and chest plates are not protective; cape does not enable user to fly.

These are, of course, extreme cases. But they underscore the importance of providing ample warning in your instructions about any potential hazard. Similarly, if malfunction can occur at any point, you should explain corrective measures, as in these examples:

If the belt slips off the drive wheel, disengage the clutch.

If any of the solution splashes into the eyes or onto exposed skin, wash immediately with cold water.

If the motor begins to whine, immediately turn off the power.

Figure 7.8 Hazard Icon

Checklist   Evaluating Instructions

A good set of instructions

___ opens with a brief introduction that identifies the procedure and explains its function;

___ lists the materials, equipment, tools, and skills required to perform the procedure;

___ provides a well-organized, step-by-step explanation of how to perform the procedure;

___ provides any appropriate warnings, cautions, or notes to enable the reader to perform the procedure without unnecessary risk;

___ is clear, accurate, and sufficiently detailed to enable the reader to perform the procedure without unnecessary difficulty;

___ employs helpful comparisons and analogies to clarify difficult concepts;

___ uses clear, simple "commands";

___ concludes with a brief summary;

___ employs effective visuals (photographs and line drawings—exploded and/or cutaway views) to clarify the text;

___ contains no typos or mechanical errors in spelling, capitalization, punctuation, or grammar.

Exercises

Exercise 7.1

As discussed in the text and mentioned on the checklist, written instructions should open with a brief introduction that identifies the procedure and explains its purpose. Write such introductions for three of the following procedures:

- Balancing a cheque book
- Creating a playlist on an MP3 player
- Measuring a person's blood pressure
- Programming a digital wristwatch
- Hemming a pair of pants

Exercise 7.2

Write instructions (and include visuals) explaining how to perform a common procedure related to your field of study or employment—for example, welding a lap joint, administering a bed bath, or restraining a potentially troublesome person.

Exercise 7.3

Write instructions (and include visuals) explaining how to perform a common indoor household chore—for example, washing laundry, cleaning a bathroom, or repairing a leaky faucet.

Exercise 7.4

Write instructions (and include visuals) explaining how to perform a common outdoor household chore—for example, mowing a lawn, sealing a blacktop driveway, or installing a rain gutter.

Exercise 7.5

Write instructions (and include visuals) explaining how to perform a common sports-related procedure—for example, waxing a pair of skis, suiting up for an ice hockey game, or performing stretching exercises.

Exercise 7.6

Write instructions (and include visuals) explaining how to perform a common procedure related to automobile maintenance and repair—for example, changing the engine oil and filter, using jumper cables, or washing and cleaning a vehicle.

Exercise 7.7

Write instructions (and include a map) explaining how to travel from your home to your college.

Exercise 7.8

Write instructions (and include visuals) explaining how to perform one of these procedures:

- Cooking a favourite meal
- Laying track on a model railroad

- Building a dog house
- Changing a baby's diaper
- Waterproofing a pair of work boots

Exercise 7.9
Consult the owner's manual accompanying a household appliance or other product you have purchased, and examine the visuals provided to facilitate assembly or proper use. How helpful are they? Write a memo to your instructor in which you discuss your findings. Be sure to include copies of the visuals.

Exercise 7.10
Consult textbooks, periodicals, and websites devoted to your field of study or employment, and find five examples of visuals designed to accompany instructions. How helpful are they? Write a memo to your instructor in which you discuss your findings. Be sure to include copies of the visuals.

mycanadiantechcommlab

Visit www.mycanadiantechcommlab.ca for everything you need to help you succeed in the job you've always wanted! Tools and resources include the following:

- Composing Space and Writer's Toolkit
- Document Makeovers
- Grammar Exercises—and much more!

Proposals

LEARNING OBJECTIVE

When you complete this chapter, you'll be able to use standard procedures to write successful solicited and unsolicited proposals.

LIKE THE VARIOUS OTHER KINDS OF WORKPLACE WRITING, proposals are a major example of business communication. Simply put, a proposal is a persuasive offer intended to secure authorization to perform a task or provide products or services that will benefit the reader. There are basically two kinds of proposals: solicited and unsolicited (that is, requested and unrequested). But there are subcategories within those broad divisions, including internal and external proposals. This is not really as complicated as it seems, however, because the conventions governing proposal writing are well-established and quite logical. This chapter explores these issues and provides examples of solicited and unsolicited proposals.

SOLICITED PROPOSALS

In this case the business, agency, or organization seeking proposals has already identified a situation or problem it wishes to address. It issues an RFP (request for proposal) that spells out the details of the project and provides instructions to outsiders for submitting bids. RFPs, many of which are quite lengthy and complex, commonly appear in trade publications, as government releases, and on the internet. An individual or organization wishing to compete for a particular contract must craft a proposal that will convincingly demonstrate its superiority to the many others received.

In one sense, however, responding to an RFP is easier than writing an unsolicited proposal because the problem or goal has already been established and there is no need to convince anyone of its existence or importance. In addition, the RFP usually provides explicit instructions regarding the format, design, and content of the proposal, so those requirements—which must be followed exactly—are already in place. Figure 8.1–8.6 shows an RFP issued by a local government, soliciting bids for a pool filtration system on a city-owned building.

UNSOLICITED PROPOSALS

In this case, the proposal originates with the writer, who has perceived a problem or need that the writer's expertise might be able to remedy. Although an unsolicited proposal (Figures 8.10–8.11, and 8.12–8.13) may face no direct competition, it's more challenging to compose because it must convince the reader of the potential benefits. In short, it must be more strategically persuasive than a solicited proposal (Figures 8.8–8.9, and 8.15–8.29), whose acceptance or rejection is often based largely on cost and time projections as well as on the writer's credentials and track record on similar projects, all of which is fairly objective information.

Figure 8.1 Request for Proposal, Page 1

REGISTER AS A PLAN TAKER

Disclaimer

Any information or changes to the requirements of this bid opportunity will be posted on the website in the form of an addendum.

IT IS **IMPORTANT** THAT YOU REGISTER SO THAT YOU MAY RECEIVE FAX NOTIFICATION OF ANY NEW ADDENDA. YOU ACKNOWLEDGE, HOWEVER, THAT SINCE THIS IS AN AUTOMATED PROCESS THE CITY CANNOT GUAR-ANTEE THAT YOU WILL BE NOTIFIED.

Failure to register may result in non-acceptance of your submission. The City of Cambridge is NOT responsible for computer malfunctions or delays; there-fore, **it is your responsibility to check the website for addenda prior to bid closing.**

Source: Courtesy of the City of Cambridge

Figure 8.2 Request for Proposal, Page 2

Proposal 2010-13

PRE-QUALIFICATION OF CONTRACTORS FOR
POOL FILTRATION SYSTEM FOR W.G. JOHNSON POOL

The City of Cambridge is calling for pre-qualification of bidders specializing in commercial grade pool filtration systems. Tenders will be issued in February of 2010 with the project construction commencing in May 2010.

Pre-Qualification of Contractors, experienced in the following disciplines, is requested:
- Commercial pool filter and pump installation along with all associated piping
- Pool liner repair and replacement
- Plumbing and pipe fitting.
- Full system commissioning and pressure testing

Interested parties are invited to submit the following documentation:
1. Completed Canadian Standard Form of Contractors' Qualification Statement (CCDC11-1996), including details of experience related to this type of work.
2. A letter from your Surety Company confirming whether you are able to provide bonding for the project.
3. A letter from an insurance company stating that the Contractor can provide a minimum of $2,000,000 Comprehensive General Liability Insurance.
4. Contractor's WSIB Certificate of Clearance and CAD7.
5. Resumes of key supervisory personnel, project manager and superintendent who would be assigned to this project.
6. Minimum of three (3) references of projects of similar scope.

Bidders should be registered with the Purchasing Division, either in person or via the plan takers section of the website.

Six (6) sealed copies of your submission, marked clearly as to their contents, are to be submitted to John Avery, Manager of Purchasing, City of Cambridge, Purchasing Division, 50 Dickson Street, 4th Floor, Cambridge, Ontario, N1R 5W8 no later than:

12:00 noon, Wednesday, February 17, 2010

The City reserves the right to reject any and all submissions. Only contractors that the City of Cambridge deems suitable to undertake this project will be invited to submit bids at a later date.

All technical questions regarding this proposal shall be directed to _____ at Stantec Consulting by email at _____ . For questions on submitting your information, contact _____ , Senior Buyer at _____ .

Submissions received after the closing time will NOT be accepted. They are to be dropped off at Purchasing Services Counter, 4th Floor, 50 Dickson Street **, Cambridge, ON.**
The onus is on the bidder to ensure that the information is received in the
proper location and before the closing time.

Tenders, Quotations and Proposals can now be viewed and/or downloaded from our website
Bid results will be posted, when applicable, on the website after opening.
http://www.cambridge.ca/cs_corporate/purchasing_tenders_list.php?

John Avery, CPPB
Manager of Purchasing and Inventory

Source: Courtesy of the City of Cambridge

Figure 8.3   Request for Proposal, Page 3

Proposal 2010-13

PRE-QUALIFICATION OF CONTRACTORS
For Pool Filtration System at W.G. Johnson Pool

GENERAL INSTRUCTIONS

1. PREAMBLE

Collaborative Structures Ltd is the Construction Manager for the projects at W.G. Johnson Pool. Collaborative Structures Ltd. will be calling tenders for the pool filtration system for W.G. Johnson Pool at an overall budgeted cost of $1,000,000.00.

2. SCOPE OF THE PROJECT

The project involves:

- The supply of labour, materials, plans (shop drawings and details as required), tools and equipments to complete the work as per the drawings and specifications prepared by Stantec Consulting
- Excavate as required around swimming pool perimeter to fully access swimming pool piping. Removal of tile and saw-cutting and concrete patching of concrete pool deck will be by others. All replacement floor tile work will be by others.
- Installation of additional skimmers, jets, and drains to meet current OBC regulations.
- Cut and repair pool walls as required.
- Removal and replacement of pool liner.
- Supply and installation of new filters, pumps, water treatments systems and all associated piping as per the plans and specifications prepared by Stantec.
- Full system commissioning and pressure testing.

3. REQUEST FOR PRE-QUALIFICATION

3.1   Submit a completed, signed and sealed CCDC Document #11, including resumes.

3.2   Confirm your firm's desire to pre-qualify for this project.

3.3   Provide a letter from your Surety Company confirming your ability to provide a 100% Performance bond and a 50% Labour and Material payment bond *for a project with construction value of up to $1,000,000.00.* Indicate the length of time you have been with this Surety Company, and provide a named reference with phone numbers.

3.4   Submit a current CAD7 WSIB Rating Form and a current WSIB Clearance Certificate.

3.5   Provide a letter from your financial institution regarding your general financial position (including the number of years with that institution, ability to fund requirements of a $1,000,000.00 project, history of NSF, general standing, etc.). Provide a named reference from your financial institution with phone number. This letter will be received "in confidence" and will be viewed only, by Purchasing Department employees of the City of Cambridge.

Source: Courtesy of the City of Cambridge

Figure 8.4   Request for Proposal, Page 4

Proposal P-2010-10
Pre-Qualification of Contractors for the
Pool Filtration System at W. G. Johnson Pool – City of Cambridge

3.6   Provide copies of your letters sent to the Financial and Bonding References authorizing them to discuss your general financial matters and bonding capacity with the City of Cambridge.

3.7   Provide identification of labour agreements, locals and expiry dates particular to this project.

3.8   Provide a summary of similar projects in <u>scope and size</u> that you have completed within the last five (5) years including the following information:

- *A brief description of the project clearly identifying commercial pool projects.*
- Include the name of the sub-contractor(s) used on each project.
- Provide the principal contact for the owner and consultant complete with their telephone numbers, fax numbers and addresses.
- Identify repeat clients in the private and public sector.

Describe in some detail (1 page maximum), including major sub trades, the two projects that are most similar to this project.

3.9   *Identify the key personnel you expect to assign to manage the respective phases of this project* – as a minimum the Construction Project Manager, Site Superintendent, and Field/Office Coordinator. Provide their resumes and a summary of their past project experience identifying the projects undertaken while in your employ or that of others.

Note: As part of the tendering process, it will be necessary for the pre-qualified Contractors to confirm on the bid form the personnel named to this project. If a named individual becomes unavailable, the contractor will be required to provide an acceptable replacement having equivalent or better experience.

Immediately prior to tendering the project, the pre-qualified Contractors will be requested to confirm that the key personnel named in their pre-qualification submission are available and will be named in their tender submission as a pre-requisite to Contractors being invited to tender. <u>Any change in key personnel named in their tender may lead to their tender being rejected.</u>

3.10   Submit a copy of your company's Health and Safety Policy.

3.11   Work is open to both union and non-union companies. State whether you are a Union or Non-Union firm. If a unionized company, what contractual agreements do you have with trade unions (if any), and when do these agreements expire?

3.12   Describe briefly all lawsuits with which your organization is involved and indicate if you are suing or being sued. Indicate your position with respect to the resolution of disputes, the use of courts for this purpose and management procedures to avoid litigation and/or arbitration.

Note: No submission will be accepted from any Contractor who has a claim or has instituted a legal proceeding against the City or against whom the City has a claim or has instituted a legal proceeding, without the prior approval of City Council. This applies whether the legal proceeding is related or unrelated to the subject matter of this pre-qualification.

Source: Courtesy of the City of Cambridge

Figure 8.5 Request for Proposal, Page 5

Page 3   Proposal P-2010-10
                              Pre-Qualification of Contractors for the
                    Pool Filtration System at W. G. Johnson Pool – City of Cambridge

4. PRE-QUALIFICATION EVALUATION

4.1 Contractors will be evaluated according to the following criteria:

4.1.1 Mandatory Criteria

1. A letter from your financial institution indicating you have the financial capacity to undertake projects of the size and nature indicated in this prequalification. (Item 3.5)

2. Submission of a letter from your Surety Company stating intent and ability to provide a 100% Performance Bond and a 50% Labour and Material Bond for the project. (Item 3.3)

3. Submission of a current CAD7 WSIB Rating Form and WSIB Clearance Certificate. (Item 3.4)

4. Similar projects in scope and size undertaken within the last 5 years, including details of the three most similar projects. (Item 3.8)

4.1.2 Evaluated Criteria   **Points**

1. Completeness of submission   10

2. Annual value of construction for the past five years   10

3. Similar projects undertaken within last five years (Item 3.8)   35

4. References   15

5. Experience of key personnel proposed to be assigned to this project. (Item 3.9)   15

6. Project Management methodology based on the response to (Item 3.11), and litigation record (Item 3.12)   10

7. Health and Safety plan and safety record (Item 3.10)   5

5. EVALUATION METHOD

5.1 Contractors not complying with ALL of the Mandatory Criteria will not be considered. Failure to provide information on any of the above categories may result in the disqualification of the submission. Unsatisfactory results on any of the areas requested will result in the firm not being pre-qualified.

5.2 *Contractors must obtain a minimum score of sixty (60) points to be eligible for shortlisting. All of those that score 60 points or higher will be short-listed for pre-qualification.*

5.3 References will be checked for all Contractors. Unsatisfactory references may result in the contractor not being pre-qualified.

5.5 An evaluation team consisting of the Project Manager, Engineer, Purchasing Manager, and various departmental staff will collectively evaluate the submissions to determine the list for pre-qualification. An interview at City Hall may be required.

Source: Courtesy of the City of Cambridge

Figure 8.6 Request for Proposal, Page 6

Page 4

Proposal P-2010-10
Pre-Qualification of Contractors for the
Pool Filtration System at W. G. Johnson Pool – City of Cambridge

6. SUBMISSION DELIVERY & OPENING

6.1   One (1) original and five (5) copies of submissions shall be delivered in a sealed package, clearly marked **"Proposal P-2010-13 Pre-qualification of Contractors for the Pool Filtration System at W.G. Johnson Pool in Cambridge Ontario"** to the address shown below not later than **12:00 noon, on Wednesday, February 17, 2010**.

The Corporation of the City of Cambridge
50 Dickson Street
4th Floor, Purchasing Department
Cambridge, Ontario N1R 5W8
Attention: Mr. John Avery, Manager of Purchasing & Inventory

Submissions must be time-stamped at the above location to be considered. Late submissions will not be accepted and will be returned unopened without exception. The time stated on the time stamp located in the above referenced office will be the only recognized timepiece for the purpose of this submission.

7. Queries/Addenda

Addenda may be issued in writing and posted on the City's website during the pre-qualification period, up to 48 hours prior to opening by the Designated Official. All addenda become part of the submission documents and must be included with the bidder's information. All questions from bidders must be in writing to the Designated Official. No questions will be taken from bidders after 48 hours prior to opening.

The Owner has no responsibility to provide addenda. All Addenda will be posted on the City of Cambridge website; www.cambridge.ca/cs_corporate/purchasing_tenders_list.php

Bidders are to check the website for addenda prior to submitting their information.

Source: Courtesy of the City of Cambridge

INTERNAL AND EXTERNAL PROPOSALS

Like most other kinds of business writing, a proposal—solicited or not—may be either an in-house document (see Figures 8.8–8.11) or an external one (see Figures 8.1–8.6 and 8.12–8.29).

Internal Proposals: These are often rather short because the writers and readers are already known to each other, and the context is mutually understood. Solicited in-house proposals are not usually written in response to a formal RFP but, rather, to a direct assignment from a manager, supervisor, or other administrator. Unsolicited in-house proposals are motivated by an employee's own perception of need—e.g., the belief that a certain policy or procedure should be adopted, modified, or abandoned.

External Proposals: As mentioned, solicited external proposals are usually in response to formal RFPs, but unsolicited external proposals—more difficult to create—obviously are not. They are motivated primarily by the desire for financial reimbursement. In effect, they might almost be seen as a form of employment application.

FORMATS OF PROPOSALS

If short proposals are in-house, they usually take the form of a memo, email, or memo report; if external, they are typically sent as a letter. Longer, more fully developed proposals can include many sections and very much resemble long reports, and are sometimes written collaboratively (see Chapter 10). Actually, then, there are eight kinds of proposals, as Figure 8.7 illustrates.

Figure 8.7
Categories of Proposals

		SOLICITED	UNSOLICITED
INTERNAL		short	short
		long	long
EXTERNAL		short	short
		long	long

OBJECTIVES OF PROPOSALS

Regardless of whether a proposal is solicited or unsolicited, internal or external, short or long, it should accomplish several objectives, some of which may overlap:

- Clearly summarize the situation or problem that the proposal is addressing. If unsolicited, the proposal must convince the reader that there is, in fact, an important unmet need.

- Provide a detailed explanation of how the proposal will correct the situation or problem. This is sometimes called the "project description" and it typically contains several parts.

- Confirm the feasibility of the project and the anticipated benefits of completing it, as well as possible negative consequences of not doing so.

- Convincingly refute any probable objections.

- Establish the writer's credentials and qualifications for the project.

- Identify any necessary resources, equipment, or support.

- Provide a reliable timeline for completion of the project. A Gantt chart (see Chapter 5) is sometimes used for this.

- Provide an honest, itemized estimate of the costs. Deliberately understating the timeline or the budget is not only unethical (see Chapter 1) but also fraudulent. Doing so can incur legal liability.

- Close with a strong conclusion that will motivate the reader to accept the proposal. A convincing cost/benefit analysis is helpful here.

As mentioned in earlier chapters, workplace communications must always be sensitive to considerations of audience, purpose, and tone. But this is especially

First impressions are extremely important. Proposals must look professional.

important in proposal writing because of its fundamentally persuasive nature. A proposal writer must be alert to the differing requirements of upward, lateral, downward, and outward communication. The phrasing should be reader-centred, using the "you" approach. And because, by definition, proposals seek to improve conditions by rectifying problems, it's important that they remain positive and upbeat in tone. The writer must refrain from assigning blame for existing difficulties and should instead focus on solutions. This is especially important when writing in-house, where a hostile climate can result if the writer neglects to consider people's needs and feelings, particularly if the proposal's recommendations might alter or otherwise affect the responsibilities of co-workers or departments.

Like any workplace document, a proposal is far more likely to succeed if well-written. Nothing tarnishes credibility more quickly than careless typos and basic errors in spelling, punctuation, or grammar. In addition, workplace writing should always be accurate, clear, and well-organized. And the wording should be simple, direct, and concise, using active verbs and everyday vocabulary, with no rambling, wordy expression. The crucial point to remember is that no amount of study from a textbook will enable you to compose your best writing on the first try. Any professional writer will tell you that the key is to revise, revise, and revise. And, finally, proofread—carefully.

In addition, a proposal should look inviting. As will be explained in Chapter 9, Short Reports, our ability to comprehend what we read is greatly influenced by its physical arrangement on the page or screen. We see a document—forming an involuntary subconscious opinion of it—before beginning to actually read. Obviously, a positive initial impression goes a long way toward fostering a more receptive attitude in a reader. Therefore, strive for a visually appealing page design by applying the principles outlined in Chapter 9.

Figures 8.8–8.29 present several sample proposals:

- A proposal from a student to her instructor, regarding a topic for her long report assignment (Figures 8.8–8.9)
- A proposal from an employee to her supervisor, regarding improvements to the company's daycare facilities (Figures 8.10–8.11)
- A proposal from a landscaping company to a real estate agency, regarding improvements to the agency's grounds (Figures 8.12–8.14)
- A proposal from a community group to a fund-granting agency, regarding improvements to a trail system in a local park (Figures 8.15–8.29)

All of these are good examples of various formats, situations, and kinds of proposals.

Figure 8.8 Solicited Internal Proposal, Page 1

George Brown College
200 King Street East
Toronto, ON M5A 3W8

MEMORANDUM

DATE: 15 October 2011

TO: Professor Wade Rosenberg
             Communications Department

FROM: Tabitha Roetz

RE: Long Report Proposal

As you know, I am pursuing a diploma in Architectural Technology
and am enrolled in your COMM 113 (Professional Communications for
AS + CMT) class to fulfill my Communications requirement. We have
been assigned to submit a short proposal identifying our choice of
topic for the long report due at the end of the semester, along with a
brief outline of the report, a preliminary bibliography, and a timeline
for completion. Here's my proposal.

Report Topic: Five Major Architectural Structures in Canada

Outline: Introduction

                 1 – Canadian Museum of Civilization – Hull, QC

                 2 – Chateau Frontenac – Quebec City, QC

                 3 – CN Tower – Toronto, ON

                 4 – Olympic Stadium – Montreal, QC

                 5 – Plus 15 Walkways – Calgary, AB

                 Conclusion

Figure 8.9 Solicited Internal Proposal, Page 2

Roetz, pg. 2

Preliminary

Bibliography: www.canada.worldweb.com/TravelArticles/
Top10//8-147309.html

www.quebeccityhotels.worldweb.com/index.html#12096

www.toronto.worldweb.com/SightsAttractions/
BuildingsTowers/index.html#9184

www.discovercalgary.com/Calgary/Transportation/
Bridges/index.html#241930

www.montreal.worldweb.com/SightsAttractions/
ArenasStadiums/index.html#15602

www.cntower.ca/media_centre/press_kit/

Timeline: Oct. 20–Nov. 23: Research

Nov. 24: Individual Conference

Nov. 25–Dec. 10: Writing

Dec. 11–13: Editing/Revising

Dec. 14: Report Due

My report will focus on the history of each building, along with its holdings and special features. Having personally visited each of these sites at least once during family vacations over the past several years, I am well acquainted with the topic and can illustrate the report with photos from my own collection. In addition, I have numerous magazine and newspaper articles, books, brochures, flyers, and other promotional materials that I can use to supplement my bibliography.

Given my longtime interest in the subject, I'm confident I can do a good job with this topic, and I'm hoping you'll approve it. Please contact me if you need any further information. My student email account is troetz.stu@georgebrown.ca, and of course I can discuss this with you after class or during your office hours.

Figure 8.10 Unsolicited Internal Proposal, Page 1

RASCO INCORPORATED
Scudder Boulevard
Victoria, BC V9A 4B2
www.rascoinc.ca

MEMO

DATE: May 22, 2011

TO: Jim Sandiford
               Site Director

FROM: Maureen Noble
               Daycare Supervisor

SUBJECT: Daycare Proposal

As you know, Rasco Incorporated's free daycare program has been a major factor in enabling the company to attract and retain a dependable, highly skilled workforce in a very competitive industry.

As you always say, however, "Good can always be better." Therefore, I have a proposal that would, if accepted, greatly improve our daycare program.

The daycare room itself is well-suited for the purpose. It is bright, roomy, and fully equipped with everything needed; it's a model of what a daycare facility should look like. My two part-time workers, Patty and Michelle, are both excellent.

In the nice weather, however, there's not much for the children to do outdoors. We often bring them outside and let them run around or play soccer in the grassy area alongside the parking lot, but that's not fully appropriate for the really young ones, and there's always the danger factor to consider. What if somebody lost control of a car?

My proposal is to install a small playground surrounded by a sturdy chain-link fence and equipped with a picnic table and a manufactured play structure with swinging, sliding, and climbing accessories. One of us could still monitor the soccer players in the area behind the building while the others supervised the playground.

Figure 8.11 Unsolicited Internal Proposal, Page 2

Noble, pg. 2

The equipment could be installed in one day by our own maintenance personnel, although the fence would have to be erected by its
supplier. The long-established Valla's Fencing in nearby Esquimalt
tells me they could do a job this size (roughly 12 m by 15 m) in a
couple of days.

Obviously, this would all cost some money, but I really think it would
be a wise investment. Here's a tentative budget, which I've estimated
after researching playground equipment on the Internet and at local
stores, and after pricing fence costs and installation charges at
several local fencing companies (including Valla's, whose quote
was the lowest).

play set	$ 1000.
picnic table	100.
surface sand	150.
chainlink fence	3750.
Total	$ 5000.

Thanks very much for considering this proposal. I'll be happy to discuss it with you in greater detail if you wish.

Figure 8.12 Unsolicited External Proposal, Page 1

GREEN THUMB
LANDSCAPING AND LAWNCARE

929 Windmill Road · Dartmouth, NS B3A 1J7
(902) 555–1234

May 12, 2010

Ms. Mary G. Chesebro
Chesebro Realty
21 West Main Street
Dartmouth, NS B3A 3K4

Dear Ms. Chesebro:

As you know, we have been maintaining the lawns at your business for several years, and everything looks very nice. But we have a suggestion about how we could make your grounds even more attractive.

During our weekly visits we've noticed that several of the trees surrounding the building might benefit from professional attention. Our proposal is as follows:

General Tree Work

Prune blue spruce located at left front of building according to following specifications:

- Remove all dead, diseased, and broken branches that are 1 in. (2.5 cm) in diameter and larger throughout crown to improve health and appearance and reduce risk of branch failure

- Reduce height approximately 8 to 10 ft. (2.5 to 3 m) to reduce risk of branch, stem, and/or root failure $275.

Prune Norway spruce located at left rear of building according to following specifications:

- Prune structurally to reduce risk of branch failure

- Subordinate co-dominant leader, remove dead and broken branches $165.

Figure 8.13 Unsolicited External Proposal, Page 2

Soil Management

Treat blue spruce, hemlock at right side of building, and hemlock behind
parking area with slow-release fertilizer to help improve health following
damage from site conditions, insects, and disease $ 265.

Total Amount: $ 705.

Here is the site plan:

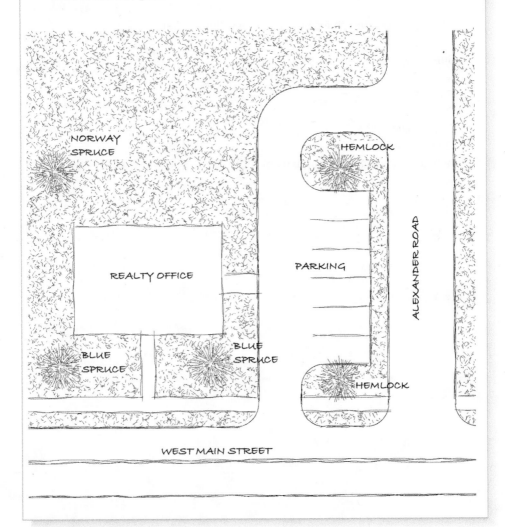

Figure 8.14 Unsolicited External Proposal, Page 3

All Green Thumb Landscaping and Lawncare jobs are performed in a
professional manner by highly trained workers provided with state-of-
the-art tools and equipment. In addition, we clean up after every job,
removing all wood, brush, and debris. We carry full liability insurance,
and all our employees are covered by workers' compensation.

If you wish to discuss this proposal, please contact our office at your
convenience. If you accept, we will send you a contract to sign and
return.

Thank you very much for being a Green Thumb client!

Sincerely,

Elvir Vlasic

Elvir Vlasic
Office Manager
(e-mail: evlasic@greenthumb.com)

Figure 8.15 Solicited External Proposal (Cover Letter, Page 1)

YELLOWSTONE SKI CLUB

P.O Box 12 Whitehorse, YT Y1A 6J6
www.yellowstoneskiclub.ca

March 16, 2011

Ms. Elizabeth Cortwright, Director
Whitehorse Philanthropic Foundation
P.O. Box 25
Whitehorse, YT Y1A 0A1

Dear Ms. Cortwright:

In response to the Whitehorse Philanthropic Foundation's recent RFP, focusing on local outdoor development projects, the Yellowstone Ski Club is submitting the enclosed proposal, which, as you will see, concerns the rehabilitation of the deteriorated trail for intermediate skiers.

For several years, our club has been formulating plans to rehab this trail. The project will involve three phases. At this point we are requesting a matching grant of $20 000 from the Foundation to complete the first part of the project, which includes the following:

- Creation of a defining entrance vista and increased visibility; improving security of the wax room area by means of landscaping, tree & brush removal, and signage

- Installation of a locking gate near the entrance to this trail—to restrict vehicle access (except for service vehicles) while allowing easy entrance for skiers

- Improved drainage provisions above and near the entrance to the trail

- Upgrade of existing parking area

- Resurfacing of roadway leading to the entrance

As a cross-country ski club, we are obviously concerned with improving the trail for that activity. But the trail offers opportunities for many other outdoor activities as well: snowshoeing and, in the summer, hiking, bicycling, bird watching, cross-country running, and the like. Unfortunately, the present conditions make the trail quite unsafe and inhibit full use. These conditions may

Figure 8.16 Solicited External Proposal (Cover Letter, Page 2)

eventually cause the trail to be closed to the public. We are committed to preventing this because we see the trail as an important community resource that must be preserved.

Your RFP lists many specific guidelines that cannot be discussed here, but all are fully addressed in the body of the proposal.

Having secured the endorsement of the Mayor's office and several other local organizations, we are confident that we can succeed with this project and are hoping that you will afford our proposal all due consideration. If you have any questions, please call me at 555-1234 or email me at f.rodgers@YSC.ca.

Thanks very much for your time.

Sincerely,

Frank Rodgers

Frank Rodgers,
Yellowstone Ski Club

Figure 8.17 Solicited External Proposal (Title Page)

CITY PARK
TRAIL RESTORATION
PROPOSAL

Submitted to

Ms. Elizabeth Cortwright, Director
Whitehorse Philanthropic Foundation

by

Yellowstone Ski Club

March 16, 2011

Figure 8.18 Solicited External Proposal (Table of Contents)

CONTENTS

Figure 8.19   Solicited External Proposal, Page 1

PROJECT SUMMARY

For several years, the Yellowstone Ski Club has been formulating plans to rehabilitate the deteriorating trail for intermediate skiers. The project will involve three phases. At this point we are requesting a matching grant of $20 000 from the Foundation to complete the first part of the project, which includes enhancement of the entrance, in part by installing gates and repaving the roadway. Funding for the second and third parts of the project will be sought from other nongovernmental sources.

PROJECT DESCRIPTION

Originally a carriage path, the present trail took shape as a public works project during the Great Depression and enjoyed considerable popularity until fairly recently. Now, however, natural deterioration has taken its toll and the trail is endangered. Broken culverts and clogged drainage ditches have allowed water runoff to erode the trail, and in many places the road surface is badly damaged. In short, potentially unsafe conditions are inhibiting full use of the trail and may eventually cause it to be closed.

The Yellowstone Ski Club is committed to preventing this because we see the trail as an important community resource that must be protected. We envision a return to the trail's former diverse-use status. We want the trail to remain a resource for cross-country skiing and other outdoor sports, but we are hopeful that the proposed improvements will also afford a broad range of other nonmotorized leisure opportunities as well.

As mentioned previously, we envision a three-part plan:

Phase One

- Creating a defining entrance vista and increased visibility; improving security of pavilion area by landscaping, tree and brush removal, and signage
- Installing of a locking gate near the entrance to this trail—to restrict vehicle access (except for service vehicles) while allowing easy entrance for skiers
- Improving drainage provisions above and near the trail
- Upgrading of existing parking area
- Resurfacing of roadway leading to the entrance

Figure 8.20 Solicited External Proposal, Page 2

Phase Two

- Replacing and backfilling 15 unsalvageable drainage culverts
- Cleaning out and repairing 7 additional salvageable culverts
- Boxing out and grading area around all 22 culverts
- Placing 2 inches of Type 3 binder to stabilize area around all 22 culverts in preparation for paving trail
- Cleaning out drainage ditches alongside trail

Phase Three

- Installing riprap (filler stone) to inhibit water runoff
- Applying two layers of surfacing—a base and a covering of fine stone mixed with rolled petroleum slurry—all along the trail

RATIONALE

This project is currently the Yellowstone Ski Club's top priority for several reasons. We are dedicated to promoting physical fitness through skiing, and the trail plays a significant role in that endeavour. The intermediate trail is part of the extensive 83 kilometres of trails that we offer. We believe that all levels of skiers need to be accommodated so that every member of the community will be encouraged to enjoy this healthy activity during the winter. We also feel that upgrading the trail will allow people to enjoy running, hiking, and other activities through the summer months. By upgrading this trail, we will also be able to offer tourists a venue for enjoying our unique climate in Canada. The Yellowstone Ski Club board believes that the project will foster positive and significant changes in the community, ones that identify and enhance local strengths and that focus on identifiable outcomes that will make a difference. Our goals are quite clearly defined and—if achieved—will certainly impact most favourably on the quality of life here in Whitehorse. Now that the area is undergoing something of a revitalization, we wish to contribute an additional dimension by championing a renewed commitment to one of our city's most valuable resources—the Yellowstone Ski Club.

Figure 8.21   Solicited External Proposal, Page 3

RFP CRITERIA

The Whitehorse Philanthropic Foundation's RFP includes specific criteria by which each proposal will be judged. What follows is a point-by-point response to these parameters.

Describe the degree to which the project provides for enhanced public enjoyment of outdoor amenities in the greater Whitehorse area.

Despite its deteriorated condition, the Intermediate Trail is used on a year-round basis. It is used primarily for running, hiking, and bicycling during the nonwinter months of April through October. From November through March, the trail is used by cross-country skiers and snowshoers. Our proposal will ensure that these activities will continue without fear of injuries caused by poor footing or surface conditions. In addition, the project will provide the high school cross-country ski and running teams with a natural training site. Until recently, the school had used the trail in this way, but for the past three years school officials have considered the trail too unsafe. This has forced the ski team to travel, creating added expense.

Describe the degree to which the project furthers a specific goal of state, regional, or local planning bodies.

The Whitehorse City Council has officially identified the Intermediate Trail problem as a high-priority issue. The Yellowstone Ski Club Board of Directors has been working closely with the Mayor's Office about this, and we have received assurances of full co-operation. (See Appendix.) Indeed, at least some of the work involved will almost certainly be performed pro bono by Whitehorse Parks Department personnel.

Figure 8.22 Solicited External Proposal, Page 4

Specify the project's Index of Need (statistically driven rating assigned by Regional Grants Office).

The Regional Grants Office has assigned a preliminary rating of 78.

Describe the degree of citizen involvement in project conception and implementation.

The project is under the direction of the Yellowstone Ski Club, an organization whose mission is to promote health and fitness through skiing. Other citizens' groups from the Whitehorse area have committed resources toward the completion of the project. Members of the Yellowstone Ski Club will provide project administration and supervision. In addition, a volunteer group consisting of employees of a large local business will provide equipment and operators for much of the tree removal, drainage ditch clearing, and drainage restoration. As mentioned previously, it is expected that additional assistance (engineering and oversight) will be provided by the City Parks Department.

Describe the degree to which the project relates to other Whitehorse-area initiatives (natural, cultural, historical, or recreational).

Our club is a large recreation area comprising 83 kilometres of trails, a wax house, three warming huts, a sauna, and a ski playground for children. Until its deterioration, the intermediate trail through the wooded area was an integral part of this multi-use area. It is our intention to restore the trail to provide a safe environment for runners, hikers, bicyclists, cross-country skiers, and snowshoers, thereby promoting greater citizen enjoyment of the natural world. The trail in question connects to other park roads, which are currently shared-use roadways for nonmotorized and motorized access to park facilities.

Describe the degree to which volunteer labour, nontraditional labour, and other certified donations will be used to accomplish the project's goals.

At least three area citizens' organizations, the Yellowstone Ski Club included, have committed resources to the completion of the trail restoration project. Two of the three will provide a considerable amount of volunteer labour and equipment. The third organization has committed up to $20 000 in financial support, pending approval of this proposal by the Whitehorse Philanthropic Foundation. In addition, the Yellowstone Ski Club is able to call upon an

Figure 8.23 Solicited External Proposal, Page 5

extensive list of volunteers who have signed up to help during other club-sponsored initiatives. A community service group affiliated with a large local corporation will supply heavy equipment and operators for much of the work.

Describe the impact the proposal will have on the cultural, social, and recreational needs of the region.

As mentioned in several other parts of this proposal, the trail restoration project is specifically designed to serve the recreational needs of the region, by ensuring the continuation of the community-oriented events. In addition, successful completion of the project will greatly enhance the opportunities for recreational running, hiking, cross-country skiing, bicycling, and snowshoeing. And restoration of the trail will permit its use by the Whitehorse schools' cross-country ski and running teams. In addition, we expect that the refurbished trail will invite use by bird watchers and other nature lovers, as part of the existing system of interlocking trails within the park.

TIMELINE

Obviously, any scheduling projections for a project of this scope must be tentative at best because the project depends on several variables, including funding and weather. The Yellowstone Ski Club is hoping to secure adequate financing through a variety of means (see Budget section of this proposal), but this may take longer than expected. In addition, the Yukon winters certainly preclude any progress during that season, leaving only the spring and fall seasons to complete work (we hope to keep the trail open for use during the summer). What follows, then, is a very optimistic timeline. We will make every effort to stay on schedule, but we realize that full completion of the project may take somewhat longer than planned.

Figure 8.24 Solicited External Proposal, Page 6

Phase One: Fall 2011

Phase Two: Spring 2012

Phase Three: Fall 2012

BUDGET

PHASE ONE

Expenses

architectural fees	$ 1000
replace culvert at entrance	2000
purchase and install main gate	6500
erect main gate brick pillars	2200
clear and pave two parking areas	5000
clean out, repair, and reline 2 culverts	3000
repave road from main gate to gate #2	9500
clear trees and landscape east area	6000
clean drainage trenches	3500
purchase and install gate #2	800
purchase and install signage at both gates	500
	$ 40 000

Funding Sources

donated labour for landscaping	$ 4000
donated labour and equipment for ditching	3500
donated wrought iron for main gate	1000
donated materials and installation of signage	500
partial contribution of architectural fees	700
cash contributions from Yellowstone Ski Club	10 300
Whitehorse Philanthropic Foundation Contribution	20 000
	$ 40 000

PHASE TWO

Expenses

replace and backfill 15 drainage culverts	$ 30 000
clean out, repair, and reline 7 drainage culverts	7500
box out and grade for blacktop at replaced culverts	5500
place 5 cm of type 3 binder at replaced culverts	4500
clean out 1.5 km of drainage ditches	11 700
	$ 59 200

Figure 8.25 Solicited External Proposal, Page 7

PHASE THREE

Expenses

pave 3 km of road 2.5 m wide, 1 cm true + 2.5 cm top	$ 42 500
	$ 42 500

Total Phase Two & Phase Three Expenses	$ 101 700

Funding Sources (Phase Two & Phase Three)

cash contributions from Yellowstone Ski Club	$ 10 000
donated labour and equipment for ditching	11 700
monies from additional grant funding	80 000
	$ 101 700

YELLOWSTONE SKI CLUB BOARD OF DIRECTORS

President: Frank Rodgers (CEO, Rodgers Industries)
Vice-President for Activities & Events: Joseph Carr (CPA, Donnelly & Co.)
Vice-President for Administration & Finance: Rev. Thomas J. Moran (Clergy)
Secretary: Position currently vacant
Treasurer: Eugene Torpey (President, Glenwood, Inc.)
Member: Robert Catanzaro, B.Ed. (Teacher, Porter Creek Secondary School)
Member: Thomas Gibbons (Athletic Director, Vanier Catholic Secondary School)
Member: Dr. Cathleen McGovern (Physician, Meyers Medical Group)
Member: Charles McCabe (Owner, McCabe's Clothiers)
Member: Jane Scerbo (Owner, Whitehorse Dry Cleaning)
Member: Robert F. Veale (Comptroller, Lincoln Co.)
Member: Grace Walsh (Principal, Golden Horn Elementary School)

Figure 8.26 Solicited External Proposal, Page 8

CONCLUSION

A recognized, long-established, high-profile local organization with a large, active membership, the Yellowstone Ski Club has been successful in eliciting project endorsements from the Mayor's Office and several major local businesses. We have also secured pledges of assistance from such groups as the Whitehorse Mountain Climbing Club, the Valley Bicycle Club, and various service clubs in the city. Given the range of expertise and the many professional affiliations represented on the club's Board of Directors, we are confident that we will be able to secure needed materials, services, and cash donations as the project moves forward. At present we are preparing a sizable grant application to be submitted to the federal government, we are planning a new 5k cross-country ski race specifically to benefit the trail project, and we intend to conduct raffles and other fundraising activities at area events. In short, we know we can succeed in this important endeavour, and we urge the Whitehorse Philanthropic Foundation to assist us by approving our grant proposal.

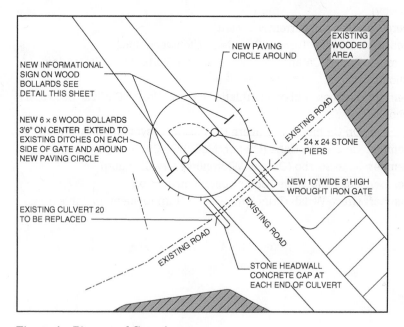

Figure 1 - Blowup of Gate Area

Figure 8.27   Solicited External Proposal, Page 9

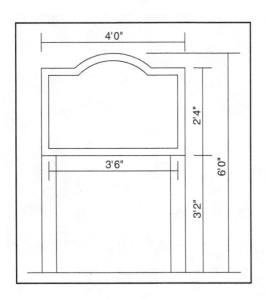

Figure 2 - Sign Detail

Figure 3 - Sketch View of Main Gate

Figure 8.28   Solicited External Proposal, Page 10

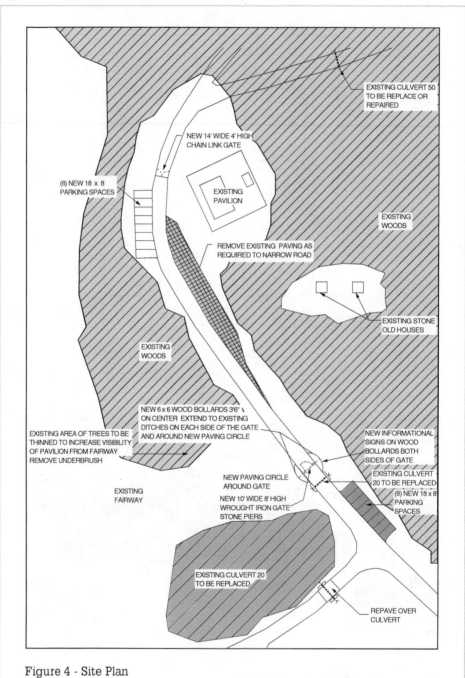

EXISTING CULVERT 50 TO BE REPLACE OR REPAIRED

NEW 14' WIDE 4' HIGH CHAIN LINK GATE

(8) NEW 18 x 8 PARKING SPACES

EXISTING PAVILION

EXISTING WOODS

REMOVE EXISTING PAVING AS REQUIRED TO NARROW ROAD

EXISTING STONE OLD HOUSES

EXISTING WOODS

NEW 6 x 6 WOOD BOLLARDS 3'6" ON CENTER EXTEND TO EXISTING DITCHES ON EACH SIDE OF THE GATE AND AROUND NEW PAVING CIRCLE

EXISTING AREA OF TREES TO BE THINNED TO INCREASE VISIBILITY OF PAVILION FROM FAIRWAY REMOVE UNDERBRUSH

NEW INFORMATIONAL SIGNS ON WOOD BOLLARDS BOTH SIDES OF GATE

EXISTING CULVERT 20 TO BE REPLACED

(8) NEW 18 x 8 PARKING SPACES

NEW PAVING CIRCLE AROUND GATE

EXISTING FAIRWAY

NEW 10' WIDE 8' HIGH WROUGHT IRON GATE STONE PIERS

EXISTING CULVERT 20 TO BE REPLACED

REPAVE OVER CULVERT

Figure 4 - Site Plan

Figure 8.29 Solicited External Proposal, Page 11

THE CITY
OF WHITEHORSE
Office of the Mayor
City Hall • Whitehorse, YT

January 5, 2011

Mr. Frank Rodgers, President
Yellowstone Ski Club
P.O. Box 12
Whitehorse, YT Y1A 6J6

Dear Frank,

Thanks very much for sharing with me the Yellowstone Ski Club's
wonderful plans to restore the intermediate trail on your grounds. I'm
sure you know of my great love for the various trails you have and
my belief that these trails are one of the city's greatest assets.

For that reason, your trail restoration project greatly appeals to me,
and I fully support your efforts.

I'm pleased that the club members are willing to undertake this project, and I ask that you keep me informed of your progress. I look forward to the day when the entire community will be able to once
again enjoy full use of the trail.

Thanks again! If I can assist in any way, please contact me.

Sincerely,

Hanna Julian

Mayor Hanna Julian

Figure 5 - Mayor's Endorsement

✓ **Checklist**   Evaluating a Proposal

An effective proposal

____ is prepared in a format (email, memo, memo report, letter, or booklet) appropriate to its nature;

____ clearly identifies the situation or problem and fully explains how the proposal addresses it;

____ confirms the feasibility of the proposal, refuting any probable objections and establishing the writer's credentials and qualifications for the project;

____ provides a reliable timeline for completion of the project; identifies any necessary resources, equipment, or support; and includes an itemized budget;

____ closes with a strong, persuasive conclusion that will motivate the reader to accept the proposal;

____ uses plain, simple language;

____ maintains an appropriate tone, neither too formal nor too conversational;

____ is well-designed and employs effective visuals—tables, graphs, charts, and the like;

____ contains no typos or mechanical errors in spelling, capitalization, punctuation, or grammar.

Exercises

Exercise 8.1
Write a proposal seeking approval from your college's student activities director to create a new campus club or organization.

Exercise 8.2
Write a proposal seeking approval from your college's athletic director to implement an improvement to the intramural sports program.

Exercise 8.3
Write a proposal seeking approval from the chair or dean in your major field of study to take an elective course not among the program's recommended electives.

Exercise 8.4
Write a proposal seeking approval from your workplace supervisor to implement a change in a particular policy or procedure.

Exercise 8.5
Write a proposal seeking approval from one of your instructors to create a peer tutoring arrangement or study group designed to enhance students' performance in the course.

Exercise 8.6
Write a proposal seeking approval from your clergyperson to create a religion-based club or interest group.

Exercise 8.7
Write a proposal seeking approval from your local library director to present a public lecture at the library on a topic you're knowledgeable about.

Exercise 8.8
Write a proposal in response to an RFP found on the internet or in a trade journal or magazine.

Exercise 8.9
Create a list identifying each of the proposals in Exercises 8.1–8.8 as solicited or unsolicited, and internal or external.

Exercise 8.10
Nearly all college-level workplace communications courses include an assignment requiring the completion of a long report. Using Figures 8.8–8.9 as a model, write a proposal seeking your instructor's approval of your chosen topic. If the topic has been assigned by the instructor, write a proposal seeking approval of your plan of approach.

PEARSON
mycanadiantechcommlab

Visit www.mycanadiantechcommlab.ca for everything you need to help you succeed in the job you've always wanted! Tools and resources include the following:

- Composing Space and Writer's Toolkit
- Document Makeovers
- Grammar Exercises—and much more!

Short Reports:

PAGE DESIGN, FORMATS, AND TYPES

LEARNING OBJECTIVE

When you complete this chapter, you'll be able to apply the basic principles of page design and format to write effective short reports of various kinds.

LIKE EMAILS AND LETTERS, REPORTS are an important form of on-the-job communications, can be internal or external documents, and follow certain standard conventions. In several respects, however, reports are quite different from memos, emails, and letters.

For example, a report is rarely just a written account of information the reader already knows. Nearly always, the report's subject matter is new information. The reader may be acquainted with the general outline of the situation the report explores but not with the details. Very often, in fact, the reader will have specifically requested the report to get those details. Reports exist for the very purpose of communicating needed information that's too complicated for a memo, email, or letter. Stated in the simplest terms, there are essentially two kinds of reports: short and long. This chapter focuses on the former, discussing the basic principles of page design, short-report formats, and several common types of short reports.

PAGE DESIGN

As we have seen, the physical characteristics of memos, emails, and letters are largely determined by established guidelines that vary only slightly. But reports, though also subject to certain conventions, are to a much greater degree the creation of individual writers who determine not only their content but also their physical appearance. This is significant because our ability to comprehend what we read is greatly influenced by its physical arrangement on the page or screen. A report, therefore, should never *look* difficult or intimidating. Consider, for example, Figure 9.1, which has been adapted from a safety manual for railroad employees.

The passage is nearly unreadable in its present state. To make it more visually appealing, the first step is to insert more space between the lines and use both uppercase and lowercase letters (see Figure 9.2).

Certainly, the revised page is far more legible. It can be improved still further, however, by organizing the content into paragraphs and adopting a ragged right margin (see Figure 9.3).

The use of varied spacing, lists, and boldface headings, as well as some minor editing, will make the content emerge even more clearly. Obviously, Figure 9.4 is easier to read than the earlier versions. Such revision is worthwhile and not particularly difficult if the following fundamental principles of effective page design are observed.

■ *Legible type:* Although many different typefaces and type sizes exist, most readers respond best to 12-point type using both uppercase and lowercase letters, like this text. Anything smaller or larger is difficult to read, as is the all-capitals approach; such options are useful only in major headings or to emphasize a particular word or phrase.

Figure 9.1 Poor Page Design

ELECTRIC SHOCK

ELECTRIC SHOCK IS NOT ALWAYS FATAL, AND RARELY IS IT
IMMEDIATELY FATAL. IT MAY ONLY STUN THE VICTIM AND
MOMENTARILY ARREST BREATHING. IN CASES OF ELECTRIC
SHOCK, BREAK CONTACT, RESTORE THE VICTIM'S BREATHING
BY MEANS OF ARTIFICIAL RESPIRATION, AND MAINTAIN
WARMTH. TO AVOID RECEIVING A SHOCK YOURSELF, EXERCISE
EXTREME CAUTION WHEN ATTEMPTING TO RELEASE THE VIC-
TIM FROM CONTACT WITH A LIVE CONDUCTOR. MANY PERSONS,
BY THEIR LACK OF KNOWLEDGE OF SUCH MATTERS, HAVE BEEN
SEVERELY SHOCKED OR BURNED WHEN ATTEMPTING TO RES-
CUE A CO-WORKER. TO RELEASE A VICTIM FROM CONTACT
WITH LIVE CONDUCTORS KNOWN TO BE 750 VOLTS OR LESS, DO
NOT TOUCH THE CONDUCTOR, AND DO NOT TOUCH THE VICTIM
OR THE VICTIM'S BARE SKIN IF THE VICTIM IS IN CONTACT WITH
THE LIVE CONDUCTOR. INSTEAD, USE A PIECE OF DRY, NONCON-
DUCTING MATERIAL SUCH AS A PIECE OF WOOD, ROPE, OR RUB-
BER HOSE TO PUSH OR PULL THE LIVE CONDUCTOR AWAY FROM
THE VICTIM. THE LIVE CONDUCTOR CAN ALSO BE HANDLED
SAFELY WITH RUBBER GLOVES. IF THE VICTIM'S CLOTHES ARE
DRY, THE VICTIM CAN BE DRAGGED AWAY FROM THE LIVE CON-
DUCTOR BY GRASPING THE CLOTHES—NOT THE BARE SKIN. IN
SO DOING, THE RESCUER SHOULD STAND ON A DRY BOARD AND
USE ONLY ONE HAND. DO NOT STAND IN A PUDDLE OR ON DAMP
OR WET GROUND. TO RELEASE A VICTIM FROM CONTACT WITH
LIVE CONDUCTORS OF UNKNOWN VOLTAGE OR MORE THAN
750 VOLTS . . .

■ *Generous margins:* Text should be framed by white space. The top and bottom
margins should both be at least 1 inch (2.5 cm) and the side margins 1.25 inches
(3.2 cm). If the report is to be bound, the left margin should be 2 inches (5.1
cm). (If the report is to be duplicated back-to-back before binding, the 2-inch
(5.1 cm) margin should be on the *right* side of the even-numbered pages.) The
right margin should not be justified; this improves legibility by creating length
variation from line to line.

Figure 9.2 Revised Page

ELECTRIC SHOCK

Electric shock is not always fatal, and rarely is it immediately fatal. It may only stun the victim and momentarily arrest breathing. In cases of electric shock, break contact, restore the victim's breathing by means of artificial respiration, and maintain warmth. To avoid receiving a shock yourself, exercise extreme caution when attempting to release the victim from contact with a live conductor. Many persons, by their lack of knowledge of such matters, have been severely shocked or burned when attempting to rescue a co-worker. To release a victim from contact with live conductors known to be 750 volts or less, do not touch the conductor, and do not touch the victim or the victim's bare skin if the victim is in contact with the live conductor. Instead, use a piece of dry, nonconducting material such as a piece of wood, rope, or rubber hose to push or pull the live conductor away from the victim. The live conductor can also be handled safely with rubber gloves. If the victim's clothes are dry, the victim can be dragged away from the live conductor by grasping the clothes—not the bare skin. In so doing, the rescuer should stand on a dry board and use only one hand. Do not stand in a puddle or on damp or wet ground. To release a victim from contact with live conductors of unknown voltage or more than 750 volts . . .

■ *Textual divisions:* Long, unbroken passages of text are very difficult to follow with attention, which is why the practice of dividing text into paragraphs was adopted centuries ago. In most workplace writing, paragraphs should not exceed five or six sentences and should be plainly separated by ample white space. If the paragraphs are single-spaced, insert double-spacing between them; if the paragraphs are double-spaced, use triple-spacing between them. To further organize content, group related paragraphs within a report into separate sections that logically reflect the internal organization of the report's information.

Figure 9.3 Second Revision

ELECTRIC SHOCK

Electric shock is not always fatal, and rarely is it immediately fatal. It may only stun the victim and momentarily arrest breathing. In cases of electric shock, break contact, restore the victim's breathing by means of artificial respiration, and maintain warmth. To avoid receiving a shock yourself, exercise extreme caution when attempting to release the victim from contact with a live conductor. Many persons, by their lack of knowledge of such matters, have been severely shocked or burned when attempting to rescue a co-worker.

To release a victim from contact with live conductors known to be 750 volts or less, do not touch the conductor, and do not touch the victim or the victim's bare skin if the victim is in contact with the live conductor. Instead, use a piece of dry, nonconducting material such as a piece of wood, rope, or rubber hose to push or pull the live conductor away from the victim. The live conductor can also be handled safely with rubber gloves. If the victim's clothes are dry, the victim can be dragged away from the live conductor by grasping the clothes—not the bare skin. In so doing, the rescuer should stand on a dry board and use only one hand. Do not stand in a puddle or on damp or wet ground.

To release a victim from contact with live conductors of unknown voltage or more than 750 volts . . .

Like the individual paragraphs, these sections should be plainly separated by proportionately greater spacing. Avoid widows and orphans when arranging paragraphs. Widows and orphans occur when a small part of the paragraph is found at the end of a page or at the top of a new page. Rearrange wording so that there is more than a line or two of a paragraph on its own. For example, you may choose to begin a new paragraph on a new page.

■   *Headings:* Separate sections of text should be labelled with meaningful headings that further clarify content and allow the reader to skim the report for specific aspects of its subject matter. Ordinarily, a heading consists of a word or phrase,

Figure 9.4 Third Revision

ELECTRIC SHOCK

Electric shock is not always fatal, and is rarely immediately fatal. It may only stun the victim and momentarily arrest breathing. In cases of electric shock, do three things:

1. Break contact.
2. Restore breathing by artificial respiration.
3. Maintain warmth.

To avoid receiving a shock yourself, exercise extreme caution when attempting to release the victim from contact with a live conductor. Many persons, lacking knowledge of such matters, have been severely shocked or burned attempting to rescue a co-worker.

Release victim from contact with live conductors known to be 750 volts or less:

- Do not touch the live conductor.
- Do not touch the victim or the victim's bare skin while the victim is in contact with the live conductor.
- Instead, use a piece of DRY, nonconducting material such as a piece of wood, rope, or rubber hose to push or pull the live conductor away from the victim. The live conductor may be handled safely with rubber gloves.
- If the victim's clothes are dry, the victim can be dragged away from the live conductor by grasping the clothing—not the bare skin. In so doing, the rescuer should stand on a dry board and . . .

not a complete sentence. (Instructional materials, however, sometimes use *questions* as headings.) The position of a heading is determined by its relative importance. A major heading is set in boldface caps and centred,

LIKE THIS

A secondary heading is set either in uppercase letters or in both uppercase and lowercase, is flush with the margin, and can be set in boldface print,

LIKE THIS

or

Like This

A subtopic heading is run into the text, separated by a period or a colon, and is sometimes indented. Set in both uppercase and lowercase letters, it can be set in bold print,

Like This. These recommendations are based on those in *The Gregg Reference Manual,* the most widely recognized authority on such matters.

Obviously, these principles are flexible, and various approaches to heading design and placement are used, some of them quite elaborate. Among the most helpful recommendations in *Gregg* is to limit a report to no more than three levels of headings.

- *Lists:* Sometimes a list is more effective than a conventional paragraph. If the purpose of the list is to indicate a definite order of importance, the items in the list should be *numbered* in descending order, with the most important item first, and the least important last. Similarly, if the list's purpose is to indicate a chronological sequence of events or actions (as in a procedures manual), the items should be numbered in sequential order. Numbers are not necessary, however, in a list of approximately equal items. In those cases, bullets (solid black dots or squares, like those used in this section), asterisks, or dashes will suffice.

- *White space:* All documents make use of white space—the blank areas of a document—to help readers focus on important aspects of the writing. White space includes the margins, but it also is the space between paragraphs and headings. Figure 9.4 illustrates how white space can improve understanding. White space can also help readers go through the document faster.

Tech Tips

Thanks to computerized word processing, nearly every workplace writer now has access to many page design features that in the past were available only through commercial print shops. As we've already seen, options such as varied spacing and type size, boldface print, capitalization, and underlining can make your documents appear much more professional. In addition, pages can be formatted in columns or other spatial arrangements.

Used selectively, these features enhance the design of a page not only by signalling major divisions and subdivisions within the content but also by creating emphasis with highlighted key words and phrases. In addition, many software packages are equipped with ready-made report templates and other features, such as headers and automatic page numbering for multipage documents, and these can be adapted to the individual writer's needs.

Even more versatile are the many DTP (desktop publishing) programs now available. These programs are ideal for creating documents that are more elaborate, such as newsletters, brochures, and manuals. By imitating traditional print-shop techniques, which required a drafting table, scissors, paste, rulers, compasses, and the like, DTP programs enable you to draw complex layouts right on the page. You can rotate bits of text to any angle; you can curve text; and you can wrap text around irregularly shaped graphics. Graphics can be enlarged, reduced, or cropped. In addition, DTP programs provide a vast range of fonts and permit very tiny gradations in spacing and type size. Interfaced with standard word-processing and graphic-design software, a good optical scanner, and a high-resolution laser printer, a DTP program such as Adobe InDesign can produce excellent, professional-quality results.

Remember to exercise restraint and maintain consistency in using these tools, however. Keep your page design relatively simple. It's very easy to get carried away and end up creating a messy and confusing document, especially if you're still relatively new to this technology. Like visual elements, page design options should never function simply as decoration but as aids to your reader's understanding. The key is to experiment with your software and thoroughly familiarize yourself with its capabilities. Soon you'll develop a more accurate sense of which page design features might genuinely help your reader.

When creating a report at work, you may be working on it over a period of time and you may be working with other people. This means that the document will probably be revised several times by you or others and that several versions may be available at the same time. Therefore, it is important to save drafts in a manner that allows you to work on the most recent revision. You may choose to title the draft and number it. The subsequent versions of the drafts will carry higher numbers, as in Formal report v1, Formal report v2, Formal report v3, etc. You may also choose to add the date that a revision was made. Whatever system you choose, make sure everyone follows the same pattern so that the current version of the document is the one people are working on.

REPORT FORMATS: MEMO, LETTER, AND BOOKLET

Many companies and organizations prepare short reports by using the fill-in-the-blanks approach typified by the form reproduced in Figure 9.5. As we have seen, however, computer technology now enables individual writers to personally design the pages of their reports. A customized report can usually be categorized into one of three report formats: memo, letter, or booklet.

Typically used for in-house purposes, the **memo report** is similar to the conventional memo but is longer (two pages or more) and is therefore divided into labelled sections. The **letter report**–typically sent to an outside reader–is formatted like a conventional business letter, except that the letter report is divided into labelled sections, much like a memo report. The **booklet report** resembles a short term paper and includes a title page. It, too, is divided into labelled sections. The booklet report is also accompanied by a cover memo (for in-house reports) or cover letter (for reports sent to outside readers). Much like the opening paragraph of a memo report or letter report, the cover memo or letter serves to orient the reader by establishing context and explaining the purpose and scope of the booklet report.

Both memo reports and booklet reports often contain visuals; letter reports sometimes do. Figures 9.6–9.16 illustrate the three formats. Written by a fictitious health inspector and his supervisor, these examples use easily understood subject matter. The three report formats can be adapted to any workplace situation, however, simply by changing the headings (and, of course, the text) to suit the subject at hand.

TYPES OF REPORTS

Like memos, emails, and letters, workplace reports are written in all kinds of situations for an enormous variety of reasons. Many reports are in a sense unique because they are written in response to one-time occurrences. On the other hand, it's not uncommon for a given report to be part of an ongoing series of weekly, monthly, or annual reports on the same subject. Generally, reports can be classified into several broad categories, but the most common categories are as follows:

- *Incident report:* Explains the circumstances surrounding a troublesome occurrence, such as an accident, a fire, an equipment malfunction, or a security breach.

- *Progress report:* Outlines the status of an ongoing project or undertaking.

- *Recommendation report:* Urges that certain procedures be adopted (or rejected).

- *Travel report:* Identifies the purpose and summarizes the results of business-related travel.

Figure 9.5 Employee Accident Report Form

EMPLOYEE ACCIDENT/FORM A

TO BE COMPLETED BY EMPLOYEE

Name _____   Home address _____

Social Insurance No. _____   Date of birth _____

Sex __M__ __F__   Department in which you work _____

Accident date _____   Day of week _____   Time _____ a.m. _____ p.m.

Date accident was reported _____   To whom _____

Location of accident _____   Witnesses _____

Description of accident (what you were doing, what equipment you
were using, etc.)

_____

_____

_____

Description of injury (include nature of injury and body part)

_____

_____

_____

Did you receive medical care on premises? _____   Describe _____

_____

_____

If you are being treated:

Name and address of physician: _____

Name and address of hospital: _____

Do you have a second job? _____

EMPLOYEE'S SIGNATURE _____   Date: _____

TO BE COMPLETED BY COMPANY NURSE

Above employee came to me on _____   regarding the above injury.

Comments:

_____

_____

_____

NURSE'S SIGNATURE _____   Date: _____

Figure 9.6   Memo Report, Page 1

Region of Waterloo
Public Health

MEMORANDUM

DATE: February 4, 2011

TO: Marjorie Witkowski, Supervisor

FROM: Richard Vaughan, Senior Inspector

SUBJECT: Restaurant Inspections

As you requested, here are the results of my most recent inspections
of food service establishments in the region, along with a week-by-
week statistical summary of inspections during January.

UNSATISFACTORY

The following establishments were found to be in substantial violation of the sanitary code.

Big Daddy's Steak House
431 Grand Avenue, Cambridge
Inspected January 28, 2010

Toxic chemicals (antifreeze, can of ant/roach killer) found on
premises. Potentially hazardous foods not kept at or above 140
degrees F (60 degrees C) during hot holding. Food not protected—
buckets of food stored on floor in cooler, food not covered in
coolers. Raw meat stored over prepared foods in cooler. Food

Figure 9.7   Memo Report, Page 2

2

build-up in storage room refrigerator. Canned goods in poor condition (dented, rusted). Bowl used as flour scoop. Box of paper towels improperly stored on floor. Nonfood contact surfaces not easily cleanable. Cardboard used as liner on food storage shelves. Restroom missing hand-wash sign. Light fixture missing shield and end caps. Kitchen ceiling tiles missing. No 2010 permit on display.

Employee Cafeteria, Paragon Insurance Co.
Airport Road, Breslau
Inspected January 30, 2010

Potentially hazardous foods not kept at or below 45 degrees F (7.2 degrees C) during cold holding. Potentially hazardous foods not kept at or above 140 degrees F (60 degrees C) during hot holding. Single-service napkins stored on kitchen floor.

Roma Pizzeria
38 Crowley Street, Ayr
Inspected January 31, 2010

Worker serving pizza slices with bare hands. Potentially hazardous foods not kept at or above 140 degrees F (60 degrees C) during hot holding. Food not protected—uncovered food in freezer, salt bucket not labelled. Hair improperly restrained—hats, nets/visors required. In-use utensils stored on paper plate. Employee (delivery driver) smoking in kitchen.

SATISFACTORY

The following establishments were found to be in essential compliance with the sanitary code, although some violations were noted.

Imperial Wok
618 Rogers Street, Waterloo
Inspected January 31, 2010

Potentially hazardous foods not kept at or above 140 degrees F (60 degrees C) during hot holding. Food not protected—jars of juice stored on kitchen floor. Improper use of utensils—scoop stored handle down in flour.

Figure 9.8 Memo Report, Page 3

3

Cuzzie's Pub
39 Railroad Street, Waterloo
Inspected January 31, 2010

Unshielded light fixture in walk-in cooler. No hand soap in restroom.

NO VIOLATIONS

The following establishments were found to be in full compliance
with the sanitary code.

University Coffee House
17 University Avenue N., Waterloo
Inspected January 28, 2010

Mister Eight Ball
49 Clinton Street, Kitchener
Inspected January 31, 2010

SUMMARY OF JANUARY 2010 INSPECTIONS

	Unsatisfactory	Satisfactory	No Violations
Jan. 7–11	3	2	2
Jan. 14–18	5	0	1
Jan. 21–25	2	3	2
Jan. 28–31	3	2	2
Totals	13	7	7

Figure 9.9 Letter Report, Page 1

Region of Waterloo Public Health

Regional Office Building, Court House Square
Kitchener, Ontario N2J 4B4

February 4, 2010

Mr. Daniel Runninghorse, Editor
The Record
29 Fairway Road
Kitchener, Ontario N2F 1P3

Dear Mr. Runninghorse:

As you may know, the Region of Waterloo Public Health department conducts
ongoing, unannounced inspections of food service establishments to ensure
their compliance with provincial codes, rules, and regulations. Since the findings
of these inspections are a matter of public record, *The Record* has in the past
printed that information in its entirety. Now that you have become the editor of
The Record, we would like you to continue this practice, which we regard as a
valuable service to the community and a validation of our efforts here at the
department.

Here are the results of recent inspections, as well as a week-by-week statistical summary of all inspections during January.

UNSATISFACTORY

The following establishments were found to be in substantial violation of the
sanitary code.

Big Daddy's Steak House
431 Grand Avenue, Cambridge
Inspected January 28, 2010

Toxic chemicals (antifreeze, can of ant/roach killer) found on premises. Potentially
hazardous foods not kept at or above 140 degrees F (60 degrees C) during hot
holding. Food not protected—buckets of food stored on floor in cooler, food not

Figure 9.10 Letter Report, Page 2

2

covered in coolers. Raw meat stored over prepared foods in cooler. Food buildup in storage room refrigerator. Canned goods in poor condition (dented, rusted). Bowl used as flour scoop. Box of paper towels improperly stored on floor. Nonfood contact surfaces not easily cleanable. Cardboard used as liner on food storage shelves. Restroom missing hand-wash sign. Light fixture missing shield and end caps. Kitchen ceiling tiles missing. No 2010 permit on display.

Employee Cafeteria, Paragon Insurance Co.
Airport Road, Breslau
Inspected January 30, 2010

Potentially hazardous foods not kept at or below 45 degrees F (7.2 degrees C) during cold holding. Potentially hazardous foods not kept at or above 140 degrees F (60 degrees C) during hot holding. Single-service napkins stored on kitchen floor.

Roma Pizzeria
38 Crowley Street, Ayr
Inspected January 31, 2010

Worker serving pizza slices with bare hands. Potentially hazardous foods not kept at or above 140 degrees F (60 degrees C) during hot holding. Food not protected—uncovered food in freezer, salt bucket not labelled. Hair improperly restrained—hats, nets/visors required. In-use utensils stored on paper plate. Employee (delivery driver) smoking in kitchen.

SATISFACTORY

The following establishments were found to be in essential compliance with the sanitary code, although some violations were noted.

Imperial Wok
618 Rogers Street, Waterloo
Inspected January 31, 2010

Potentially hazardous foods not kept at or above 140 degrees F (60 degrees C) during hot holding. Food not protected—jars of juice stored on kitchen floor. Improper use of utensils—scoop stored handle down in flour.

Figure 9.11 Letter Report, Page 3

Cuzzie's Pub
39 Railroad Street, Waterloo
Inspected January 31, 2010

Unshielded light fixture in walk-in cooler. No hand soap in restroom.

NO VIOLATIONS

The following establishments were found to be in full compliance with the sanitary code.

University Coffee House
17 University Avenue N., Waterloo
Inspected January 28, 2010

Mister Eight Ball
49 Clinton Street, Kitchener
Inspected January 31, 2010

SUMMARY OF JANUARY 2010 INSPECTIONS

	Unsatisfactory	Satisfactory	No Violations
Jan. 7–11	3	2	2
Jan. 14–18	5	0	1
Jan. 21–25	2	3	2
Jan. 28–31	3	2	2
Totals	13	7	7

Please feel free to call me at your convenience if you have questions regarding these inspections or any other matters relating to the Region of Waterloo Public Health department. Unless I hear otherwise, I will continue to provide inspection results on a weekly basis.

Sincerely,

Marjorie Witkowski

Marjorie Witkowski
Supervisor

Figure 9.12 Booklet Report, Cover Memo

Region of Waterloo Public Health

MEMORANDUM

DATE: February 11, 2010

TO: Janet Butler, Commissioner

FROM: Marjorie Witkowski, Supervisor

SUBJECT: Inspections Report

As you requested, here is a complete report on the results of Richard Vaughan's inspections of food service establishments in the region during late January, along with a week-by-week statistical summary of his inspections during that month.

Figure 9.13 Booklet Report, Title Page

**INSPECTIONS OF FOOD SERVICE ESTABLISHMENTS
IN THE REGION OF WATERLOO, ONTARIO
JANUARY 27–31, 2010**

Report Submitted to

Janet Butler
Commissioner of Public Health

by

Marjorie Witkowski
Supervisor, Regional Health Department

February 11, 2010

Figure 9.14 Booklet Report, Page 1

INTRODUCTION

In keeping with its mandate to safeguard the public welfare, the Region of Waterloo Public Health department conducts ongoing, unannounced inspections of the region's food service establishments to ensure their compliance with provincial codes, rules, and regulations. This report provides the results of seven inspections conducted by Senior Inspector Richard Vaughan during the period of January 27–31 of this year, along with a week-by-week statistical summary of Mr. Vaughan's 26 total inspections during January.

UNSATISFACTORY

The following establishments were found to be in substantial violation of the sanitary code.

Big Daddy's Steak House
431 Grand Avenue, Cambridge
Inspected January 28, 2010

Toxic chemicals (antifreeze, can of ant/roach killer) found on premises. Potentially hazardous foods not kept at or above 140 degrees F (60 degrees C) during hot holding. Food not protected—buckets of food stored on floor in cooler, food not covered in coolers. Raw meat stored over prepared foods in cooler. Food buildup in storage room refrigerator. Canned goods in poor condition (dented, rusted). Bowl used as flour scoop. Box of paper towels improperly stored on floor. Nonfood contact surfaces not easily cleanable. Cardboard used as liner on food storage shelves. Restroom missing handwash sign. Light fixture missing shield and end caps. Kitchen ceiling tiles missing. No 2010 permit on display.

Employee Cafeteria, Paragon Insurance Co.
Airport Road, Breslau
Inspected January 30, 2010

Potentially hazardous foods not kept at or below 45 degrees F (7.2 degrees C) during cold holding. Potentially hazardous foods not kept at or above 140 degrees F (60 degrees C) during hot holding. Single-service napkins stored on kitchen floor.

Figure 9.15 Booklet Report, Page 2

2

Roma Pizzeria
38 Crowley Street, Ayr
Inspected January 31, 2010

Worker serving pizza slices with bare hands. Potentially hazardous foods
not kept at or above 140 degrees F (60 degrees C) during hot holding.
Food not protected—uncovered food in freezer, salt bucket not labelled.
Hair improperly restrained— hats, nets/visors required. In-use utensils
stored on paper plate. Employee (delivery driver) smoking in kitchen.

SATISFACTORY

The following establishments were found to be in essential compliance
with the sanitary code, although some violations were noted.

Imperial Wok
618 Rogers Street, Waterloo
Inspected January 31, 2010

Potentially hazardous foods not kept at or above 140 degrees F
(60 degrees C) during hot holding. Food not protected—jars of juice
stored on kitchen floor. Improper use of utensils—scoop stored handle
down in flour.

Cuzzie's Pub
39 Railroad Street, Waterloo
Inspected January 31, 2010

Unshielded light fixture in walk-in cooler. No hand soap in restroom.

NO VIOLATIONS

The following establishments were found to be in full compliance with
the sanitary code.

University Coffee House
17 University Avenue N., Waterloo
Inspected January 28, 2010

Figure 9.16   Booklet Report, Page 3

Mister Eight Ball
49 Clinton Street, Kitchener
Inspected January 31, 2010

SUMMARY OF JANUARY 2010 INSPECTIONS

	Unsatisfactory	Satisfactory	No Violations
Jan. 7–11	3	2	2
Jan. 14–18	5	0	1
Jan. 21–25	2	3	2
Jan. 28–31	3	2	2
Totals	13	7	7

Of course, an individual report can serve more than one purpose; overlap is not uncommon. An incident report, for example, may well conclude with a recommendations section intended to minimize the likelihood of recurrence. In every situation, the writer must consider the purpose and intended audience for the report. Content, language, tone, degree of detail, and overall approach must be appropriate to the circumstances, and the report headings, formatting, visuals, and other features must suit the role of the particular report. The following pages discuss the four common report types in detail.

Incident Report

An incident report creates a written record of a troublesome occurrence. The report is written either by the person involved in the incident or by the person in charge of the area where it took place. Such a report may be needed to satisfy government regulations, to guard against legal liability, or to draw attention to unsafe or otherwise unsatisfactory conditions in need of correction. Accordingly, an incident report must provide a thorough description of the occurrence and, if possible, an explanation of the cause(s). In addition, it often includes a section of recommendations for corrective measures.

When describing the incident, always provide complete details:

- Names and job titles of all persons involved, including onlookers
- Step-by-step narrative description of the incident
- Exact location of the incident
- Date and exact time of each major development
- Clear identification of any equipment or machinery involved
- Detailed description of any medical intervention required, including names of ambulance services and personnel, nurses, physicians, hospitals, or clinics
- Reliable statements (quotation or paraphrase) from persons involved
- Outcome of the incident

To avoid liability when discussing possible causes, use qualifiers such as *perhaps, maybe, possibly,* and *it appears.* Do not report the comments of witnesses and those involved as if those observations were verified facts; often they are grossly inaccurate. Attribute all such comments to their sources, and identify them as speculation only. Furthermore, exclude any comments unrelated to the immediate incident. Although you're ethically required to be as complete and accurate as possible, don't create an unnecessarily suspicious climate by relying on secondhand accounts or reporting verbatim the remarks of persons who are obviously angry or distraught, as in this example:

Ronald Perkins suffered a severed index finger when his left hand became caught in a drill press after he tripped on some wood that another employee had carelessly left on the floor near the machine. According to Perkins, this was "pretty typical of how things are always done around here."

A more objective phrasing might look something like this:

Ronald Perkins suffered a severed index finger when his left hand became caught in a drill press. Perkins said he had tripped on wood that was lying on the floor near the machine.

Similarly, the recommendations section of an incident report should not seek to assign blame or highlight incompetence but to encourage the adoption of measures that will decrease the likelihood of repeated problems. Consider, for example, the incident report in Figures 9.17–9.18, prepared in memo format.

✳ Progress Report

A progress report provides information about the status of an ongoing project or activity that must be monitored to ensure successful completion within a specified period. Sometimes called status reports or periodic reports, progress reports are submitted either upon completion of key stages of a project or at regular, pre-established intervals—quarterly, monthly, weekly, or sometimes as often as every day. They are written by the individual(s) directly responsible for the success of the undertaking. The readers of these reports are usually in the management sector of the organization, however, and may not be familiar with the technical details of the situation. Rather, their priority is successful completion of the project within established cost guidelines. Therefore, the information in a progress report tends to be more general than specific, and the language tends to be far less technical than that of other kinds of reports. Most progress reports include the following components:

- **Introduction:** Provides context and background, identifying the project, reviewing its objectives, and alerting the reader to new developments since last report.
- **Work completed:** Summarizes accomplishments to date. This section can be organized in either of two ways: if the report deals with one major task, a chronological (or timeline) approach is advisable; if it deals with several related projects, the report should have subdivisions by task.
- **Work remaining:** Summarizes all uncompleted tasks, emphasizing what is expected to be accomplished first.
- **Problems:** Identifies any delays, cost overruns, or other unanticipated difficulties. If all is well, or if the problems are of no particular consequence, this section may be omitted.
- **Conclusion:** Summarizes the status of the project and recommends solutions to any major problems.

Figure 9.17   Incident Report (Memo Format), Page 1

Southeast Insurance Company

MEMORANDUM

DATE: October 16, 2011

TO: Jonathan Purdy
                 Physical Plant Supervisor

FROM: Bonnie Cardillo
                 Nurse

SUBJECT: Incident Report

John Fitzsimmons, a claims adjuster, slipped and fell in the front lobby of
the building, striking his head and momentarily losing consciousness.

DESCRIPTION OF INCIDENT

At approximately 2:55 p.m. on Thursday, October 15, Fitzsimmons was
returning from his break when he slipped and fell in the front lobby, striking his head on the stone floor and momentarily losing consciousness.
According to Beverly Barrett, the receptionist, the floor had just been
mopped and was still wet. She paged Mike Moore, the security officer,
who in turn paged me. When I arrived at approximately 3:00 p.m.,
Fitzsimmons had revived. I immediately checked his vital signs, which
were normal. He refused further medical attention and returned to work.
I advised him to contact me if he experienced any subsequent discomfort,
but to my knowledge there has been none.

Figure 9.18 Incident Report (Memo Format), Page 2

2

RECOMMENDATIONS

Two ideas come to mind.

Perhaps we should remind all employees to contact me first (rather than Security) in situations involving personal injury. The sooner I'm contacted, the sooner I can respond. Obviously, time can be an important factor if the problem is serious.

To prevent other occurrences of this nature, perhaps the maintenance staff should be provided with large, brightly coloured warning signs alerting employees and the public alike to the presence of wet floors. I see these signs in use at the mall, the hospital, and elsewhere, and they do not appear expensive. I have noted also that many are bilingual, bearing both the English warning "Caution: Wet Floor" and the French equivalent. No doubt they can be ordered from any of the catalogues regularly received by your office.

If properly prepared and promptly submitted, progress reports can be invaluable in enabling management to make necessary adjustments to meet deadlines, avert crises, and prevent unnecessary expense. Figures 9.19–9.22 present a progress report on capital projects, prepared in booklet format with a cover memo.

Recommendation Report

A recommendation report assesses a troublesome or unsatisfactory situation, identifies a solution to the problem, and persuades decision makers to pursue a particular course of action that will improve matters. Such reports are sometimes unsolicited. Generally, however, a recommendation report is written by a knowledgeable employee who has been specifically assigned the task. As with most kinds of reports, the content can vary greatly depending on the nature of the business or organization and on the nature of the situation at hand. In nearly all cases, however, recommendation reports are intended to enhance the quality of products or services, maximize profits, reduce costs, or improve working conditions.

In the case of a solicited report, the writer should attempt to get a written request from the individual who wants the report and then carefully study it to determine the exact parameters of the situation in question. If unsure of any aspect of the assignment, the writer should seek clarification before continuing. As discussed in Chapter 1, it's vital to establish a firm sense of purpose and audience before you attempt to compose any workplace writing. A clear and focused written request—or the discussion generated by the lack of one—will provide guidance in this regard.

Because recommendation reports are persuasive in nature, they are in several respects trickier to write—and to live with afterward—than reports intended primarily to record factual information. Tact is important. Because your report essentially is designed to improve existing conditions or procedures, you should guard against appearing overly critical of the present circumstances. Focus more on what *will be* than on what *is*. Emphasize solutions rather than problems. Do not assign blame for present difficulties except in the most extreme cases. A very helpful strategy in writing recommendation reports is to request input from co-workers, whose perspective may give you a more comprehensive understanding of the situation you're assessing.

Recommendation reports are structured in various ways, but almost all include three basic components:

- *Problem:* Identifies not only the problem itself but also, if possible, its causes and its relative urgency.
- *Solution:* Sets forth a recommendation and explains how it will be implemented; also clearly states the advantages of the recommendation, including relevant data on costs, timing, and the like.
- *Discussion:* Summarizes briefly the report's key points and politely urges the adoption of its recommendation.

Figure 9.19 Progress Report (Booklet Format), Cover Memo

FALLKILL INDUSTRIES, INC.

M E M O R A N D U M

DATE: November 10, 2011

TO: Judith Ayres,
                   Accounting Department

FROM: John Daly,
                   Physical Plant

SUBJECT: Progress Report on Capital Projects

As requested, here is the progress report on the five capital projects identified as high-priority items at last spring's long-range planning meeting:

- Replacement of front elevator in Main Building
- Replacement of all windows in Main Building
- Installation of new fire alarm system in all buildings
- Installation of emergency lighting system in all buildings
- Renovation of "B" Building basement

Please contact me if you have any questions.

Figure 9.20 Progress Report (Booklet Format), Title Page

FALLKILL INDUSTRIES, INC.

PROGRESS REPORT

on

CAPITAL PROJECTS

by

John Daly
Physical Plant

Submitted to

Judith Ayres
Accounting Department

November 10, 2011

Figure 9.21 Progress Report (Booklet Format), Page 1

INTRODUCTION

Fallkill Industries, Inc., is currently involved in several major capital projects that were identified as high-priority items at last spring's long-range planning meeting: replacement of the front elevator and all windows in the Main Building, installation of a new fire alarm system and emergency lighting system in all buildings, and renovation of the "B" Building basement. Progress has been made on all of these projects, although there have been a few problems.

WORK COMPLETED

Elevator Replacement

Equipment has been ordered from Uptown Elevator. The pump has arrived and is in storage. We have asked Uptown for a construction schedule.

Window Replacement

Entrance and window wall: KlearVue Window Co. has completed this job, but it is unsatisfactory. See "Problems" section on following page. Other windows: Architect has approved submittal package, and Cavan Glass Co. is preparing shop drawings. Architect has sent Cavan Glass Co. a letter stating that work must begin no later than April 3, with completion in July.

Fire Alarm System

First submittal package from Alert-All, Ltd., was reviewed by architect and rejected. A second package was accepted. The alarm system is on order.

Emergency Lighting System

BriteLite, Inc., has begun installation in the Main Building. BriteLite will proceed on a building-by-building basis, completing one before moving on to another.

Basement Renovation

First submittal package from Innovation Renovation was reviewed by architect and rejected. Innovation Renovation is preparing a second package to reduce HVAC costs. Work will begin in June.

Figure 9.22 Progress Report (Booklet Format), Page 2

2

WORK REMAINING

Elevator Replacement
Construction schedule must be received from Uptown Elevator. Work must begin.

Window Replacement
Entrance and window wall: problems with KlearVue Window Co. must be resolved. See "Problems" section below. Other windows: shop drawings must be received from Cavan Glass Co. and approved. Work must begin.

Fire Alarm System
System must be received. Work must begin. Work will be completed during downtime (10:00 p.m. to 6:00 a.m.) to minimize disruption.

Emergency Lighting System
BriteLite, Inc., must complete installation in the Main Building, then move on to other buildings. Bulk of this work will be done during downtime.

Basement Renovation
Final submittal package must be received from Innovation Renovation and approved. Work must begin.

PROBLEMS

Window Replacement
Entrance and window wall: KlearVue Window Co. is still responsible for replacing one window that has a defect in the glass. In addition, the architect refuses to accept three of the five large panes in the window wall due to excessive distortion in the glass. The architect has sent several letters to KlearVue but has received no response. The remaining balance on this contract ($18 750) is therefore being held, pending resolution of these problems.

CONCLUSION

Although none of the five capital projects targeted at the spring meeting has in fact been satisfactorily completed, all but one are moving forward through expected channels. The one troublesome item—the unsatisfactory windows—should be resolved. If KlearVue continues to ignore the architect's inquiries, perhaps our attorneys should attempt to get a response.

Figures 9.23 and 9.24 present a recommendation report prepared in letter format. The report focuses on enabling a feed manufacturing company to avert fiscal problems by cutting costs at one of its mills.

Travel Report

There are two kinds of travel reports: field reports and trip reports. The purpose of both is to create a record of—and, by implication, justification for—an employee's work-related travel. The travel may be directly related to the performance of routine duties (a field visit to a customer or client, for example), or it may be part of the employee's ongoing professional development (such as a trip to a convention, trade show, or off-site training session). Submitted to the employee's immediate supervisor, a travel report not only describes the employee activity made possible by travelling but also assesses the activity's value and relevance to the organization.

Travel reports are usually structured as follows:

- *Introduction:* Provides all basic information, including destination, purpose of travel, arrival and departure dates and time, and mode of travel (personal car, company car, train, plane).

- *Description of activity/service performed:* Not an itinerary but, rather, a selectively detailed account. The degree of detail is greater if readers other than the supervisor will have access to the report and expect to learn something from it. In the case of a field report, any problems encountered should be detailed, along with corrective actions taken.

- *Cost accounting:* Usually required for nonroutine travel. The employee accounts for all money spent, especially if the employer provides reimbursement.

- *Discussion:* An assessment of the usefulness of the travel and, if applicable, recommendations regarding the feasibility of other such travel in the future. In the case of a field report, suggestions are sometimes made based on the particulars of the situation.

Figures 9.25 and 9.26 present the two kinds of travel reports, both in memo format.

❈ Lab Report

When you are writing a lab report, it is important to remember all the required components, which include the following:

- *A title page:* Includes the name of the experiment, the people who participated in the experiment, and the date of the experiment. If you are unsure of the

Figure 9.23 Recommendation Report (Letter Format), Page 1

COOPER & SONS FEED COMPANY

"Serving Livestock Breeders Since 1932"

Belmore Mill • Huron-Bruce Line, Belmore, ON N0B 2V0 • (519) 555-1234

February 12, 2012

Ms. Mary Cooper, CEO
Cooper & Sons Feed Company
Main Office
123 High Street
Regina, SK S4S 1B2

Dear Ms. Cooper:

Here is the report you requested, outlining a proposed expense management plan that will enable the Belmore Mill to cut costs.

PROBLEM

Because of the recent closings of several large family-run farms in the surrounding area, our profit margin has shrunk. We must therefore reduce the Belmore Mill's annual operating budget by at least $70 000 for it to remain viable.

SOLUTION

Inventory Reduction
Reduce inventory by $50 000, thereby creating savings on 10% interest expense.
Saving: $5000.

Elimination of Hourly Position
Based on seniority, eliminate one customer service position, distributing responsibilities between the two remaining employees.
Saving: $15 500 in wages plus $2500 in benefits; total, $18 000.

Figure 9.24 Recommendation Report (Letter Format), Page 2

2

Elimination of Salaried Position
Eliminate plant manager position, distributing responsibilities between
the two assistant managers.

Saving: $36320 in salary plus $7264 in benefits; total, $43584.

Reduction of Remill Costs
Each load returned from farm for remill costs an average of $165 and
creates 3.5 hours of overtime work. Lowering our error rate from 2 per
month to 1 per month will save $1980 annually. In addition, this will
raise the ingredient value we capture on these feeds by 50%
(6 ton/month × 12 months × $100 increased value) or $7200.

Saving: total, $9200.

DISCUSSION

Adoption of the above measures will result in a total annual savings of
$75 784. This more than meets the requirements.

The principal negative impact will be on personnel, and we regret the
necessity of eliminating the two positions. It should be noted, however,
that the situation could be much worse. The hourly customer service
employee can be rehired after the scheduled retirement of another customer service worker next year. Also, the retrenched plant manager can
be offered a comparable position at the Cooper & Sons mill in Canmore,
where business is booming and several openings currently exist.

Therefore, the above measures should be implemented as soon as possible to ensure the continued cost-effectiveness of the Belmore Mill.

Thank you for considering these recommendations. I appreciate having
the opportunity to provide input that may be helpful in the company's
decision-making process.

Sincerely,

John Svenson

John Svenson
Operations Assistant

Figure 9.25 Field Report (Memo Format)

ACE TECHNOLOGIES CORP.

MEMORANDUM

DATE: November 17, 2011

TO: Joseph Chen, Director
                  Sales & Service

FROM: Thomas Higgins
                  Service Technician

SUBJECT: Travel to Jane's Homestyle Restaurant (Account #2468)

INTRODUCTION

On Monday, November 10, I travelled by company truck to Jane's
Homestyle Restaurant in Fredericton to investigate the owner's complaint
regarding malfunctioning video monitors (Ace Cash Register System
2000). I left the plant at 9:00 a.m. and was back by 10:30 a.m.

SERVICE PERFORMED

All three video monitors were functioning erratically. When I examined
them, however, the problem turned out to be very simple. Because of
how the Jane's Homestyle Restaurant counter area is designed, the key-
pad must be positioned farther away from the monitor than usual. As a
result, the 38 cm cable (part #012) that creates the interface between
the two units is not quite long enough to stay firmly in place, making
the connection unstable.

After explaining the problem to the restaurant manager, I provided a
temporary "quick fix" by duct-taping the connections. When I returned
to the plant, I instructed the shipping department to send the restaurant
three 50 cm replacement cables (part #123) by overnight delivery.

DISCUSSION

This incident demonstrates the need for thorough testing of systems
when they're installed, taking into account the environments where
they'll be used. We might check whether other customers have experienced similar difficulties. Maybe all System 2000 units should be
installed with longer cable.

Figure 9.26 Trip Report (Memo Format)

ACE TECHNOLOGIES CORP.

MEMORANDUM

DATE: November 17, 2011

TO: Floyd Danvers, Director
             Human Resources

FROM: Thomas Higgins
             Service Technician

SUBJECT: Travel to Northweston Marriott for Seminar

INTRODUCTION

On Thursday, November 6, and Friday, November 7, I travelled by company car to the Northweston Marriott to attend a seminar entitled "Workplace Communications: The Basics," presented by a corporate training consultant, Dr. George J. Searles. I left the plant at 8:00 a.m. and was back by 5:00 p.m. both days.

ACTIVITIES

The seminar consisted of four half-day sessions, as follows:
- Workplace Communications Overview (Thursday a.m.)
- Review of Mechanics (Thursday p.m.)
- Memos and Letters (Friday a.m.)
- Reports (Friday p.m.)

There were 21 participants from a variety of local businesses and organizations, and the sessions were a blend of lecture and discussion, with emphasis on clear, concise writing. The instructor distributed numerous handouts that illustrated the points under consideration.

COSTS

The program cost $800, paid by the company. Aside from two days' lunch allowance ($30 total) and use of the company car (60 kilometres total), there were no other expenses.

DISCUSSION

This was a very worthwhile program. I learned a lot from it. Since it would be quite difficult, however, to summarize the content here, I've appended a complete set of the handouts distributed by the instructor. As you will see when you examine these materials, the focus of the program was quite practical and hands-on. I recommend that other employees be encouraged to attend the next time this program is offered in our area.

format, be sure to ask your instructor about what he or she prefers. The name of the experiment should be clear, concise, and descriptive. For example, you should include the lab experiment number and a short title describing the experiment.

- *An abstract:* Provides a summary of the purpose of the experiment, key findings, and major conclusions, as well as the significance of the experiment. Abstracts may also include information about methodology. Again, if you are unsure what to include, ask your instructor if you are at school or your boss if you are out in the workforce. People have varying needs when asking for reports, so it is best to meet their needs when drafting a report.

- *An introduction:* Includes—according to the University of Toronto Engineering Communication Centre—the experiment objectives as well as the background to the experiment. This background can include previous research, theory, or formulas. The introduction is brief and contains only necessary information for the readers.

- *A methods and materials, or equipment section:* Can be a bulleted list of what was required to conduct the process. Make sure it is accurate and that nothing has been left out.

- *An experimental procedures section:* Is written in chronological (time) order. You must describe what you did and how you did it in the exact sequence that you performed the events.

- *Results:* Contains graphics, such as tables and figures. See Chapter 5 for more information about how to create and use visuals properly.

- *A discussion section:* Explains your results, including reasons for results that differ from those predicted. You will also analyze your results and provide an interpretation of them for the audience. This section of the report is important.

- *References:* Must be completed according to the format your instructor (or boss) requires. For further discussion of common citation formats, see Chapter 10, Long Reports.

- *Appendices:* Contain raw data so that someone reading your report can see how you obtained and interpreted your data. Singular is *appendix.*

Note: The information above based on Engineering Communication Centre, University of Toronto. "Online Handbook: Laboratory Reports." n.d. Web. 24 Feb. 2009.

LAB REPORT

GROUP MEMBERS: _____ **CLASS:** _____

SUPERVISOR: _____ **DATE:** _____

TITLE: _____
_____

RESEARCH QUESTION:
_____
_____

OBSERVATIONS: _____
_____
_____
_____

HYPOTHESIS: _____
_____

EXPERIMENT:

MATERIALS AND
APPARATUS: _____
_____

METHOD: _____
_____
_____
_____

RESULTS: _____
_____
_____
_____

CONCLUSIONS: _____
_____
_____
_____
_____

Completing reports can be straightforward, such as filling in the blanks, but others require more input from the writer; however, all reports follow a specific format.

✓ Checklist   Evaluating a Memo Report

A good memo report

___ follows standard memo report format;

___ includes certain features:

☐ TO line, which provides the name and often the title and/or department of the receiver

☐ FROM line, which provides the name and often the title and/or department of the sender

☐ DATE line

☐ SUBJECT line, which provides a clear, accurate, but brief indication of what the memo report is about

___ is organized into separate, labelled sections, covering the subject fully in an orderly way;

___ includes no inappropriate content;

___ uses clear, simple language;

___ maintains an appropriate tone, neither too formal nor too conversational;

___ employs effective visuals—tables, graphs, charts, and the like—where necessary to clarify the text;

___ uses white space effectively

___ contains no typos or mechanical errors in spelling, capitalization, punctuation, or grammar.

✓ Checklist   Evaluating a Letter Report

A good letter report

___ follows a standard letter format (full block is best);

___ includes certain features:

☐ Sender's complete address

☐ Date

☐ Receiver's full name and complete address

☐ Salutation, followed by a colon

☐ Complimentary close ("Sincerely" is best), followed by a comma

☐ Sender's signature and full name

☐ Enclosure notation, if necessary

____ is organized into paragraphs, covering the subject fully in an orderly way:

☐ First paragraph establishes context and states the purpose

☐ Middle paragraphs constitute the report, separated into labelled sections that provide all necessary details

☐ Last paragraph politely achieves closure

____ includes no inappropriate content;

____ uses clear, simple language;

____ maintains an appropriate tone, neither too formal nor too conversational;

____ employs effective visuals—tables, graphs, charts, and the like—where necessary to clarify the text;

____ uses white space effectively;

____ contains no typos or mechanical errors in spelling, capitalization, punctuation, or grammar.

✓ **Checklist**   Evaluating a Booklet Report

A good booklet report

____ is accompanied by a cover memo or letter;

____ includes a title page that contains the following:

☐ Title of the report

☐ Name(s) of author(s)

☐ Name of company or organization

☐ Name(s) of person(s) receiving the report

☐ Date

____ is organized into separate, labelled sections, covering the subject fully in an orderly way;

____ includes only appropriate content;

____ uses clear, simple language;

____ maintains an appropriate tone, neither too formal nor too conversational;

____ employs effective visuals—tables, graphs, charts, and the like—where necessary to clarify the text;

____ uses white space effectively;

____ contains no typos or mechanical errors in spelling, capitalization, punctuation, or grammar.

Exercises

Exercise 9.1
Write a report either to your supervisor at work or to the campus safety committee at your college, fully describing the circumstances surrounding an accident or injury you've experienced at work or at college and the results of that mishap. Include suggestions about how similar situations might be avoided in the future. Use the memo report format, and include visuals if appropriate.

Exercise 9.2
Write a report to the local police department regarding the rush-hour traffic patterns at a major intersection near campus. Observe for one hour during either the morning or evening rush period on one typical weekday. Record the number and kinds of vehicles (car, truck, bus, motorcycle) and the directions in which they were travelling, along with an estimate of pedestrian traffic. Also record, of course, any accidents that occur. Evaluate the layout of the intersection (including lights, signs, and so forth) in terms of safety, and suggest improvements. Use the booklet format and include visuals.

Exercise 9.3
Write a report to your communications instructor, outlining your progress in class. List attendance, grades, and any other pertinent information, including an objective assessment of your performance so far and the final grade you anticipate receiving. Use the memo format and include visuals.

Exercise 9.4
Write a report to the chair or dean of your program, urging that a particular college policy be modified. Be specific about the reasons for your proposal. Justify the change and provide concrete suggestions about possible alternative policies. Use the memo format and include visuals if appropriate.

Exercise 9.5
Write a report to your instructor, discussing any recent vacation trip you have taken. Summarize your principal activities during the trip, and provide an evaluation of how successful the vacation was. Use the letter format and include visuals.

Exercise 9.6
Write a report to a classmate, outlining the performance of your favourite sports team over the past three years. Using statistical data, be as factual and detailed as your knowledge of the sport will permit. Attempt to explain the reasons for the team's relative success or lack of it. Use the booklet format and include visuals.

Exercise 9.7

Write a report to the student services director or the physical plant director at your college, evaluating a major campus building with respect to accessibility to the physically challenged. Discuss the presence or absence of special signs, doors, ramps, elevators, restroom facilities, and the like. Suggest additional accommodations that should be provided if such needs exist. Use the booklet format and include visuals.

Exercise 9.8

Team up with a classmate of the opposite sex, and write a report to the physical plant director analyzing the differences, if any, between the men's and women's restroom facilities in the main building on your campus. Suggest any changes or improvements you think might be necessary. Use the booklet format and include visuals.

Exercise 9.9

Have you ever been the victim of, or witness to, a minor crime on campus? Write a report to the college security director, relating the details of that experience and offering suggestions about how to minimize the likelihood of similar occurrences in the future. Use the letter format and include visuals if appropriate.

Exercise 9.10

Write a report to your classmates in which you evaluate three nearby restaurants featuring similar cuisine (for example, seafood, Chinese, or Italian) or three nearby stores that sell essentially the same product (for example, athletic shoes, books and music, or clothing). Discuss such issues as selection, quality, price, and service. Use the booklet format and include visuals.

PEARSON
mycanadiantechcommlab

Visit www.mycanadiantechcommlab.ca for everything you need to help you succeed in the job you've always wanted! Tools and resources include the following:

- Composing Space and Writer's Toolkit
- Document Makeovers
- Grammar Exercises—and much more!

Long Reports:
FORMAT, COLLABORATION, AND DOCUMENTATION

LEARNING OBJECTIVE

When you complete this chapter, you'll be able to create well-designed long reports and to correctly document the sources of your information.

IN BUSINESS, INDUSTRY, AND THE PROFESSIONS, important decisions are made every day. Some concern routine matters, and others are more complicated, involving considerable risk and expense. Suppose, for example, that a hospital administration is debating whether to add a new wing to the main building, or perhaps a police department wants to switch to a different kind of patrol car, or a successful but relatively new business venture must decide whether to expand now or wait a few years. Each situation requires in-depth study before a responsible decision can be reached. The potential advantages and drawbacks of each alternative have to be identified and examined, as well as the long-range effects. This is where the long report comes into play. This chapter discusses how to prepare such a report, explaining its formatting components, the dynamics of group-written reports, and some standard procedures for documenting sources.

FORMAT

Obviously, both the subject matter and the formatting of long reports will vary from one workplace to another, and in the academic context, from one discipline to another and even from one instructor to another. Nevertheless, most long reports share the components described in the following paragraphs.

Transmittal Document

Prepared according to standard memo or business letter format (see Chapter 3), the transmittal document accompanies a long report, conveying it from whoever wrote it to whoever requested it. The transmittal document says, in effect, "Here's the report you wanted," and very briefly summarizes its content. The memo format is used for transmitting in-house reports, whereas the letter format is used for transmitting reports to outside readers. Often the transmittal document serves as a cover sheet, although sometimes it's positioned immediately after the report's title page. Figure 10.1 is a sample transmittal memo.

Title Page

In addition to the title itself, this page includes the name(s) of whoever prepared the report, the name(s) of whoever requested it, the names of the companies or organizations involved, and the date. In an academic context, the title page includes the title, the name(s) of the student author(s) and the instructor who assigned the report, the course name (along with the course number and section number), the college or university, and the date. Figure 10.2 is a sample title page prepared for a workplace context.

Figure 10.1 Drug-Testing Report, Transmittal Memo

PARAMOUNT CONSTRUCTION, INC.

MEMORANDUM

DATE: July 9, 2012

TO: Rosa Sheridan
             Director, Human Resources

FROM: William Congreve
             Administrative Assistant

SUBJECT: Drug-Testing Report

As you may recall, we recently decided that I should prepare a
report on drug testing in the Canadian workplace to help us explore
the feasibility of introducing a program at Paramount. Here is the
report. If you have any questions, I would be happy to provide
further details.

Figure 10.2 Drug-Testing Report, Title Page

DRUG TESTING
IN THE WORKPLACE

by

William Congreve
Administrative Assistant

Submitted to

Rosa Sheridan
Director of Human Resources

Paramount Construction, Inc.
Calgary, Alberta

July 9, 2012

Abstract

Sometimes called an executive summary, this is simply a brief synopsis—a greatly abbreviated version of the report (see Chapter 4). An effective abstract captures the essence of the report, including its major findings and recommendations. In the workplace, the abstract assists those who may not have time to read the entire report but need to know what it says. Sometimes the abstract is positioned near the front of the report; at other times it appears at the end. For a 10- to 20-page report, the abstract should not be longer than one page and can be formatted as one long paragraph. Figure 10.3 offers an example of a concise abstract.

Table of Contents

As in a book, the table of contents for a long report clearly shows each numbered section of the report, along with its title and the page on which it appears. Many also show subdivisions within sections. When fine-tuning a report before submitting it, check to ensure that the section numbers, titles, and page numbers used in the table of contents are consistent with those in the report itself (see Figure 10.4).

List of Illustrations

This list resembles the table of contents, but rather than referring to text sections, it lists tables, graphs, charts, and all other visuals appearing in the report—each numbered and titled—and their page numbers. As with the table of contents, always check to ensure that your illustrations list accurately reflects the visual contents of the report and the corresponding labelling/captions (see Figure 10.5).

Glossary

A "mini-dictionary," the glossary defines all potentially unfamiliar words, expressions, or symbols in your report. Not all reports need a glossary; it depends on the topic and the intended audience. But if you are using specialized vocabulary or symbols that may not be well known, it's best to include a glossary page with terms alphabetized for easy reference and symbols listed in the order in which they appear in the text (see Figure 10.6).

Text

One major difference between a long report and an academic term paper is that a report is divided into sections, usually numbered, and each with its own title. As mentioned previously, it's important that these divisions within the text be accurately reflected in the table of contents.

Every long report also includes an introduction and a conclusion. The introduction provides an overview of the report, identifying its purpose and scope, and explaining the procedures used and the context in which it was written. The conclusion summarizes the main points in the report and lists recommendations, if any.

Figure 10.3 Drug-Testing Report, Abstract

ABSTRACT

Paramount Construction is considering introducing a mandatory drug-testing program. Although intended to reduce the costs associated with workplace substance abuse, drug testing is quite controversial. Some experts argue that the extent of workplace drug abuse has been greatly exaggerated and that drug-testing programs—first introduced in large numbers in the 1980s—are a needless violation of employees' privacy. Most drug-testing programs rely on EMIT, a test that often yields inaccurate results, thus necessitating the use of confirmatory GC/MS testing to reduce the possibility of false positives. Drug testing appears to be least problematic when used to screen applicants for employment rather than administered to established employees. To avoid costly lawsuits and other setbacks, progressive companies observe several key features of successful drug-testing protocol: a clear policy statement, strict guidelines for specimen collection, use of NIDA-certified laboratories, confirmation of all positive test results, and employee assistance services. Paramount probably should introduce a drug-testing program, beginning by testing job applicants only, rather than the existing workforce, but we should first establish an Employee Assistance Program (EAP). In addition, we should seek assistance from an outside (NIDA) consultant.

Figure 10.4 Drug-Testing Report, Table of Contents

iii

TABLE OF CONTENTS

Figure 10.5 Drug-Testing Report, List of Illustrations

iv

LIST OF ILLUSTRATIONS

Figure 10.6 Drug-Testing Report, Glossary

v

GLOSSARY

CDC	Centers for Disease Control
EAP	Employee Assistance Program
EMIT	Enzyme Multiplied Immunoassay Technique
enzymes	Organic catalysts produced by living cells but capable of acting independently; complex colloidal substances that can induce chemical changes in other substances without undergoing change themselves
false negative	Test result that incorrectly indicates the absence of the substance(s) tested for
false positive	Test result that incorrectly indicates the presence of the substance(s) tested for
GC/MS	Gas Chromatography/Mass Spectrometry
immunoassay	Analysis of a substance to determine its constituents and the relative proportions of each
mass spectrum	Identifiable pattern of electromagnetic energy given off by a substance under specific test conditions
metabolites	Drug by-products that remain in the body after the effects of the drug have worn off
MRO	Medical Resource Officer, a licensed physician knowledgeable about substance abuse
NIDA	National Institute on Drug Abuse

Visuals

A major feature of many reports, visuals (see Chapter 5) sometimes appear in a separate section—an appendix—at the end of a report. A better approach, however, is to integrate visuals into the text, as this is more convenient for the reader. Either way, you should draw the reader's attention to pertinent visuals (stating, for example, "See Figure 5"), and every visual must be properly numbered and titled, with its source identified. The numbering/titling system must be the same system used in the list of illustrations.

Pagination

Number your report pages correctly. There are several pagination systems in use. Generally, page numbers (1, 2, 3, and so on) begin on the introduction page and continue until the last page of the report. Front-matter pages (abstract, table of contents, list of illustrations, glossary, and anything else that precedes the introduction) are numbered with lowercase Roman numerals (i, ii, iii, iv, and so on). There is no page number on the transmittal document or the title page, although the latter "counts" as a front-matter page, so the page immediately following the title page is numbered as ii. The best position for page numbers is in the upper right corner because that location enables the reader to find a particular page simply by thumbing through the report. Notice the page numbering throughout the sample report in this chapter (Figures 10.1–10.20).

For longer reports, employees often work together to create documents.

COLLABORATION

A memo, letter, or short report nearly always is composed by one person working individually. This is sometimes true of long reports as well. However, since the subject matter of long reports is often complex and multifaceted, such reports are often written collaboratively. Indeed, nearly all workplace writers are called on to collaborate at least occasionally. Teamwork is common in the workplace because it provides certain obvious advantages. For example, a group that works well together can produce a long report *faster* than one person working alone. In addition, the team possesses a broader perspective and a greater range of knowledge and expertise than an individual. To slightly amend the old saying, two heads—or more—are better than one. In addition, with the increasing sophistication of *groupware* (word-processing and document design programs created specifically for collaborative use), teamworking has become easier and faster than ever.

Nevertheless, collaboration can pose problems if the members of a group have difficulty interacting smoothly. Real teamwork requires everyone involved to exercise tact, courtesy, and responsibility. The following factors are essential to successful collaboration:

1. Everyone on the team must fully understand the purpose, goals, and intended audience of the document.

2. There must be uniform awareness of the project's confidentiality level, especially if individual team members must consult outside sources for data, background information, or other material.

3. Team members must agree to set aside individual preferences in favour of the group's collective judgment.

4. A team leader must be in charge of the project—someone whom the other members are willing to recognize as the coordinator. Ideally, the leader is elected from within the group (although sometimes the leader is appointed by someone at a higher level of authority). The leader must be not only knowledgeable and competent but also a "people person" with excellent interpersonal skills. The leader has many responsibilities:

    - Schedules, announces, and conducts meetings
    - Helps establish procedural guidelines, especially regarding progress assessment
    - Monitors team members' involvement, providing encouragement and assistance
    - Promotes consensus and mediates disagreements
    - Maintains an accurate master file copy of the evolving document

    In short, the leader operates in a managerial capacity (much like a professor in a college class), ensuring a successful outcome by keeping everyone on task and holding the whole effort together.

5. The team must assign clearly defined roles to the other members, designating responsibilities according to everyone's talents and strengths. For example, the group's most competent researcher takes charge of information retrieval. Someone trained in drafting or computer-assisted design agrees to format the report and create visuals. The member with the best keyboarding skills (or clerical support) actually produces the document. The best writer is the overall editor, making final judgments on matters of organization, style, mechanics, and the like. If an oral presentation is required, the group's most confident public speaker assumes that responsibility. A given individual might assume more than one role, but everyone must feel satisfied that the work has been fairly distributed.

6. Once the project has begun, the team meets regularly to assess its progress, prevent duplication of effort, and resolve any problems that arise. All disagreements or differences of opinion are reconciled in a productive manner. In any group undertaking, a certain amount of conflict is inevitable and indeed necessary to achieve consensus. This interplay, however, should be a source of creative energy, not antagonism. Issues must be dealt with on an objectively intellectual level, not in a personal or emotional manner. To this end, the group should adopt a code of interaction designed to minimize conflict and maximize the benefits of collaboration. Here are some guidelines:

- Make a real effort to be calm, patient, reasonable, and flexible—in short, *helpful.*

- Voice all reservations, misgivings, and resentments rather than letting them smoulder.

- Direct criticism at the issue, not the person ("There's another way of looking at this" rather than "You're only looking at this one way"), and try not to *interpret* criticism personally.

- Make an effort to really *listen* to others' remarks and not interrupt.

- Paraphrase others' statements to be sure of their meaning ("What you're saying, then, is . . .").

- Identify strengths in other people's work before mentioning weaknesses ("This first section is very well written, but I have a suggestion for revising the second section").

- Avoid vague, unhelpful criticism by addressing specifics ("In paragraph 3, it's unclear whether Dept. A or Dept. B will be in charge" rather than "Paragraph 3 is unclear"). This is especially important when providing *written* feedback.

- Try not to concentrate on picky, inconsequential fine points. Although glaring errors in spelling, grammar, and the like should certainly be corrected, the focus should be on the big picture.

- Accentuate the positive rather than the negative ("Now that we've agreed on the visuals, we can move on" instead of "We can't seem to agree on anything but the visuals").

- Suggest rather than command ("Maybe we should try it this way" instead of "Do it this way!") and offer rather than demand ("If you'd like, I'll . . . " instead of "I'm going to . . . ").

- Be aware of your body language, which can send negative signals that impede progress by creating resistance on the part of your teammates.

- In cases of major conflict, the leader must mediate to prevent the group from bogging down. One solution is to table the problematic issue and move on, addressing it at a later meeting after everyone has been able to consider it in greater depth. If there's a severe clash between two group members, it's usually best for the leader to meet privately with them to reach compromise.

7. All members of the group must complete their fair share of the work in a conscientious fashion and observe all deadlines. Nothing is more disruptive to a team's progress than an irresponsible member who fails to complete work punctually or who vanishes for long periods of time. To maintain contact between regularly scheduled meetings of the group, members should exchange phone numbers and/or email addresses. If all team members are sufficiently tech savvy, they can maintain contact through synchronous electronic discussion in real time using a virtual conference room or multiuser domain (MUD) accessible via the internet. But exchanges in such settings should be brief and to the point, as lengthy comments take too long to write and read, thus inhibiting the free and spontaneous flow of ideas so necessary to productive collaboration. Another option is to use file transfer protocol (FTP) to create a common website to which group members can post drafts for review by their teammates. In any case, electronic communication should be seen simply as a way to keep in touch between meetings and should not become a substitute for frequent face-to-face interaction.

Regardless of how the team goes about its work, however, it's extremely helpful to the eventual editor if all sections of the document have been prepared according to uniform procedures. Therefore, unless the workplace has adopted an organization-wide style manual that governs such matters, the team should formulate its own guidelines. The editor then does not have to waste valuable time imposing conformity on various members' work but can concentrate instead on more important matters such as organization and content. To be useful, however, the guidelines should not be too extensive. Their purpose is simply to ensure that all members are preparing their drafts in a consistent way. Here are 10 areas to consider:

- Margins: Usually, 1-inch or 1½-inch (2.5 cm or 3.8 cm) margins are used.
- Fonts: Simple fonts are the most legible; the standard Microsoft Word font for documents is Times New Roman.

- Type size: 12-point type is the norm, although headings can be larger.

- Spacing: Double-spacing is best for drafts (to facilitate editing), but final versions of documents are often single-spaced.

- CAPITALS, **bold face**, *italics*, and <u>underlining</u>: There must be agreement on when and how to use these options.

- Abbreviations, acronyms, and numbers: Again, the team must agree on their use.

- Page numbers: Position numbers in the upper-right corners of all draft pages.

- Placement and labelling of visuals: For recommendations, see Chapter 5.

- Headings: Depending on the nature of the document, headings can take many forms, including single words, phrases, statements, questions, and commands. As with all other format features, however, there should be uniformity in all sections.

- Documentation: If documentation is required, the same system should be used throughout.

Theoretically, a group can handle the writing of a report or other document in one of three ways:

- The whole team writes the report collectively, and then the editor revises the draft and submits it to the group for final approval or additional revisions.

- One person writes the entire report, and then the group—led by the editor—revises it collectively.

- Each team member writes one part of the report individually, and then the editor revises each part and submits the complete draft to the whole group for final approval or additional revisions.

Of these alternatives, the first is the most truly collaborative but is also extremely difficult and time consuming, requiring uncommon harmony within the group. The second method is preferable but places too great a burden on one writer. The third approach is the most common and is certainly the best, provided the editor seeks clarification from individuals whenever necessary during the editing process. For this reason, the third approach is the one that underlies most of what's been said here. Note, however, that in all three approaches the whole group gets to see and comment on the report in its final form. Because everyone's name will be on it, no one should be surprised when the finished product is released. Collaboration is, after all, a team effort with the goal of producing a polished document approved by all members of the team.

DOCUMENTATION

Documentation is simply a technical term for the procedure whereby writers identify the sources of their information. In the workplace and in popular periodicals, this is often accomplished by inserting the pertinent information directly into the text, as in this example:

> As journalist James Fallows says in his article "Microsoft Reboots" in the December 2006 issue of the *Atlantic Monthly*, "the debut of a new operating system usually leads to a surge in PC sales, as people who have been waiting to upgrade buy machines with the new software installed" (168).

This straightforward approach eliminates the need for a bibliography (list of sources) at the end of the piece. Documentation in academic writing, however, nearly always includes both a bibliography and parenthetical citations identifying the origin of each quotation, statistic, paraphrase, or visual within the text.

Documentation is necessary to avoid *plagiarism*—the use of someone else's work without proper acknowledgment. As the Modern Language Association (MLA) handbook explains, the term derives from the Latin *plagiarius*, meaning "kidnapper." Plagiarism means "Using another person's ideas, information, or expressions without acknowledging that person's work . . . ." It also means "Passing off another person's ideas, information, or expressions as your own to get a better grade or gain some other advantage . . . " (52). In several highly publicized recent cases, plagiarism has resulted in the firing of journalists at the *New York Times* and other publications. Similarly, the president of a prestigious northeastern college in the United States was forced to resign a few years ago after delivering a speech (later posted on the college's website) that included material borrowed from internet sources but not documented as such. Not surprisingly, then, "students exposed as plagiarists suffer severe penalties, ranging from failure in the assignment or in the course to expulsion from school" (53).

Here are the MLA's useful guidelines for recognizing and avoiding plagiarism: You have plagiarized if

- You took notes that did not distinguish summary and paraphrase from quotation, and then you presented wording from the notes as if it were all your own.
- While browsing the web, you copied text and pasted it into your paper without quotation marks or without citing the source.
- You presented facts without saying where you found them.
- You repeated or paraphrased someone's wording without acknowledgment.
- You took someone's unique or particularly apt phrase without acknowledgment.
- You paraphrased someone's argument or presented someone's line of thought without acknowledgment.

- You bought or otherwise acquired a research paper and handed in part or all of it as your own.

You can avoid plagiarism by

- Making a list of the writers and viewpoints you discovered in your research and using this list to double-check the presentation of material in your paper.

- Keeping the following three categories distinct in your notes: your ideas, your summaries of others' material, and exact wording you copy.

- Identifying the sources of all material you borrow—exact wording, paraphrases, ideas, arguments, and facts.

- Checking with your instructor when you are uncertain about your use of sources.

Bibliography

There are several standard ways to format a list of citations. The MLA format, which titles the list "Works Cited," and the American Psychological Association (APA) format, which titles the list "References," are the most commonly taught in college courses, although a great many others do exist: American Chemical Society (ACS), American Institute of Physics (AIP), American Mathematical Society (AMS), and the Council of Science Editors (CSE), to name just a few. Here is a typical bibliography entry formatted according to the MLA (7th edition) and APA (6th edition) guidelines:

MLA   Baron, Naomi S. *Alphabet to Email: How Written English Evolved and Where It's Heading.* London: Routledge, 2000. Print.

APA   Baron, N. S. (2000). *Alphabet to email: How written English evolved and where it's heading.* London: Routledge.

Notice the differences between the two formats. Perhaps the most obvious is the placement of the date of publication. (If a publication date is not provided, use "n.d.") But variations also exist with respect to capitalization, punctuation, and abbreviation. In both systems, however, double-spacing is used between the entries, and book titles—like the titles of newspapers, magazines, journals, and other periodicals—are italicized. In both formats, entries appear in alphabetical order by authors' last names or, in the case of an anonymous work, by the first significant word of the title.

There are many other kinds of sources besides a single-author book, however, and each requires a slightly different handling. Some of the most common citations are as follows:

Book by Two Authors

MLA   Willis, Tracey R., and Gemma C. Siringo. *Academic Advisement for the 21st Century.* 2nd ed. Washington: NEA, 2006. Print.

APA   Willis, T. R., & Siringo, G. C. (2006). *Academic advisement for the 21st century* (2nd ed.). Washington, DC: National Education Association.

Book by Three Authors

MLA   Whitman, William C., William M. Johnson, and John A. Tomczyk. *Refrigeration* & *Air Conditioning Technology.* 5th ed. Clifton Park: Thomson Delmar, 2005. Print.

APA   Whitman, W. C., Johnson, W. M., & Tomczyk, J. A. (2005). *Refrigeration* & *air conditioning technology* (5th ed.). Clifton Park, NY: Thomson Delmar.

Book by a Corporate Author

MLA   American Welding Society. *Welding Inspection Handbook.* 3rd ed. Miami: AWS, 2000. Print.

APA   American Welding Society. (2000). *Welding inspection handbook* (3rd ed.). Miami, FL: Author.

Edited Book of Articles

MLA   Stangor, Charles, ed. *Stereotypes and Prejudice: Essential Readings.* Philadelphia: Psychology Press, 2000. Print.

APA   Stangor, C. (Ed.). (2000). *Stereotypes and prejudice: Essential readings.* Philadelphia: Psychology Press.

Article in an Edited Book

MLA   Allport, Gordon. "The Nature of Prejudice." *Stereotypes and Prejudice: Essential Readings.* Ed. Charles Stangor. Philadelphia: Psychology Press, 2000. 20–48. Print.

APA   Allport, G. (2000). The nature of prejudice. In C. Stangor (Ed.), *Stereotypes and prejudice: Essential readings* (pp. 20–48). Philadelphia: Psychology Press.

Article in a Newspaper

MLA   Clark, Nicola. "One Word for Airplane Makers: Plastics." *New York Times* 16 June 2007: C3. Print.

APA   Clark, N. (2007, June 16). One word for airplane makers: plastics. *The New York Times,* p. C3.

Anonymous Article in a Newspaper

MLA   "Nuclear Power Sets off a Debate in the Senate." *Wall Street Journal* 15 June 2007: A2. Print.

APA   Nuclear power sets off a debate in the Senate (2007, June 15). *The Wall Street Journal,* p. A2.

Article in a Weekly or Biweekly Magazine

MLA   Hobson, Katherine. "Injury-Free Workouts." *U.S. News* & *World Report* 25 June 2007: 62–70. Print.

APA   Hobson, K. (2007, June). Injury-free workouts. *U.S. News* & *World Report, 142,* 62–70.

Article in a Monthly or Bimonthly Magazine

MLA   Sovoboda, Elizabeth. "The Fuel Cell." *Popular Science* July 2007: 76–82, 99. Print.

APA   Sovoboda, E. (2007, June). The fuel cell. *Popular Science, 271,* 76–82, 99.

Anonymous Article in a Magazine

MLA   "Beyond the Prius." *The Economist* 16 June 2007: 72. Print.

APA   Beyond the Prius. (2007, June 16). *The Economist, 383,* 72.

Article in a Trade Journal or Academic Journal

MLA   Fahey, Richard. "Clean Drinking Water for All." *Civil Engineering* 77.4 (2007): 45–54. Print.

APA   Fahey, R. (2007). Clean drinking water for all. *Civil Engineering, 77*(4), 45–54.

Personal Interview

MLA   Britton, William. Personal interview. 10 Nov. 2008.

APA   Financial officer William Britton (personal communication, November 10, 2008) stated that the "total cost of the project may be well over a million dollars."

Note: In APA style, all personal communications (conversations, interviews, and the like) are excluded from the list of references. Such sources are documented only within the text, as in the above example.

Online Sources

Internet Site

MLA   American Federation of Labor—Congress of Industrial Organizations. *AFL-CIO: America's Union Movement,* 2007. Web. 21 June 2007.

APA   American Federation of Labor - Congress of Industrial Organizations. (2007). *America's union movement.* Retrieved from http://www.aflcio.org

The date of access at the end of the entry in MLA documents the date that you viewed the online source. The date is no longer required by the APA format. Note that MLA no longer requires the URL, but if your instructor wishes you to add it, place the URL in angled brackets after the date of access.

Link Within an Internet Site

MLA   American Federation of Labor—Congress of Industrial Organizations. "Workers' Rights." *AFL-CIO: America's Union Movement.* 2007. Web. 21 June 2007.

APA   American Federation of Labor - Congress of Industrial Organizations. (2007). Workers' rights. *AFL-CIO: America's union movement.* Retrieved from http://www.aflcio.org/issues/iobseconomy/workersrights

Article in a Newspaper

MLA   Labaton, Stephen. "Microsoft to Alter Windows Vista." *New York Times.* 20 June 2007. Web. 22 June 2007.

APA   Labaton, S. (2007, June 20). Microsoft to alter Windows Vista. *The New York Times.* Retrieved from http://www.nytimes.com

Article in a Magazine

MLA   Krisher, Tom. "Chrysler to Boost Fuel Efficiency." *TIME* 21 June 2007. Web. 15 May 2008.

APA   Krisher, T. (2007, June 21). Chrysler to boost fuel efficiency. *TIME.* Retrieved from http:www.time.com

Article in a Database

MLA   Oh, William. "Preventing Damage to Motor Bearings." *HPAC Engineering* 79.4 (2007): 46–49. *Academic Search Premier.* Web. 10 May 2007.

APA   Oh, W. (2007). Preventing damage to motor bearings. *HPAC Engineering, 79*(4), 46–49. Retrieved from Academic Search Premier database.

Note: For APA if the document has a doi number, include this rather than the database name.

Email Message

MLA   Russo, Linda. "Re: Thursday's Meeting." Message to the author. 15 Jan. 2009. Email.

APA   Human Resources director Linda Russo (personal communication, January 15, 2009) agrees that Thursday's meeting "did not fully accomplish its objectives."

Note: In APA style, personal communications (email, conversations, interviews, and the like) are excluded from the list of references. Such sources are documented only within the text, as in the above example.

The examples just given follow the basic formats recommended by the MLA and the APA for documenting online sources. As you can see, both styles provide essentially the same information used to identify print sources: the author's name (if known), the title of the work, and, in some cases, the URL or web address at which the work appeared. But electronic sources are of many different kinds, not all of which easily lend themselves to these formats. For a more complete explanation of how electronic (and print) sources are handled, you should consult the two organizations' handbooks, readily available in most libraries:

MLA Handbook for Writers of Research Papers. 7th ed. New York: MLA, 2009. Print.

American Psychological Association. (2009). *Publication manual of the American Psychological Association* (6th ed.). Washington, DC: Author.

Because technology is changing so rapidly, the methods for citing these sources also change. Help is available on the internet itself. Numerous websites exist to assist you in preparing correct bibliography entries in various styles, including MLA and APA. Typically these sites employ a "fill in the blanks" approach. You provide the information, and the computer does the rest, creating a bibliography entry based on the publication data you've given. Of course, you must be careful to enter the data correctly for the program to work. Here are two such sites:

www.citationmachine.net

www.easybib.com

Even more conveniently, the 2007 edition of Microsoft Word includes a documentation feature that works much the same way. To access it, simply go to the Reference tab on the tool bar, and click on Manage Sources.

Parenthetical Citations

Every time you use a source within the body of a report, whether quoting directly or paraphrasing in your own words, you must identify the source by inserting parentheses. The contents and positioning of these parentheses vary somewhat depending on whether you're using MLA or APA style. Here are examples of how to cite quotations:

MLA "Email has emerged as a medium that allows communication in situations where neither speech nor writing can easily substitute" (Baron 259).

APA "Email has emerged as a medium that allows communication in situations where neither speech nor writing can easily substitute" (Baron, 2000, p. 259).

If you mention the author's name in your own text, neither MLA nor APA requires that the name appear in the parentheses, although the APA system then requires *two* parenthetical insertions:

MLA As Baron observes, "Email has emerged as a medium that allows communication in situations where neither speech nor writing can easily substitute" (259).

APA As Baron (2000) observes, "Email has emerged as a medium that allows communication in situations where neither speech nor writing can easily substitute" (p. 259).

When you're paraphrasing, the differences between the two styles are as follows:

MLA Email is sometimes more practical than speech or writing (Baron 259).

APA Email is sometimes more practical than speech or writing (Baron, 2000).

MLA As Baron observes, email is sometimes more practical than speech or writing (259).

APA As Baron (2000) observes, email is sometimes more practical than speech or writing.

To credit a quote from an unsigned source (such as the two "Anonymous Article" examples shown on page 246) do it as follows:

MLA   "Even if the Prius is pushed aside by other forms of hybrid, it has done wonders for Toyota's reputation" ("Beyond" 72).

APA   "Even if the Prius is pushed aside by other forms of hybrid, it has done wonders for Toyota's reputation" ("Beyond the Prius," 2007, p. 72).

To credit a paraphrase from an unsigned source, follow these examples:

MLA   Whatever its future, the Prius has greatly enhanced Toyota's status as an industry leader ("Beyond" 72).

APA   Whatever its future, the Prius has greatly enhanced Toyota's status as an industry leader ("Beyond the Prius," 2007).

The purpose of parenthetical citations is to enable readers to find your sources on the Works Cited or References page, in case they wish to consult those sources in their entirety. As the *MLA Handbook* explains, "Documentation . . . tends to discourage the circulation of error, by inviting readers to determine for themselves whether a reference to another text presents a reasonable account of what that text says" (126).

Obviously, proper documentation is an important part of any report or other paper that has drawn on sources beyond the writer's own prior knowledge. Figures 10.7–10.20 show the remainder of a correctly prepared report, *Drug Testing in the Workplace*, with documentation prepared according to MLA guidelines (you saw the preliminary sections of this report in Figures 10.1–10.6). As mentioned earlier, actual reports written in the workplace may employ other styles of documentation. But the *format* of this report is fairly typical of the kind used in the workplace and in most college courses focusing on workplace communications. Once you've mastered this format, you can adapt it to a wide range of situations, whatever documentation system you may be using.

Tech Tips

The MLA Handbook says it quite well:

> Assessing Internet resources is a particular challenge. Whereas the print publications that researchers depend on are generally issued by reputable publishers, like university presses, that accept responsibility for the quality and reliability of the works they distribute, relatively few electronic publications currently have comparable authority. (34)

Consequently, you must exercise great selectivity when gathering information online. Here are some questions to ask when evaluating electronic sources:

- Who has posted or sponsored the site? An individual? An organization? A special interest or advocacy group? What are their credentials or qualifications? The final suffix in the URL indicates a site's origins:

.com	Commercial enterprise
.org	Nonprofit organization
.edu	College, university, or other educational institution
.gov	Government agency
.mil	Military group
.net	Network

.ca   Sites from Canada

.uk   Sites from Great Britain

.au   Sites from Australia

Sometimes it's helpful to enter the individual's or group's name in a search engine to see what related sites emerge. This often reveals affiliations and biases that have an impact on credibility.

■ Does the site itself provide links to related sites? Does it credit its own sources?

■ Is the information presented in a reasonably objective fashion, or does the site seem to favour or promote a particular viewpoint or perspective?

■ Does the site provide an email address or other contact information that you can use to seek more information?

■ What is the date of the posting? Is the information current?

■ How well written is the site? How well designed? In short, does it seem to be the work of professionals or of amateurs?

✔ Checklist   Evaluating a Long Report

An effective long report

___ is accompanied by a transmittal document (memo or letter);

___ includes certain components:

☐ Title page that includes the title of the report, name(s) of author(s), name of company or organization, name(s) of person(s) receiving the report, and the date

☐ Abstract that briefly summarizes the report

☐ Table of contents, with sections numbered and titled and page numbers provided

☐ List of illustrations, each numbered and titled, with page numbers provided

☐ Glossary, if necessary

___ is organized into sections numbered and titled in conformity with the table of contents, covering the subject fully in an orderly way;

___ is clear, accurate, and sufficiently detailed to satisfy the needs of the intended audience;

___ uses plain, simple language;

___ maintains an appropriate tone, neither too formal nor too conversational;

___ employs effective visuals—tables, graphs, charts, and the like—each numbered and titled in conformity with the list of illustrations;

___ includes full documentation (bibliography and parenthetical citations) prepared according to MLA or APA format;

___ contains no typos or mechanical errors in spelling, capitalization, punctuation, or grammar.

Figure 10.7 Drug-Testing Report, Page 1

I - INTRODUCTION

Since the founding of the company in 1952, Paramount Construction has always sought to achieve maximum productivity while providing safe, secure, and conducive work conditions for our employees. In keeping with these goals, management has determined that it may now be time for Paramount to take a more active role in the war against drugs by adopting measures to ensure a substance-free workplace. One such measure that has been suggested is the creation of a mandatory drug-testing policy for all new and established employees, and this idea is currently under consideration.

As figure 1 illustrates, our industry incurs a number of fatal occupational injuries. While it is lower than in other occupations, it is still significant. According to the Center to Protect Workers' Rights, the number of deaths has not increased significantly since the 1990s, but this may be due to lack of accurate reporting (33). Therefore, U.S. statistics will also be used in this report.

In the U.S. many construction fatalities resulted from falls, as shown in figure 2 and figure 3. When we consider the number of Canadians who admit to drug use (see figure 4), it's certainly possible that at least some of these fatalities can be attributed to drug-related impairment.

Drug testing first became popular in North America after President Reagan's Executive Order 12564 in 1986 mandated the testing of federal employees in jobs entailing safety risks. The Drug Free Workplace Act, passed by Congress in 1988, along with the rapid evolution of reliable testing technology, further accelerated the spread of testing (Knudsen 623). But drug testing has always been somewhat controversial, and we need to carefully consider all aspects of the subject before reaching a determination about whether we should adopt the practice here in Canada. This report, compiled after an in-depth review of recent professional literature on the subject, is intended as a first step in that process.

II - KINDS OF TESTING

Although there are no truly definitive figures on the percentage of employers that require drug testing in Canada, most estimates in the U.S are at least 50%, with larger companies (which can better afford testing programs) contributing disproportionately to that number (Hawkins 42). Among companies that test, several approaches are used: pre-employment, routine, reasonable suspicion/post-accident, return to work, and random (Brunet 6–7).

Figure 10.8 Drug-Testing Report, Page 2

2

Pre-Employment: Required of successful job applicants about to be hired, as a condition of employment. Indeed, some employers don't even bother to confirm a positive pre-employment test result, even though most guidelines strongly recommend such confirmation of all positive results (Hawkins 44). Sometimes a follow-up test is required after the new worker's probationary period or when the worker is being transferred or promoted. Pre-employment testing is the most common kind (White 1895).

Mining, quarrying, and oil	49.9/100,000
Logging and forestry	42.9/100,000
Fishing and trapping	35.6/100,000
Agriculture	28.1/100,000
Construction	20.6/100,000
Finance and insurance	0.2/100,000

Figure 1. Fatal Occupational Injuries by Industry from Sharpe, Andrew
and Jill Hardt. "Five Deaths a Day: Workplace Fatalities in Canada,
1993–2005," *Centre for the Study of Living Standards.* Web. Dec. 2006.
Courtesy of Centre for the Study of Living Standards.

Figure 10.9   Drug-Testing Report, Page 3

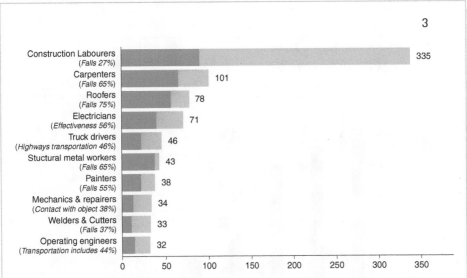

3

* *Selected occupations had a minimum of 40 fatalities and 45,000 employed workers in 2001.*
Note: Data exclude fatalities resulting from September 11 terrorist attacks.

Figure 2. Construction Occupations with Most Fatalities from United States Centers
for Disease Control, "Construction Fatalities 2001: Census of Fatal Occupational
Injuries," eLCOSH: Electronic Library of Construction Occupational Safety and Health,
Web. 15 June 2007.

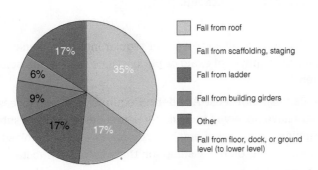

Fall from roof

Fall from scaffolding, staging

Fall from ladder

Fall from building girders

Other

Fall from floor, dock, or ground
level (to lower level)

Figure 3. Falls by Detailed Event from CDC, "Construction Fatalities."

Figure 10.10 Drug-Testing Report, Page 4

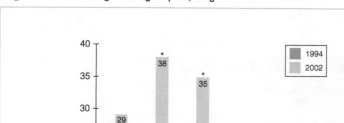

4

Data sources: 2002 Canadian Community Health Survey; 1994 Canada's Alcohol and Other Drugs Survey
* Significantly higher than estimate for 1994 (p < 0.05)
E2 Coefficient of variation 25.1% to 33.3%
F Coefficient of variation greater than 33.3%

Figure 4. Percentage of Population Aged 15 or Older Who Used Cannabis in Past Year, by Age Group, 1994, and 2002 adapted from Michael Tjepkema, "Use of Cannabis and Other Illicit Drugs," Health Reports 15.4 (2004) Web. 9 March 2010.

Routine: Required of all employees at regular intervals, sometimes as part of an annual physical exam or performance review and sometimes more often.

Reasonable Suspicion/Post-Accident: Required of all employees whose supervisors have observed behaviours that seem to indicate substance abuse. Similarly, required of employees who have been involved in a workplace accident, on the assumption that controlled substances may have been a cause.

Return to Work: Required of all returning employees who have been off the job because of a prior violation and have completed a treatment program. This assumes, of course, that the company offers such a program as part of its EAP.

Figure 10.11 Drug-Testing Report, Page 5

5

In the U.S., many companies do not, opting instead for immediate termination of anyone who fails a drug test, even if it's a first offense.

Random: Required of some employees without prior notification. "Computer-based, random-name generated software keeps the process completely objective. Consequently, some employees might be tested several times in a row, or they may not be tested for a long period of time—it's the nature of random testing. It is for this reason, however, that random testing both decreases and deters drug usage—employees don't know when they'll be tested" (Swartley 25). Because of its haphazard nature, this approach is the most effective. But it's also the most controversial, drawing fire from civil libertarians, labour unions, and workers themselves. As a result, it's the least common kind of testing (White 1895).

III - METHODS OF TESTING

Simply put, drug testing is done by analyzing biological specimens for drugs or drug metabolites in the body of the test subject. Typically, an initial immunoassay test such as an EMIT is used, followed by a confirmatory GC/MS test if the first test is positive. Several different kinds of specimens can be analyzed: sweat, saliva, blood, hair, and urine (Brunet 4–5).

Sweat: A sweat specimen can be obtained by having the test subject wear an adhesive patch that in effect soaks up the person's perspiration, which can then be tested for drug residue. This test is almost impossible to falsify, but its critics contend that the patch is susceptible to outside contamination that can produce false positives as well as false negatives. In any case, it's not widely used (Hawkins 45).

Saliva: A saliva specimen can be obtained by placing in the subject's mouth a small, specially designed sponge that soaks up oral fluids, which can then be tested for drugs or drug residue. Like the sweat test, this procedure is fairly reliable and quite noninvasive, but it has not yet gained wide acceptance.

Blood: A blood specimen can be obtained through the usual clinical procedure and is quite reliable, but has the disadvantage of being highly invasive. In addition, it requires "stringent medical conditions, because of the risk of blood-borne infectious diseases" (White 1893). For these reasons, it is not widely used.

Hair: A hair specimen can be easily obtained by simply cutting some off the subject's head, starting near the scalp. Analysis of such a 3.5-cm

Figure 10.12 Drug-Testing Report, Page 6

6

specimen will provide an accurate 90-day drug history. Thousands of employers are using this kind of test, but it's controversial because results can be skewed by certain shampoos, airborne contaminants, and the like. In addition, (National Institute on Drug Abuse) (NIDA) research has revealed that certain drug molecules bind more readily to darker hair, thus putting some racial and ethnic groups at a disadvantage. As one Substance Abuse and Mental Health Services Administration official put it, "If two employees use cocaine, the blond may barely test negative, and the other will get caught" (Hawkins 46).

Urine: A urine specimen is readily obtainable, and an uncontaminated sample is generally reliable. But the urine test is the easiest to falsify because the subject is usually afforded privacy while producing the sample. Obviously, then, this allows for various ways to alter, dilute, or even substitute for the sample. Nevertheless, the urine test remains by far the most popular method of testing. Despite its relative unreliability, urine is "preferred over blood samples because it requires a less invasive procedure, contains the metabolite . . . and is available in greater quantities" (Brunet 4).

IV - ARGUMENTS IN FAVOUR

At first glance, the question of whether to test for drugs in the workplace seems quite uncomplicated. Obviously, a drug-free workplace is preferable to one in which employees' performance—and safety—may be compromised by substance abuse. And statistics seem to bear this out. According to several sources, drug abusers are one-third as productive as nonabusers, three times more likely to be late, almost four times more likely to be in a workplace accident, and five times more likely to file a workers' compensation claim. Indeed, in the U.S., where such statistics are available, 47% of all such claims are drug-related, with drug-related problems costing businesses an estimated $75 billion to $100 billion (U.S. dollars) annually (Swartley 24, 28). As figure 5 shows, our own industry, along with mining, is the hardest hit by workers' compensation costs in the U.S., where these recent statistics are available. It is easy to extrapolate the same results in Canada. Not surprisingly, drug testing has gained increased acceptance over the years, with most people expressing support for testing, especially of employees in safety-sensitive positions (Brunet 27).

Figure 10.13 Drug-Testing Report, Page 7

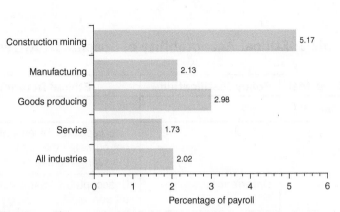

Figure 5. Workers' Compensation Costs, by Industry from United States Centers for Disease Control, "Employer Spending on Workers' Compensation, by Industry, 2000," eLCOSH: Electronic Library of Construction Occupational Safety and Health, Web. 15 June 2007.

V - ARGUMENTS AGAINST

Although drug testing certainly enjoys great intuitive appeal, there exists a number of arguments against the practice. Most fundamentally, it's been said that drug testing creates an adversarial climate in the workplace, leading to distrust and lowered morale. Along those lines, ethicists and civil libertarians—particularly the Human Rights Commission—have been quick to remind us that drug testing is an invasion of privacy and can even be seen as an infringement on human rights. See table 1. They have also pointed out that the oft-cited statistics about drug users' productivity deficits, tardiness, absenteeism, and accident involvement derive from the so-called Firestone Study of 1972, which has never been documented and can be fairly categorized as an example of "junk science." Indeed, it would appear that no such study ever actually existed (Zimmer 7; White 1896).

Opponents argue that employers have been influenced not only by faulty data, but also by sensationalized media accounts and pressure from government agencies and the powerful—because it is highly profitable—testing industry itself. In addition, even the National Academy of Science has admitted that "when post-accident drug screening reveals . . . marijuana, it does not mean that marijuana . . . played a causal role" (Zimmer 9) because tests do not measure impairment; rather, by detecting metabolites they reveal past use, which

Figure 10.14 Drug-Testing Report, Page 8

Table 1: Ethical Acceptability of Specific Drug Tests

Type of Drug Test	Policy Justification	Ethical Determination
Pre-employment		
	Symbolic	Unacceptable: Benefits of testing do not outweigh the harms, especially the infringement of personal privacy
	Deterrence	Unacceptable: Same rationale as above
	Public and Worker Safety	Not addressed in ethics literature
Existing Workforce		
Universal	Productivity	Unacceptable: Economic interests of employers are secondary to the autonomy interests of workers
	Treatment	Unacceptable: Protecting individual's autonomy is a stronger moral duty than beneficence
	Public and Worker Safety	Not addressed in ethics literature
Random	Deterrence	Unacceptable: "With no showing of a significant problem there is too little evidence that there will be any deterrent effect or any progress made to combat drug use" (DeCew 22)
	Public and Worker Safety	Acceptable: Preventing harm to third parties overrides individual privacy considerations
For Cause	Treatment	Acceptable: Beneficence is an acceptable rationale if person is in danger
	Public and Worker Safety	Acceptable: If the safety of others is in jeopardy and a problem is evident, then the privacy concerns of the individual are trumped by the need to prevent harm

Source: James R. Brunet, *Drug Testing in Law Enforcement Agencies: Social Control in the Public Sector* (New York: LFB Scholarly Publishing, 2005), Print.

Figure 10.15 Drug-Testing Report, Page 9

9

may have occurred up to three weeks prior to the incident (see table 2). As one researcher puts it, "Drug testing is not necessarily a measure of performance impairment, but instead may reveal illegal behavior" (Knudsen 623). We have known for some time that workplace accidents are caused by a number of other factors besides impairment. (See table 3.)

Table 2: Approximate Duration of Detectability of Selected Drugs in Urine

Drugs	Approximate Duration of Detectability
Amphetamines	2 days
Barbiturates	1–7 days
Benzodiazepines	3 days
Cocaine metabolites	2–3 days
Methadone	3 days
Codeine	2 days
PCP	8 days
Cannabinoids	
Single use	3 days
Moderate smoker (4 times/week)	5 days
Heavy Smoker (daily)	10 days
Chronic heavy smoker	21 days

Source: Mark A. Rothstein, "Drug Testing in the Workplace: The Challenge to Employment Relations and Employment Law," *Ethical Theory and Business*, Eds. Tom L. Beauchamp and Norman E. Bowie (Upper Saddle River, N.J.:Prentice Hall, 1997), 292–309. Print.

And the actual tests themselves have been criticized as unreliable. "The accuracy of some on-site urine tests can be as low as 52 percent" (Hawkins 41). Indeed, a CDC study of 13 testing facilities found error rates approaching 100%, which led to the creation of strict accreditation criteria that labs must now meet for NIDA certification (Brunet 33). As with anything, however, employers can choose among a wide range of testing instruments, and the cost varies accordingly. Unfortunately, "the least expensive drug tests, favoured by employers, are also the most error-prone" (Hawkins 41). But even if an employer chooses a NIDA-certified lab, there is still the problem of employees attempting to beat the test. There are a variety of products sold on the open market for this purpose, and countless internet websites dispense related advice and information.

Figure 10.16 Drug-Testing Report, Page 10

Table 3: Percentage of Job Injuries Associated With Each Variable

Variable		Injuries [% (N)]	Total N	Injuries Associated with Variable
Trouble sleeping	No	5.7(12)	210	77.8
	Yes	15.4(42)	273	
Noise and dirt	No	6.2(20)	324	62.3
	Yes	22.0(33)	150	
Danger	No	6.8(26)	380	50.9
	Yes	28.1(27)	96	
Shift work	No	8.2(31)	365	41.5
	Yes	21.8(22)	101	
Worry	No	9.0(35)	387	34.0
	Yes	19.8(18)	91	
Boredom	No	9.1(37)	408	28.8
	Yes	21.7(15)	69	
Conflict	No	9.1(42)	419	28.3
	Yes	25.0(15)	60	
Illicit drug use	No	9.8(43)	440	20.4
	Yes	25.6(11)	43	

Source: Scott MacDonald, "The Role of Drugs in Workplace Injuries: Is Drug Testing Appropriate?" *Journal of Drug Issues 25* (1995), 703–722. Print.

"The more usual methods of attempting to avoid detection are through use of diuretics and laxatives, adulteration, and substitution" (White 1898).

VI - CHARACTERISTICS OF AN EFFECTIVE PROGRAM

Employers agree that for any drug-testing program to succeed, every effort must be made to safeguard against error (and attendant liability) and to minimize any potentially negative impact on employee morale. To this end, most progressive companies design their programs according to the NIDA guidelines. Some key features are as follows:

Clear policy statement: Using input from human resources, employee relations, union and legal department representatives, and employees

Figure 10.17 Drug-Testing Report, Page 11

11

themselves, a clear, comprehensive policy statement must be written. The statement should spell out the company's standards of employee conduct, details of how and under what circumstances testing will occur, and what steps will be taken in response to a positive test result.

Strict guidelines for specimen collection: A company may choose to collect specimens in-house (usually at the company's health or medical facility) or off site, at a hospital or clinic or at a facility specializing in such procedures. In any case, it is absolutely crucial that collection be conducted according to the strictest NIDA standards. "Because the first few links in the chain of custody are forged here . . . many experts feel that choosing your collection site merits greater attention than choosing your lab" (Brookler 130).

NIDA-certified laboratory: To become NIDA-certified, a lab must meet the most stringent standards of accuracy and protocol, especially regarding the chain of custody governing the handling of specimens. In short, NIDA-certified laboratories are the most reliable and certainly the most credible in court.

Confirmation of positive results: Positive test results should be confirmed by means of a GC/MS follow-up test. "Without the GC/MS confirmation, you aren't legally defensible" (Brookler 129). In the event of a positive confirmation, the case must then be referred to the company's Medical Review Officer (MRO), who searches for alternative medical explanations for the positive test result before providing final confirmation. The MRO may refer the case back to management only after the employee has been given the opportunity to meet with the MRO. At most companies, the MRO is a contract employee.

Employee assistance program: Because substance abuse is recognized as a disease, many employers now provide employee assistance programs (EAP). Rather than being terminated, employees who test positive may instead be referred for counselling. In such instances, the rehabilitation option is usually presented as a condition of continued employment. This approach, which stresses rehabilitation rather than punishment, is consistent with nationwide trends.

Figure 10.18 Drug-Testing Report, Page 12

12

VII - CONCLUSION

Certainly, the whole subject of drug testing in the workplace is rather complicated, but several things do seem clear:

> Substance abuse costs employers, both directly and indirectly. Substance abuse in employees leads to reduced productivity, additional costs of hiring and training workers, and administrative costs of absenteeism and worker's compensation claims. It can also result in loss of customers and sales, and damage your organization's reputation. . . . The right drug and alcohol testing program protects employees, customers, and your bottom line. It can increase employee productivity and retention, decrease absenteeism, and save you money. (Current 34)

Paramount Construction probably should introduce a testing program, but the way to begin would be to require testing of job *applicants* only—at least at first. This would enable us to become gradually acquainted with the procedures and problems involved, without the risk of alienating employees already on board. We might expand the program at a later date, but not in the form of random testing, which has been shown to engender resentment and legal challenges. Any testing of the established workforce should be done only on a for-cause basis—in response to habitual absenteeism, erratic behaviour, on-the-job accidents, and the like. And we definitely should establish provisions for an EAP before any testing occurs. The next step should be to call in an outside consultant, preferably from NIDA, to provide guidance.

Figure 10.19 Drug-Testing Report, Page 13

13

WORKS CITED

Brookler, Rob. "Industry Standards in Workplace Drug Testing." *Personnel Journal* April 1992: 128–132. Print.

Brunet, James R. *Drug Testing in Law Enforcement Agencies: Social Control in the Public Sector*. New York: LFB Scholarly Publishing, 2005. Print.

Current, Bill. "New Solutions for Ensuring a Drug-Free Workplace." *Occupational Health & Safety* 71.4 (2002): 34–35. Print.

The Center to Protect Workers' Rights. "Inconsistent Data on Safety and Health in Construction." *The Construction Chart Book*. 2009. Web. 3 August 2010.

DeCew, Judith Wagner. *In Pursuit of Privacy: Law, Ethics, and the Rise of Technology*. Ithaca: Cornell UP, 1997. Print.

Hawkins, Dana. "Drug Tests Are Unreliable." *Drug Testing*. Ed. Cindy Mur. Farmington Hills, MI: Greenhaven, 2006. 41–46. Print.

Kerns, Dennis L., and William I. Stopperan. "Keys to a Successful Program." *Occupational Health & Safety* 69.10 (2000): 230–233. Print.

Knudsen, Hannah K., Paul M. Roman, and J. Aaron Johnson. "Organizational Compatibility and Workplace Drug Testing: Modeling the Adoption of Innovative Social Control Practices." *Sociological Forum* 18.4 (December 2003): 621–640. Print.

Minchin, R. Edward, Jr., Charles R. Glagola, Kelu Guo, and Jennifer L. Languell. "Case for Drug Testing of Construction Workers." *Journal of Management in Engineering* 22.1 (2006): 43–50. Print.

Figure 10.20 Drug-Testing Report, Page 14

14

Swartley, Judith A. "Workplace Drug Testing Is Cost Effective." *Drug Testing.*

Ed. Cindy Mur. Farmington Hills, MI: Greenhaven, 2006. 23–28. Print.

White, Tony. "Drug Testing at Work: Issues and Perspectives." *Substance*

Use & Abuse 38. 11–13 (2003): 1891–1902. Print.

Zimmer, Lynn. *Drug Testing: A Bad Investment.* New York: ACLU, 1999.

Print.

Exercises

Exercise 10.1
Rewrite the transmittal memo (Figure 10.1) and the title page (Figure 10.2), as if the report were your own work submitted as an assignment in your workplace communications course.

Exercise 10.2
Create a table of contents for a report on one of these aspects of your college:

- Degree or certificate program in your field of study
- Student Services provisions
- Athletic program
- Affirmative Action guidelines
- Physical Plant

Exercise 10.3
Rewrite the "Works Cited" in Figures 10.19 and 10.20, using APA format.

Exercise 10.4
Guided by the table of contents on the following page, team up with two or three other students to write a collaborative report entitled "Radar: History, Principles, Applications."

Exercise 10.5
Practically all workplace communications courses include a long report assignment at some point during the semester, usually near the end. Specific features of the project, however, vary greatly from instructor to instructor. Write a long report designed to satisfy your instructor's course requirements.

mycanadiantechcommlab

Visit www.mycanadiantechcommlab.ca for everything you need to help you succeed in the job you've always wanted! Tools and resources include the following:

- Composing Space and Writer's Toolkit
- Document Makeovers
- Grammar Exercises—and much more!

TABLE OF CONTENTS

Oral Presentations:

PREPARATION AND DELIVERY

LEARNING OBJECTIVE

When you complete this chapter, you'll be able to prepare and deliver successful oral presentations.

IF YOU'RE LIKE MOST PEOPLE, you dread the prospect of having to stand in front of an audience and make a speech. You feel unsure of yourself and fear you'll appear awkward or foolish. Nevertheless, you should make a real effort to overcome such misgivings. The ability to present your ideas clearly and forcefully to a group of listeners is a valuable skill that equips you for leadership in the workplace, where it is often necessary to address groups of supervisors, co-workers, clients, or customers. The skill is also quite useful in community contexts, such as club gatherings, town meetings, school board hearings, and other public forums. It's certainly helpful in the college setting, too, where oral reports are becoming a requirement in more and more courses.

A good speech is the result of three elements: preparation, composure, and common sense. The same can be said of the employment interview, which will be discussed in Chapter 12. In many respects, the two endeavours are similar. Both are examples of oral communication, both are fairly formal speaking situations, and both place essentially the same demands on you. The main difference, of course, is that in a job interview you're usually speaking to one or two listeners, whereas in an oral presentation you are generally addressing a group. After reading this chapter, you should be able to prepare and deliver successful oral presentations.

PREPARATION

A successful oral presentation nearly always is based on thorough preparation. This involves some preliminary activities followed by actual rehearsal of the speech.

Preliminaries

Preparing for an oral presentation is much like preparing to write. Just as if you were about to compose a memo, letter, or written report, you must first identify your purpose. Are you simply trying to inform your listeners, or are you attempting to entertain them? Are you perhaps seeking to persuade them of something or motivate them to action? In any case, you need a plan that enables you to achieve your goal.

It's crucial to assess your audience. What are your listeners' backgrounds and interests? How about their perspective on your topic? In short, what might influence their expectations or responses? Unless you gear your remarks to your audience, you probably won't connect satisfactorily with your listeners. For example, a mayoral candidate addressing a gathering of senior citizens would be foolish to focus a campaign speech on long-range outcomes the listeners may never live to see. Such a group would respond better to a presentation of the candidate's short-term goals, particularly those related to that audience's immediate concerns—crime prevention, perhaps, or health care. Just as you do in written communications, you must always bear in mind the nature of your audience when preparing your remarks.

It's also helpful to get a look in advance at the room where you will be speaking. This ensures that you'll be somewhat more at ease during the presentation because you'll be on familiar turf. If you're planning to use audiovisual equipment, you should acquaint yourself with it as well. Nothing is more embarrassing than suddenly discovering that there's no convenient electrical outlet for your overhead projector, or that expected equipment is defective or unavailable. Guard against such setbacks by checking everything when you visit the site beforehand.

Of course, you must be thoroughly familiar with your subject matter. Gather information about the topic and assemble an arsenal of facts, figures, and examples to support your statements. This requires some research and homework—an essential part of your preparation. You must know not only how to approach and organize the material but also how to *develop* it. Nobody wants to listen to a speaker who has nothing to say or who rambles on and on with no apparent direction or focus.

Therefore, the opening of your speech must include a clear statement of purpose, informing the audience about what to expect. From there you must follow a logical path, covering your material in a coherent, step-by-step fashion, dealing with one main idea at a time, in an orderly sequence. And, as in written communication, you should provide effective transitions to facilitate progress from point to point. For all this to happen, you must write out your entire speech ahead of time. Because it's best, however, to actually *deliver* the speech from notes or note cards, a finely polished, letter-perfect piece of writing is not absolutely necessary.

But you do need to have a well-developed and well-organized draft from which you can select key points and supporting details for your notes or note cards. You must also ensure that your notes or cards are plainly legible so you can glance down and easily see them on the lectern as you deliver the speech. Prepare your notes or cards using a bold, felt-tipped pen, and write substantially larger than you normally do. It's very damaging to your presentation if you have to pause to decipher your own handwriting, or if you have to bend over or pick up your notes or cards to see them clearly. Figure 11.1 is a page from the draft of an oral presentation about various applications of radar technology. Figure 11.2 shows notes based on that same information, and Figure 11.3 depicts note cards.

Rehearsal

As important as the preliminaries are, rehearsal is the most important part of your preparation. Many people skip this step, figuring they'll wing it when the time comes and rely on their wits. Unless you're a very experienced speaker, however, this almost never works. Before attempting to deliver an oral presentation, you *must* practise it. You need not recruit a practice audience (although it certainly helps), but you must at least recite the speech aloud several times. This reveals which parts of the presentation seem the most difficult to deliver and establishes how *long* the speech really is. You don't want to run noticeably shorter or longer than the allotted

Figure 11.1 Draft Page of an Oral Presentation

As we have seen, radar has obvious military value and has been used to detect and track enemy planes, submarines, missiles, and so on. Permanent Ballistic Missile Early Warning Systems (BMEWS) are in place at various strategic locations around the globe: Clear, Alaska; Thule, Greenland; Fylingdale Moor, England; and elsewhere. An impressive recent development is Relocatable Over-the-Horizon Radar (ROTHR), which can bounce high-frequency signals in the 5–28 MHz range off the ionosphere to scan an area from 500 to 1800 nautical miles away. But radar has many nonmilitary applications as well.

Radar permits astronomers to measure interplanetary distances precisely and to collect much data that otherwise might be unavailable, by obtaining radar echoes from the major bodies of the solar system . . . and deriving as much information as possible from them. Since radar can ascertain surface textures and details and can find objects as small as insects or as large as mountains, it's obviously very useful in making maps of distant, restricted, or otherwise inaccessible places—even planets.

Obviously, radar can be nearly as useful to civilian aviators as it is to the military by detecting storms and other aircraft and by determining location and altitude. Indeed, one of the first applications of radar was in radio altimeters. And, of course, air traffic controllers use radar extensively to prevent "runway incursions" and other mishaps.

Figure 11.2 Oral Presentation Notes

Permanent Ballistic Missile Early
Warning Systems (BMEWS):
   Clear, Alaska
      Thule, Greenland
         Fylingdale Moor, England

Relocatable Over-the-Horizon Radar (ROTHR): bounces
high-frequency signals off ionosphere; can scan areas
500–1800 nautical miles away.

Astronomers: measure interplanetary distances, collect solar system data.

Cartographers: make maps—even of planets; can find
objs as small as insects or as large as mts.

Aviators: detect storms, other planes; determine
location, altitude; air traffic control, prevent "runway
incursions."

Figure 11.3   Note Cards

Permanent Ballistic Missile Early Warning

Systems (BMEWS):

   Clear, Alaska

     Thule, Greenland

       Fylingdale Moor, England

Relocatable Over-the-Horizon Radar (ROTHR):

bounces high-frequency signals off ionosphere;

can scan areas 500–1800 naut. miles away.

time because that would violate the audience's expectations. Remember that speeches tend to run shorter in actuality than in rehearsal; the pressures of live performance generally speed up the delivery. If aiming for a 5-minute presentation, you need 7 or 8 minutes in rehearsal. If you're expected to speak for half an hour, your rehearsal might take 40 to 45 minutes.

In addition to preparing your speech, you must prepare *yourself*. All the common-sense advice that you will see presented in Chapter 12 concerning the employment interview applies equally here. Get a good night's sleep. Shower. Eat, but do not consume any alcoholic beverages. Dismiss any troubling thoughts from your mind. Wear clothing appropriate for the occasion. If you are not sure what is appropriate, verify this with your instructor before the presentations are scheduled to begin. All this preparation will contribute to your general sense of confidence and well-being, thereby helping you develop composure and deliver the presentation to the best of your ability.

DELIVERY

The key to successfully delivering your oral presentation in public is to relax. Admittedly, this is more easily said than done but not as difficult as it may seem. Most audiences are at least reasonably receptive, so you need not fear them. In the classroom setting, for example, all your listeners will soon be called on to present their own orals or will have done so already. This usually makes them sympathetic and supportive. It's simply not true that everyone in the room is scrutinizing your every word and gesture, hoping you'll perform poorly. (At any given moment, in fact, a certain percentage of the audience is probably not paying attention at all!) Nevertheless, there are several areas of concern you may wish to consider when delivering an oral presentation.

Introductions and Conclusions

Since first impressions are so important, a good oral presentation must begin with an effective introduction. Here are four useful strategies for opening your speech.

- *Ask the audience a pertinent question.* This is an effective introduction because it immediately establishes a connection between you and your listeners—especially if somebody responds. But even if no one does, you can provide the answer yourself, thereby leading smoothly into your discussion. In a presentation titled "Tourist Attractions in Toronto," for example, you might open with this query: "Does anyone here know the name of the street the CN Tower is on?"

- *Describe a situation.* There's something in human nature that makes us love a story, especially if it involves conflict. The enduring appeal of fairy tales, myths, and legends, and even soap operas and sentimental country-western lyrics proves the point. You can capitalize on this aspect of your listeners' collective psychology by opening your presentation with a brief story that somehow relates to your subject. A speaker attempting to explore the dangers of tobacco, for example, might begin like this: "My friend Jane, a wonderful young woman with a bright future, had been smoking a pack a day since 10th grade. Finally, at age 25, she had decided to quit. But when she went to the doctor for her annual physical, she learned that it was already too late. Tragically, Jane died of lung cancer less than a year later."

- *Present an interesting fact or statistic.* This will help you grab the audience's attention by demonstrating that you're familiar with your topic. The annual edition of *World Almanac and Book of Facts* is an excellent source of statistical information on diverse topics, but there are many other resources. Any qualified librarian can direct you to government documents, corporate reports, computer databases, and other useful resources. Even though statistics can be deceptive, people like what they perceive as the hard reality of such data and therefore find numbers quite persuasive. A speech intended to demonstrate the need for truly universal health care in Canada, for example, might open with this observation: "When travelling in another Canadian province or territory outside your own province, did you know that you may not receive free health care?"Although many websites are untrustworthy, the internet is another good source of statistics if used judiciously. One useful site is Statistics Canada at www.statcan.gc.ca.

■ *Use a quotation.* Get a "big name"–Shakespeare, Martin Luther King, Jr., Pierre Elliott Trudeau, the Bible–to speak for you. Find an appropriate saying that will launch your own remarks with flair. Many useful books of quotations exist, but *Bartlett's Familiar Quotations* (available in virtually any good bookstore or library) is the best known, and for good reason. Bartlett includes nearly 100 quotes on the subject of money alone, for example. *Bartlett's* is available–along with *Simpson's Contemporary Quotations* and the *Columbia World of Quotations*–on the web at www.bartleby.com.

The conclusion to your talk is as important as the introduction. Always sum up when you reach the end of an oral presentation. Repeat your key points and show clearly how they support your conclusion. Like an airplane rolling smoothly to a stop on the runway rather than crashing to the ground after reaching its destination, you should not end abruptly. You can accomplish this by returning the audience to the starting point. When you reach the end of your speech, refer to the question, scenario, fact, statistic, or quotation with which you opened. This creates in your listeners the satisfying sense of having come full circle, returning them to familiar territory.

Another common concluding tactic is to ask whether members of your audience have any questions. If so, you can answer them, and then your work is done. If no questions are forthcoming, the audience has in effect ended the speech for you. Because this creates the sense of a letdown, however, you can instead have an accomplice or two in the audience ask questions to which you have prepared responses in advance. Although staged, this is a common practice among professional speakers. Whatever form of conclusion you choose, always close by thanking the audience members for their time and attention.

If you are presenting in a group, all members should participate in the presentation. It is often best to have each member responsible for a certain segment of the presentation. For example, one person can present the introduction and conclusion, while other members present the body of information. Practice is extremely important when presenting as a group, as you want to present the information as seamlessly as possible. Each member should know when his or her turn is. Oral cues, such as introducing the next speaker with a statement such as "And now Abdul will discuss the effects of noise pollution," can help people remember their turn. By practising, all group members are also assured that the necessary information is presented. Finally, when presenting as a group, all members should be listening attentively to the person presenting. If your group does not pay attention to the presenter, how can you expect the audience to pay attention?

If you are part of a panel discussion, you need to make sure that you are prepared to present your information, but you also need to be aware of what other members are saying. Be an active listener by bringing a note pad with you so that you can record comments, observations, or notes about what others are saying. You may want to incorporate what others have said into your own presentation. Make sure you are aware of the order of the presenters so that you know when it is your turn to speak, and finally, be prepared to answer questions from the audience.

Vocal Factors

Obviously, the *voice* is the principal instrument of any oral presentation. Therefore, pay attention to your vocal qualities. Speak at a normal rate of speed, neither too fast nor too slow, and at a normal volume, neither too loud nor too soft. Pronounce each word clearly so the audience can understand your entire speech without straining. When using a microphone, be sure it's approximately one foot away from your mouth—any farther, and it may not pick up your voice adequately; any closer, and your overly amplified *b*s and *p*s may create an annoyingly explosive sound. In addition, try to maintain the normal rhythms of everyday conversation. Nothing is more boring than listening to a speech delivered in an unvarying monotone. Conversely, it's irritating to be subjected to an overly theatrical delivery characterized by elaborate gestures or exaggerated vocal effects. The key is to be natural, as if you were speaking to one or two people rather than to a whole group.

At the same time, an oral presentation is certainly a more formal speaking situation than a social conversation is. Therefore, you should provide more examples and illustrations than you ordinarily might, along with more transitional phrases than usual. In addition, make a conscious effort to minimize verbal "ticks," those distracting little mannerisms that characterize everyday speech: *um, y'know, okay? right?* and the like. Listening to a tape recording of your oral presentation enables you to assess the degree to which you need to work on your vocal mannerisms. Though you don't want to sound stiffly artificial, you should stay away from the more colourful vernacular. Avoid slang, expletives, and conspicuously substandard—"I ain't got no"—grammar. Achieving the right level of formality can be challenging, but practising the presentation a few times helps.

Finally, make sure you complete your thoughts and fully explain your ideas for the audience. In conversations, speakers may leave thoughts unfinished or trail off rather than completing an idea. This is often not problematic, as the listener can immediately ask the speaker questions to confirm understanding of the topic. In oral presentations, however, listeners may not be able to ask immediate questions. Therefore, you need to make sure you complete all your thoughts and provide all the information the audience needs in order to understand your presentation as you mean it.

Physical Factors

Although your voice is obviously important, your audience *sees* you as well as hears you. Audience members respond to your body language as much as to your words. As you would in an employment interview, you must create a favourable physical impression. Get rid of any chewing gum long before stepping up to the lectern. Stand up straight behind the lectern; don't slump or lean over it. Control your hand motions. Do not fold your arms, drum with your fingertips, click a ballpoint pen, or cling rigidly to the lectern with a stiff-armed, white-knuckled grip. Refrain from touching your face or hair, tugging at your clothes, or scratching your body. You can gesture occasionally to make a point but only if such movements are spontaneous, as in casual conversation. In short, your hands should not distract the audience from what you're saying. Your feet, too, can create problems. Resist the tendency to tap your feet, to shift from one leg to the other, or to stray purposelessly from the lectern. Plant your feet firmly on the floor and stay put.

In the academic setting, your professors (much like many workplace supervisors) may impose certain regulations concerning proper attire for oral presentations. Baseball caps, for example, are sometimes prohibited, along with various other style and dress affectations, such as those mentioned in the "Interview" section of Chapter 12. Whether in a classroom or on the job, you should observe any such guidelines, even if you feel they're overly restrictive.

Eye Contact

As much as possible, *look* at your audience. This is probably the hardest part of public speaking, but it's imperative. Unless you maintain eye contact with audience members, you'll lose their attention. Keep your head up and your eyes directed forward. If you find it impossible to actually look at your listeners, fake it. Look instead at desk tops, chair legs, or the back wall. You must create at least the *illusion* of visual contact.

Holding your listeners' attention is one—although certainly not the only—reason you should absolutely avoid the dreadful error of simply reading to your audience from the text of your speech. Few practices are more boring, more amateurish, or more destructive of audience–speaker rapport. As mentioned in the section about preparation, you should deliver your presentation from notes or note cards rather than from a polished text to force yourself to adopt a more conversational manner. But keep your papers or cards out of sight, lying flat on the lectern. Do not distract the audience by nervously shuffling them.

Audiovisuals

To greatly enhance your oral presentation, consider using audiovisual aids in conjunction with the various visuals (tables, graphs, charts, pictures) discussed in Chapter 5. Audiovisual tools can be helpful to both you and your audience by illustrating key points throughout your talk. If the room where you are speaking is equipped with a chalkboard or dry-erase board, take advantage of it as appropriate. A flip chart–a giant, easel-mounted pad of paper that you write on with felt-tip markers–is another useful option. You may also choose to use large display posters prepared in advance, but you must remember to bring along tape or thumbtacks to secure them for viewing.

Whether using a chalkboard, flip chart, or poster to make your point, remember to position yourself *next to* it, not in front of it; you must not block the audience's view. Remember, as well, to face the audience rather than the display. Be sure your writing is plainly legible from a distance; write in large, bold strokes, using colour for emphasis and incorporating the other design principles outlined in Chapter 5. Make sure your drawings and text are easy to see even from the back of the room. Follow this rule of thumb: the image must be at least one-sixth as large as the distance from which it will be seen. For example, a graph viewed from 12 metres should be 2 metres wide.

For lettering, use the following chart:

Distance	Size of Lettering
Up to 3 m	2 cm
6 m	2.5 cm
9 m	3.2 cm
12 m	3.8 cm
15 m	4.4 cm
18 m	5 cm

Although they require more preparation time, you may want to create a Power-Point presentation or create transparencies that can be projected onto a screen. They lend your presentation a great deal of credibility by making it much more professional and polished. One advantage is that you can control the size of the images on the screen, enlarging them as necessary to create displays that are easily visible even in a relatively big room.

Here are some basic guidelines to bear in mind when using PowerPoint slides or transparencies in conjunction with an oral presentation:

■ Make certain beforehand that you know how to use an overhead projector or digital video processor (DVP). (Transparencies must not be reversed, upside down, or out of sequence.)

- Do not include too much information on a PowerPoint slide or transparency. Keep it simple. Use brief phrases instead of full sentences, and limit each screen to four or five main points. Similarly, do not use more than two type sizes, fonts, or styles on a given screen. Maintain consistency throughout a presentation, using capitalization, underlining, spacing, and other elements the same way on each screen. Figure 11.4 depicts a series of inconsistently formatted screens, and Figure 11.5 depicts the same screens consistently formatted.

- To draw the audience's attention to a detail on the screen, use a laser pointer rather than a yardstick or conventional pointer, which are effective only for pointing out details on chalkboards, posters, maps, and the like. Presentation software, of course, affords a variety of imaginative highlighting methods.

- Avoid the glaring "empty white screen" effect; turn off your DVP or transparency projector once you're done with it, or if you'll not be referring to it for more than a minute or two.

Depending on the length, scope, and topic of your speech, you may decide to supplement your remarks with videotape or sound recordings, provided they're of good quality. Relevant physical objects can also be displayed or passed around. If you were explaining how to tune a guitar, for example, you would certainly want to demonstrate the procedure on an actual instrument. Similarly, if you were explaining the workings of a particular tool or other device, ideally you would provide one (or more) for the audience to examine.

Of all the options available, however, the presentation software packages that have become so popular in recent years are perhaps the most helpful. Microsoft PowerPoint is by far the preferred choice, but there are also online programs, such as at http://prezi.com, that allow you to make a presentation that is not static. These software programs greatly facilitate the creation of tables, graphs, bulleted lists, and other images for use on transparencies. The software is at its best, though, when images are exhibited by a liquid crystal display (LCD) projector connected to a laptop or other computer controlled by the speaker. This technology provides a wide variety of type sizes, fonts, colours, clip art, backgrounds, three-dimensional effects, and other format features, as well as sound and animation. In addition, static images and streaming video can be imported from the internet and other outside sources to create multimedia presentations. Although some training is required to fully exploit the technology's potential, anyone can easily learn the fundamentals. Before creating PowerPoint slides, make sure you read the Tech Tips found on page 286. Figures 11.6 through 11.11 depict a series of PowerPoint slides outlining responses to several kinds of workplace emergencies.

Speakers using PowerPoint or other software sometimes employ the "slow reveal" strategy, whereby information is projected a bit at a time rather than all at once, gradually adding onto or "building" the content. This can be done by using animation.

Figure 11.4 Inconsistent Format

CULVERTS

- **Replace/repair**
- **Restore drainage capacity**
- **Return roadway to original elevation**

Drainage Ditches

- Remove Trees and Brush
- Restore Drainage Patterns
- Add Riprap to Control Flow

<u>GATE SYSTEM</u>

- *install locking gates*
- *provide pedestrian access alongside gates*
- *install signs at entry gate*

Figure 11.5 Consistent Format

CULVERTS

- Replace/repair

- Restore drainage capacity

- Return roadway to original elevation

DRAINAGE DITCHES

- Remove trees and brush

- Restore drainage patterns

- Add riprap to control flow

GATE SYSTEM

- Install locking gates

- Provide pedestrian access alongside gates

- Install signs at entry gate

Figure 11.6 First PowerPoint Slide

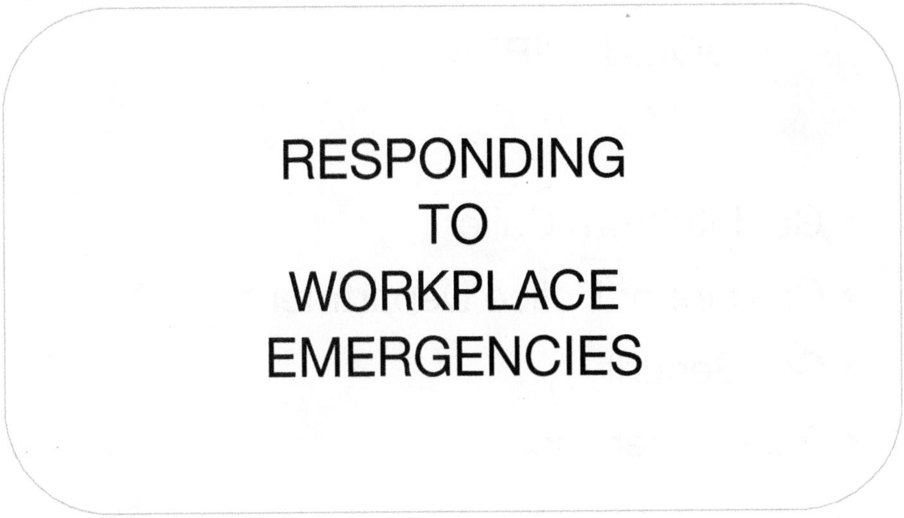

RESPONDING TO WORKPLACE EMERGENCIES

Figure 11.7 Second PowerPoint Slide

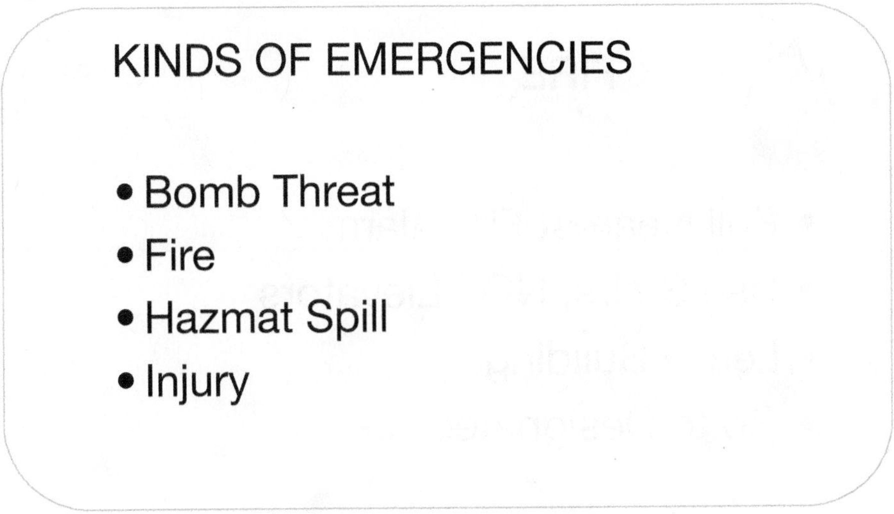

KINDS OF EMERGENCIES

- Bomb Threat
- Fire
- Hazmat Spill
- Injury

Figure 11.8 Third PowerPoint Slide

BOMB THREAT

- Get Info from Caller
- Call Fire or Police Department
- Call Security
- Alert Supervisor

Figure 11.9 Fourth PowerPoint Slide

FIRE

- Pull Nearest Fire Alarm
- Use Stairs, NOT Elevators
- Leave Building
- Go to Designated Area

Figure 11.10 Fifth PowerPoint Slide

HAZMAT SPILL

- Alert Others in Area
- Get Away from Spill
- Call 911
- Call Security

Figure 11.11 Sixth PowerPoint Slide

INJURY

- Call 911
- Call Company Nurse
- Call Security
- Provide Aid and Comfort

Thus, the audience can concentrate on each point rather than reading ahead and losing track of the speaker's comments. This is just one of PowerPoint's many useful features, which include an array of techniques borrowed from Hollywood filmmakers. To move from one slide to the next, for example, PowerPoint is able to "wipe" the screen as if it were a windshield; one image is pushed from view while another moves in behind it. Similarly, the Dissolve option causes the slow fading out of one image and the gradual fading in of its successor, sometimes with a superimposition of images at the midpoint of the transition. Among the program's most commonly used capabilities is the Fly In option, which makes a word or image appear to be airborne, "landing" on the screen like a lobbed dart, often accompanied by a sound effect.

A well-crafted PowerPoint component adds a high degree of professionalism to any oral presentation, revealing that the speaker is up-to-date and knowledgeable about current practices. As with any visual components of oral or written communications, however, you should use electronic options selectively and with restraint, not just for the sake of appearing tech-savvy but to genuinely enrich and enhance the content. A common mistake is to overload the presentation with special effects, creating a jumpy, hyperactive quality that deflects the audience's attention away from the content. An opposite but equally unproductive approach is to outline the entire speech on PowerPoint and then simply read aloud from these too-numerous slides while facing away from the audience. This can literally put listeners to sleep. Instead, you should use PowerPoint slides simply as background, greatly expanding on their content by presenting a fully developed speech delivered in accordance with the established principles of effective public performance. You want your audience to consider PowerPoint not as a substitute for the speech but as a tool for better delivering it. The purpose of any audiovisual aid is to reinforce and clarify, rather than overshadow, the speaker's remarks.

Remember, too, that electronic delivery systems can malfunction or present other unexpected difficulties. If you plan to use PowerPoint in an upcoming presentation, rehearsal (actually using the technology) is even more crucial than it would be otherwise. Even if everything appears to be ready, you should never approach a PowerPoint presentation without a backup plan. It's always a good idea to have a full set of printed copies of your slides to distribute to the audience in case of an equipment failure or other last-minute problem.

You can create handouts in a variety of ways with PowerPoint. You can, for example, have from one to six slides on a page. You can also choose to have blank lines beside slides so that audience members can take additional notes. Some presenters deliver the handouts at the beginning of a presentation, while others hand them out at the end. Handing them out at the beginning, though, allows your audience to follow along and pay attention to you, rather than trying to take notes and keep up with the presentation. A final option is emailing your PowerPoint slides to the audience

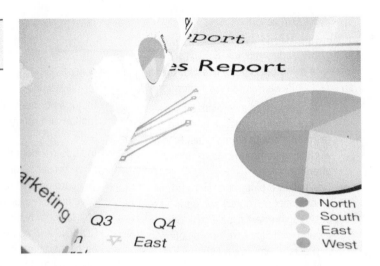

Handouts can help enhance oral presentations.

members before the presentation so that they have a chance to look at the presentation before they attend.

Enthusiasm

Try to deliver your oral presentations in a lively, upbeat, enthusiastic manner. This actually makes your job easier, since a positive attitude on your part will help to foster a more receptive attitude on the part of the audience. If your listeners sense that you'd rather be elsewhere, they will probably "tune out." When that occurs, you receive no encouraging feedback, and knowing you've lost your audience makes it even more difficult to continue. If you sense, however, that the audience is following along, this reinforcement in turn fuels your performance. That cannot happen, however, unless you project in an engaging way. From the start, *you* establish the tone. Therefore, it makes sense to adopt a positive attitude when giving an oral presentation, not only for the audience's sake but also to serve your own purposes.

The many factors that contribute to a good delivery may seem like a lot to keep track of. If you're like most speakers, however, you probably have real difficulty in only one or two areas. An especially useful strategy is to videotape your rehearsal to determine what you should work on to improve your delivery. As stated at the start of the chapter, a successful oral presentation is the result of preparation, composure, and common sense. If you take seriously the recommendations offered in this chapter and practise the strategies and techniques suggested, your performance as a public speaker will improve greatly.

Tech Tips

Here are some basic guidelines for creating an effective PowerPoint presentation:

- Don't get carried away with all the options at your disposal; exercise restraint. As with so many aspects of workplace communications, less is often more.
- Don't allow a patterned, textured, or incompatibly coloured background to obscure your text. Use a dark background with light text for projection in a darkened room; use a light background with dark text for projection in a lighted room.
- Use relatively large print for greater legibility: 30- to 34-point for text, 44- to 50-point bold for headings.
- Use consistent formatting features on all slides.
- Avoid large segments of running text. Use lists and outlines instead.
- Include no more than 5 items of information and no more than 15 words per slide.
- Include no more than 25 slides in any given presentation.
- To guard against technical difficulties, have a backup plan that provides several options. Not all computers have a CD drive and some, as a result, will not be compatible with your flash. As well, some computers don't have internet access. Therefore, you should email your PPT presentation to yourself and bring an electronic version on CD and/or flash drive. And bring hard-copy handouts for distribution in case all else fails.

Checklist   Evaluating a Public Speaker

A good public speaker

____ opens with an interesting, attention-getting introduction;

____ follows a clear and logical pattern of organization;

____ provides enough detail to fully develop the subject;

____ closes with a smooth, satisfying conclusion;

____ speaks in a firm, clear, expressive voice;

____ makes frequent eye contact with the audience;

____ appears physically relaxed and composed, with no distracting mannerisms;

____ maintains an appropriate level of formality, neither too casual nor too solemn;

____ delivers in an alert, engaging manner;

____ satisfies but does not exceed the appropriate length for the presentation.

 **Exercises**

Exercise 11.1
Prepare and deliver a 5- to 10-minute oral presentation on one of the following autobiographical topics:

- A Childhood Memory
- My Brush with Danger
- An Angry Moment
- A Very Satisfying Accomplishment
- My Career Goals
- What I Expect My Life to Be Like in 10 Years

Exercise 11.2
Prepare and deliver a 5- to 10-minute oral presentation that summarizes a book, an article, a lecture, a film, or a television broadcast related to your field of study or employment (see Chapter 4).

Exercise 11.3
Prepare and deliver a 5- to 10-minute oral presentation that provides a specific mechanism description related to your field of study or employment (see Chapter 6). Present an actual example of such a mechanism, along with any audiovisual aids that may be helpful to your audience.

Exercise 11.4
Prepare and deliver a 5- to 10-minute oral presentation describing a process related to your field of study or employment (see Chapter 6). Present any audiovisual aids that may be helpful to your audience.

Exercise 11.5
Prepare and deliver a 5- to 10-minute oral presentation describing a procedure related to your field of study or employment (see Chapter 6). Present any audiovisual aids that may be helpful to your audience.

Exercise 11.6
Prepare and deliver a 5- to 10-minute oral presentation providing instructions related to your field of study or employment (see Chapter 7). Present any audiovisual aids that may be helpful to your audience.

Exercise 11.7
Prepare and deliver a 5- to 10-minute oral presentation based on Exercise 9.10. Present any audiovisual aids that may be helpful to your audience.

Exercise 11.8
Prepare and deliver a 5- to 10-minute oral presentation based on Exercise 6.18. Present any audiovisual aids that may be helpful to your audience.

Exercise 11.9

Prepare and deliver a 5- to 10-minute oral presentation based on Exercise 4.8. Present any audiovisual aids that may be helpful to your audience.

Exercise 11.10

Prepare and deliver a 5- to 10-minute oral presentation about an employer in your field of study. Include the main products or services this company provides. Discuss how long the employer has been in business. Provide information about the corporate headquarters (such as where it is situated). Discuss the workforce and any skills or credentials potential employees need. Present any audiovisual aids that may be helpful to your audience.

PEARSON
mycanadiantechcommlab

Visit www.mycanadiantechcommlab.ca for everything you need to help you succeed in the job you've always wanted! Tools and resources include the following:

- Composing Space and Writer's Toolkit
- Document Makeovers
- Grammar Exercises—and much more!

Job Application Process:

LETTER, RÉSUMÉ, INTERVIEW, AND FOLLOW-UP

LEARNING OBJECTIVE

When you complete this chapter, you'll be able to write an effective job application letter and résumé and you'll also be able to interview and follow up successfully.

THE EMPLOYMENT OUTLOOK TODAY is quite challenging, with many qualified applicants vying for every available position, and all indicators suggest that the competition will continue to get tougher. Therefore, it's now more important than ever to fully understand the process of applying for a job. Essentially, it involves four components: an effective application letter, an impressive résumé, a strong interview, and a timely follow-up.

Some job announcements provide only a phone number or an address, with no mention of a written response. In such cases you will likely complete a standard questionnaire like the one shown in Figures 12.1 and 12.2, instead of submitting a letter and résumé. Generally, however, these are not the most desirable positions. The better openings, those that pay more and offer greater opportunity for advancement, typically require you to respond in writing, either by mail, by fax, or online. This enables employers to be more selective by automatically eliminating applicants unable to compose a letter and résumé or too unmotivated to do so.

It's important to understand that employers require a written response partly to secure a representative sample of your *best work*. Therefore, the physical appearance of your job application correspondence is crucially important. You may be well qualified, but if your letter and résumé are sloppy, crumpled, handwritten, poorly formatted, or marred by mechanical errors, they will probably be discarded unread. Unless your keyboarding skills and sense of page design are well developed, you might consider hiring a professional typist to prepare your documents. If your résumé is saved in an electronic file, it can be easily customized to match each position for which you apply and, if you're applying online, can be sent as an email attachment. But you cannot expect software, or a typist, to work from scratch. You must understand the basic principles governing the preparation of job application correspondence. This chapter provides you with that knowledge, along with information about how to interview and follow up successfully.

APPLICATION LETTER

Prepared in a conventional format and three-part structure, a job application letter is no different from any other business letter (see Chapter 3). It should be neatly typed on 8½-by-11-inch (216-by-279-mm) white paper and should be framed by ample (1- to 1½-inch or 2.5- to 3.8-cm) margins. In nearly every case, the letter should be no longer than one page. The writer's address, the date, the reader's name and address, the salutation, and the complimentary close are handled just as they would be in any other letter, except that all punctuation should be included. Most employment counsellors agree that open punctuation and/or an "all caps" inside address should be avoided in an application letter because some personnel directors dislike these practices.

Figure 12.1 Job Application Questionnaire, Page 1

SUPER DUPER GROCERY SHOPPE

APPLICATION FOR EMPLOYMENT   DATE: _____

PERSONAL

NAME _____

ADDRESS _____

CITY   PROVINCE   POSTAL CODE

PHONE   SOC. INSUR. #

HOW LONG AT THIS ADDRESS? _____

DESIRED EMPLOYMENT LOCATION:

_____

POSITION APPLIED FOR: FULL OR PART TIME

DAYS AVAILABLE: S M T W T F S

HOURS AVAILABLE: _____

DATE AVAILABLE TO START: _____

ARE YOU OVER 16 YEARS OF AGE?   YES NO

HAVE YOU EVER BEEN EMPLOYED BY US BEFORE?   YES NO

IF SO, UNDER WHAT NAME, WHAT LOCATION & WHEN?

_____

DO YOU POSSESS A VALID DRIVER'S LICENCE?   YES ____ NO ____

IF YES, CLASS _____   PROVINCE _____   EXP. DATE _____

HAVE YOU EVER BEEN CONVICTED OF A CRIME, JOB-RELATED OR OTHER?   YES ____ NO ____

IF YES, PLEASE EXPLAIN _____

_____

NONE OF THE ABOVE CIRCUMSTANCES REPRESENTS AN AUTOMATIC BAR TO EMPLOYMENT. EACH CASE IS CONSIDERED AND EVALUATED ON INDIVIDUAL MERITS IN RELATION TO THE DUTIES AND RESPONSIBILITIES OF THE POSITION(S) FOR WHICH YOU ARE APPLYING.

EDUCATION

SCHOOL	NAME & LOCATION OF SCHOOL	COURSE OF STUDY	NO. OF YEARS COMPLETED	DID YOU GRADUATE?	DEGREE OR DIPLOMA
HIGH SCHOOL					
COLLEGE/ UNIVERSITY					
BUSINESS/ TRADE/ TECHNICAL					

Figure 12.2   Job Application Questionnaire, Page 2

LIST YOUR LAST 3 EMPLOYERS, STARTING WITH YOUR PRESENT ONE

<table>
<tr><td rowspan="18">EMPLOYMENT HISTORY</td><td>LENGTH OF EMPLOYMENT</td><td colspan="2">NAME OF EMPLOYER</td></tr>
<tr><td>FROM   TO</td><td colspan="2">ADDRESS OF EMPLOYER</td></tr>
<tr><td>ENDING SALARY</td><td>NAME OF SUPERVISOR</td><td>PHONE</td></tr>
<tr><td colspan="3">DUTIES</td></tr>
<tr><td colspan="3">REASON FOR LEAVING</td></tr>
<tr><td>LENGTH OF EMPLOYMENT</td><td colspan="2">NAME OF EMPLOYER</td></tr>
<tr><td>FROM   TO</td><td colspan="2">ADDRESS OF EMPLOYER</td></tr>
<tr><td>ENDING SALARY</td><td>NAME OF SUPERVISOR</td><td>PHONE</td></tr>
<tr><td colspan="3">DUTIES</td></tr>
<tr><td colspan="3">REASON FOR LEAVING</td></tr>
<tr><td>LENGTH OF EMPLOYMENT</td><td colspan="2">NAME OF EMPLOYER</td></tr>
<tr><td>FROM   TO</td><td colspan="2">ADDRESS OF EMPLOYER</td></tr>
<tr><td>ENDING SALARY</td><td>NAME OF SUPERVISOR</td><td>PHONE</td></tr>
<tr><td colspan="3">DUTIES</td></tr>
<tr><td colspan="3">REASON FOR LEAVING</td></tr>
</table>

MAY WE CONTACT YOUR PRESENT EMPLOYER?	YES ____ NO ____

REFERENCES

LIST BELOW 3 PEOPLE OTHER THAN RELATIVES AND PAST EMPLOYERS WHOM YOU HAVE KNOWN FOR AT LEAST 1 YEAR

NAME _____ ADDRESS _____ PHONE _____
AFFILIATION _____

NAME _____ ADDRESS _____ PHONE _____
AFFILIATION _____

NAME _____ ADDRESS _____ PHONE _____
AFFILIATION _____

Applicant's Statement
I certify that answers given herein are true and complete to the best of my knowledge.
I authorize investigation of all statements contained in this application for employment as may be necessary in arriving at an employment decision. This application for employment shall be considered active for a period of time not to exceed 6 months. Any applicant wishing to be considered for employment beyond this time period should inquire as to whether or not applications are being accepted at that time.
I hereby understand and acknowledge that, unless otherwise defined by applicable law, any employment relationship with this organization is of an "at will" nature, which means that the Employee may resign at any time and the Employer may discharge Employee at any time with or without cause. It is further understood that this "at will" employment relationship may not be changed by any written document or by conduct unless such change is specifically acknowledged in writing by an authorized executive of this organization. In the event of employment, I understand that false or misleading information given in my application/interview may result in discharge. I understand, also, that I am required to abide by all rules and regulations of the employer.

Signature of Applicant _____ Date _____

Ideally, the job posting will provide the name and title of the person to contact, as in the following example:

> **ELECTRICIAN:** Permanent, full time. College diploma, experience preferred. Good salary, benefits. Cover letter and résumé to: Maria Castro, Director of Human Resources, The Senior Citizens' Homestead, 666 Grand Ave., Vancouver, BC V6B 4A2. Equal opp'ty employer.

Sometimes, however, the ad doesn't mention an individual's name but provides only a title—Personnel Manager, for example—or simply the company's name. In such cases you should call the employer and explain that you are interested in applying for the job and would like to know the name and title of the contact person. Be sure to get the correct spelling and, unless the name plainly reveals gender, determine whether the individual is a man or a woman. This ensures that your letter will be among the only personalized ones received, thereby creating a more positive first impression. For various reasons, some ads reveal almost nothing—not even the name of the company—and simply provide a box number at the newspaper or the post office, like this:

> **ACCOUNTING ASSISTANT:** Computer skills and one year hands-on experience with A/R & A/P required. Reply to Box 23, The Record, 25 Fairway Road, Kitchener, ON N2A 4E2.

In such an instance, set up the inside address in your letter as follows:

> The Record
> 25 Fairway Road
> Kitchener, ON N2A 4E2

When there is no way to identify whom you are addressing, use "Dear Employer" as your salutation. This is a bit more original than such unimaginative greetings as the impersonal "To Whom It May Concern," the gender-biased "Dear Sir," or the old-fashioned "Dear Sir or Madam." Again, your letter will stand out from the others received, suggesting you are more resourceful than the other applicants.

Incidentally, newspaper classified sections are always larger on Saturday than on weekdays because of Saturday's larger readership. Also, most papers are now online, so you can easily review job postings from all over the country. This is convenient if you're interested in relocating to a particular place. Here are websites for some of Canada's major newspapers:

Calgary Herald	www.calgaryherald.com
The Chronicle Herald (Nova Scotia)	www.thechronicleherald.ca
Edmonton Journal	www.edmontonjournal.com

Financial Post (Toronto)	www.financialpost.com
The Gazette (Montreal)	www.montrealgazette.com
The Globe and Mail	www.theglobeandmail.com
The Guardian (Charlottetown)	www.theguardian.pe.ca
The Kingston Whig Standard	www.thewhig.com
Leader Post (Regina)	www.leaderpost.com
National Post	www.nationalpost.com
Ottawa Citizen	www.ottawacitizen.com
The Province (Vancouver)	www.theprovince.com
The Star Phoenix (Saskatoon)	www.thestarphoenix.com
The Sudbury Star	www.thesudburystar.com
The Telegram (St. John's)	www.thetelegram.com
Telegraph-Journal (Saint John)	telegraphjournal.canadaeast.com
Times Colonist (Victoria)	www.timescolonist.com
The Toronto Star	www.thestar.com
Vancouver Star	www.vancouverstar.com
The Windsor Star	www.windsorstar.com
Winnipeg Free Press	www.winnipegfreepress.com
Whitehorse Daily Star	www.whitehorsestar.com
Yellowknifer	www.nnsl.com/yellowknifer/yellowknifer.html

For links to international newspapers, go to www.thebigproject.co.uk/news.htm or www.onlinenewspapers.com.

In your opening paragraph, directly state your purpose: that you are applying for the job. Strangely, many applicants fail to do this. Wordy and ultimately pointless statements—for example, "I read with great interest your classified advertisement in the Tuesday edition of my hometown newspaper, the *Daily Gazette*"—invite the reader to respond, "So? Do you *want* the job, or what?" Instead, compose a one-sentence opening that comes right to the point: "As an experienced sales professional, I am applying for the retail position advertised in the *Daily Gazette*." This approach suggests that you're a confident, focused individual—and therefore a desirable applicant.

Always mention the job *title*, as the employer may have advertised more than one. Also indicate how you learned of the job opening. Most employers find this information helpful in monitoring the productivity of their various advertising efforts, and they appreciate the courtesy. If you learned of the opening by word of mouth, however, do *not* mention the name of the person who told you about it, even if you have been given permission to do so. The individual may not be well regarded by the employer, and because you have no way of knowing this, you should not risk the possibility of an unfortunate association. In such a situation, use a sentence like this one: "*It has come to my attention that you have an opening for an electrician,* and I am applying for the job."

In the middle section, which can be anywhere from one to three paragraphs, provide a narrative summary of your experience, education, and other qualifications. Go into some depth, giving sufficient information to make the employer want to read your résumé, which you should refer to specifically. But avoid *excessive* detail. Dates, addresses, and other particulars belong in the résumé, not the letter. Be sure to mention, however, any noteworthy attributes—specialized licences, security clearances, computer skills, foreign language fluency—that may set you apart from the competition. Do not pad the letter with vague claims that you cannot document. "I have five years of continuous experience as a part-time security guard" scores a lot more points than "I am friendly, co-operative, and dependable." Never mention weaknesses, and always strive for the most upbeat phrasing you can devise. "I'm currently unemployed," for example, creates a negative impression; the more positive "I am available immediately" turns this circumstance to your advantage.

The purpose, of course, is to make the employer recognize your value as a prospective employee. Using the "you" approach explained in Chapter 1, gear your letter accordingly. Without indulging in exaggeration or arrogant self-congratulation, explain why it would be in the employer's best interests to hire you. Sometimes a direct, straightforward statement such as this can be quite persuasive: "With my college education now completed, I am very eager to begin my career in banking and will bring a high level of enthusiasm and commitment to this position."

Your closing paragraph—no longer than two or three sentences—should briefly thank the employer for considering you and request an interview. Nobody has ever received a job offer on the strength of a letter alone. The letter leads to the résumé, the résumé (if you're lucky) secures an interview, and the interview (if you're *really* lucky) results in a job offer. By mentioning both the résumé and the interview in your letter, you indicate that you're a knowledgeable person familiar with conventions of the hiring process.

Understand, however, that even one mechanical error in your letter may be enough to knock you out of the running. You must make absolutely certain that there are no typos, spelling mistakes, faulty punctuation, or grammatical blunders—none whatsoever! Check and double-check to ensure that your letter (along with your résumé) is mechanically perfect.

Figure 12.3 is an effective application letter in response to the classified ad for an electrician on page 293. Figure 12.4 depicts the same letter as an email transmittal submitted in response to an online job posting. The accompanying résumé, shown in Figure 12.5, enables you to see how the résumé and letter interrelate.

Figure 12.3 Application Letter

55 Cortland Avenue
Vancouver, BC V6F 6T2
April 2, 2011

Ms. Maria Castro
Director of Human Resources
The Senior Citizens' Homestead
666 Grand Avenue
Vancouver, BC V6B 4A2

Dear Ms. Castro:

As an experienced electrician about to graduate from college with a three-year diploma in electrical engineering technology, I am applying for the electrician position advertised in the *Vancouver Star*.

In college I have maintained an 84% average while serving as vice-president of the Technology Club and treasurer of the Minority Students' Union. In keeping with my ongoing commitment to community service, last year I joined a group of volunteer workers renovating the Vancouver Youth Club. Under the supervision of a licensed electrician, I helped rewire the building and acquired a great deal of practical experience during the course of this project. The combination of my academic training and the hands-on knowledge gained at the Youth Club equips me to become a valued member of your staff. Past and current employers, listed on the enclosed résumé, will attest to my strong work ethic. I can provide those individuals' names and phone numbers on request.

Thank you very much for considering my application. Please phone or email me to arrange an interview at your convenience.

Sincerely,

James Carter

James Carter

Figure 12.4 Email Application

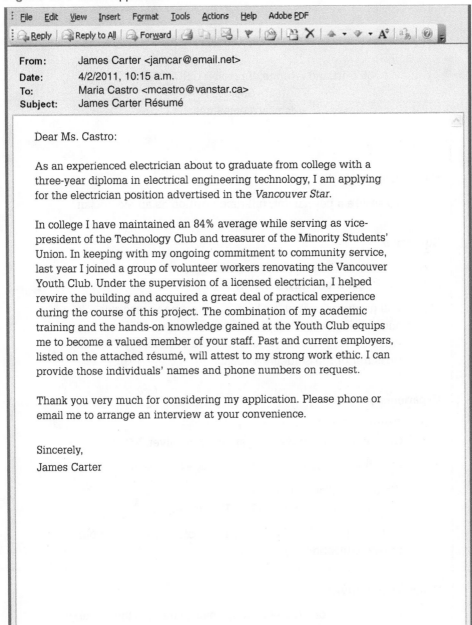

File   Edit   View   Insert   Format   Tools   Actions   Help   Adobe PDF

Reply | Reply to All | Forward

From: James Carter <jamcar@email.net>
Date: 4/2/2011, 10:15 a.m.
To: Maria Castro <mcastro@vanstar.ca>
Subject: James Carter Résumé

Dear Ms. Castro:

As an experienced electrician about to graduate from college with a three-year diploma in electrical engineering technology, I am applying for the electrician position advertised in the *Vancouver Star*.

In college I have maintained an 84% average while serving as vice-president of the Technology Club and treasurer of the Minority Students' Union. In keeping with my ongoing commitment to community service, last year I joined a group of volunteer workers renovating the Vancouver Youth Club. Under the supervision of a licensed electrician, I helped rewire the building and acquired a great deal of practical experience during the course of this project. The combination of my academic training and the hands-on knowledge gained at the Youth Club equips me to become a valued member of your staff. Past and current employers, listed on the attached résumé, will attest to my strong work ethic. I can provide those individuals' names and phone numbers on request.

Thank you very much for considering my application. Please phone or email me to arrange an interview at your convenience.

Sincerely,
James Carter

Figure 12.5 Résumé

James Carter

55 Cortland Avenue, Vancouver, BC   V6F 6T2
(613) 555-2557
jamcar@email.net

Career Objective

To secure a permanent, full-time position as an electrician.

Education

Vancouver Community College (2008–present)
1155 East Broadway, Vancouver, BC

Will graduate in May 2011 with a diploma in electrical engineering technology. Have maintained an 84% average while serving as vice-president of the Technology Club and treasurer of the Students' Union.

Experience

Counter Clerk (2008–present)
Quik Stop Grocery, 255 Bergen St., Vancouver, BC

Part-time position to help meet college expenses.

Warehouse Worker (2005–2008)
S. Lewis & Sons, 13 North Rd., Vancouver, BC

Full-time job held after high school, before deciding to pursue college education.

Community Activities

Assistant Minor Hockey League coach, church choir member, volunteer for Vancouver Youth Club renovation project (helped rewire building).

RÉSUMÉ

As Figure 12.5 illustrates, a résumé is basically a detailed list or outline of a job applicant's work history and other qualifications. The following categories of information typically appear:

- Contact Information
- Career Objective
- Education
- Work Experience
- Military Service
- Computer Literacy
- Specialized Skills or Credentials
- Honours and Awards
- Community Activities

Of course, few résumés include all these categories. Not everyone has served in the military, for example, or received awards. Not everyone is active in the community or possesses special skills. But practically anyone can assemble an effective résumé. The trick is to carefully evaluate your own background, identify your principal strengths, and emphasize those attributes. A person with a college degree but little relevant experience, for example, would highlight the education component. Conversely, someone with a great deal of experience but relatively little formal schooling would emphasize the employment history. Both individuals, however, would follow these well-established guidelines:

1. The résumé, like the application letter, should be visually attractive. It should be printed on 8½-by-11-inch (216-by-279-mm) white paper. Use capitalization, boldface, and white space skilfully to create an inviting yet professional appearance. Unless you're applying online, you can lay out your résumé in any number of ways, but it must *look* good. Experiment with a variety of layouts until it does.

2. The various categories of information must be clearly labelled and distinct from one another so the employer can quickly review your background without having to labour over the page or screen. Indeed, most employers are unwilling to struggle with a confusing résumé and will simply move on to the next one.

3. All necessary details must appear—names, addresses, dates, and so on—and must be presented in a consistent manner throughout. For example, do not abbreviate words like *Avenue* and *Street* in one section and then spell them out elsewhere. Adopt one approach to abbreviation, capitalization, spacing, and other such matters.

4. Use reverse chronological order in categories such as Education and Work Experience. List the most recent information first and then work backward through time.

5. A printed résumé should be no longer than one page unless the applicant's background and qualifications truly warrant a second. This is not usually the case, except among applicants with 10 or more years of work experience. If your résumé does have two pages, include your name at the top of the second page.

6. Some employers and websites provide online "fill in the blanks" résumé forms for electronic submission. The design of the form will govern the length of your online résumé. Otherwise, do not exceed three or four screens. Some employers, rather than providing online forms, request that you submit a scannable résumé online. This type of résumé is discussed in detail later in the chapter.

7. Like your letter, your résumé must be mechanically perfect, with absolutely no errors in spelling, punctuation, or grammar. Edit for careless blunders—typos, inconsistent spacing, and the like.

Here are some detailed pointers concerning the various categories of a résumé:

■ *Contact information:* Such irrelevant personal details as birth date, religion, marital status, social insurance number, and so forth simply waste space. Include *only* your name, address, phone number, and email address. Your contact information should appear at the top of the page or screen and need not be labelled. *Note:* Many email addresses are somewhat silly (for example, bigsexydood@sympatico.ca). If yours falls into this category, you should set up a "professional" email account specifically for job-search purposes. Similarly, you should ensure that the message on your answering machine or cellphone also conveys an appropriate impression. And if you maintain a personal website, it should contain absolutely nothing that potential employers might find juvenile or irresponsible.

■ *Career objective:* A brief but focused statement of your career plans can be useful. But if you wind up applying for a wide range of positions, you must revise it to suit each occasion. Whether to include this category depends on your individual circumstances, and whether you have room for it.

■ *Education:* In reverse chronological order, provide the name and address of each school you've attended, and mention your program of study and any degrees, diplomas, or certificates received, along with dates of attendance. You may wish to list specific classes completed, but this consumes a lot of space and is not necessary. Do not list any schooling earlier than high school, and high school itself should be omitted unless you're attempting to "beef up" an otherwise skimpy résumé.

- *Work experience:* Besides the Education section, this is the most important category in the résumé. For each position you've held, provide your job title, dates of employment, the name and address of your employer, and—if they are not evident from the job title—the duties involved. Some résumés also include the names of immediate supervisors. As in the Education section, use reverse chronological order. If you have worked at many different jobs, some for short periods, you may list only your most important positions, omitting the others or lumping them together in a one-sentence summary like this: "At various times I have also held temporary and part-time positions as service station attendant, counter clerk, and maintenance worker."

- *Military service:* If applicable, list the branch and dates of your service, the highest rank you achieved, and any noteworthy travel or duty. Some applicants, especially those with no other significant employment history, list military activity under the Work Experience category.

- *Computer literacy:* This is a highly valued attribute—indeed, a necessary one—in today's technology-driven workplace. Mention specific word-processing and other software with which you're familiar (for example, Microsoft Word and Excel or Adobe Photoshop).

- *Specialized skills or credentials:* Include licences, certifications, security clearances, foreign language competency, proficiency with certain machines—any "plus" that does not fit neatly elsewhere.

- *Honours and awards:* These can be academic or otherwise. In some cases—if you received a medal while in the military, for example, or made the college honour roll—it's best to include such distinctions under the appropriate categories. But if the Kiwanis Club awarded you its annual scholarship or you were cited for heroism by the mayor, these honours would probably be highlighted in a separate category.

- *Community activities:* Volunteer work or memberships in local clubs, organizations, or church groups are appropriate here. Most helpful are well-known activities, such as Scouts and the like. Include full details: dates of service or membership, offices held, if any, and special projects or undertakings you initiated or coordinated. Obviously, community activities often bear some relationship to applicants' pastimes or hobbies. Employers are somewhat interested in this because they are seeking individuals who can not only perform the duties of the job but also "fit in" easily with co-workers. But don't claim familiarity with an organization or activity you actually know little about. You're likely to get caught because many interviewers like to open with some preliminary conversation about an applicant's interests outside the workplace.

- *References:* Employers no longer require applicants to list the names of references on their résumés, or even to include a "References available on request" line. Nevertheless, you'll probably be asked for references if you become a finalist for a position, so you should mention near the end of your application letter that you're ready to provide them. But never identify someone as a reference without the person's permission. Before beginning your job search, identify at least three individuals qualified to write recommendation letters for you, and ask them whether they'd be willing to do so. Select persons who are familiar with your work habits and who are likely to comment favourably. Teachers and former supervisors are usually the best choices for recommendations because their remarks tend to be taken the most seriously. You must be absolutely certain, however, that anyone writing on your behalf will have nothing but good things to say. Tentative, halfhearted praise is worse than none at all. If someone seems even slightly hesitant to serve as a reference, you should find somebody more agreeable. One way to determine whether someone is indeed willing to compose an enthusiastic endorsement is to request that a copy of the recommendation be sent to you as well as to the employer. Anyone reluctant to comply with such a request is probably not entirely supportive. In any case, securing copies of recommendation letters enables you to judge for yourself whether any of your references should be dropped from your list. Better to suffer the consequences of a lukewarm recommendation once than to be undermined repeatedly without your knowledge. Usually, however, anyone consenting to write a letter on your behalf (and provide you with a copy) will give an affirmative evaluation that will work to your advantage.

Traditional Résumé

A traditional résumé can be organized in accordance with any one of three basic styles: chronological, functional, or a combination of both.

A **chronological résumé** (sometimes called an archival résumé) is the most common and the easiest to prepare. Figures 12.5 and 12.6 typify this style. Schooling and work experience are presented in reverse chronological order, with the names and addresses of schools and employers indicated, along with the dates of attendance and employment. Descriptions of specific courses of study and job responsibilities are provided as part of the Education and Work Experience categories. This style is most appropriate for persons whose education and past experience are fairly consistent with their future career plans, or for those seeking to advance within their own workplace.

A **functional résumé**, on the other hand, highlights what the applicant has done, rather than where or when it has been done. The functional résumé is skills-based, summarizing in general terms the applicant's experience and potential for adapting to new challenges. Specific chronological details of the person's background are included but are not the main focus. Moreover, the list of competencies occupies considerable space on the page and may therefore crowd out other categories of information. In Figure 12.7, for example, the Service category has necessarily been

Figure 12.6 Chronological Résumé

Carole A. Greco

61 Stebbins Drive
Mildmay, ON N0G 2V0
(519) 555-5555
cagrec@email.net

OBJECTIVE: A permanent position in financial services.

EDUCATION: Applied Degree (Accounting) May 2012
Conestoga College, Kitchener, ON
86% average; Condors soccer team captain

EXPERIENCE: Intern (Fall 2011)
Sterling Insurance Company, Kitchener, ON

Contacted and met with prospective clients,
answered client inquiries, performed general office
duties.

Administrative Assistant (Summers 2009–2011)
RBC, Walkerton, ON

Researched financial investment data, organized trust
account information, screened and answered customer
inquiries, composed business correspondence.

Student Council Treasurer (Fall 2010–Spring 2011)
Conestoga College, Kitchener, ON

Maintained $300 000 budget funding 35 campus
organizations, approved and verified all disbursements,
administered Student Council payroll.

SERVICE: Volunteer of the Year, 2009
Canadian Red Cross, Walkerton, ON

Figure 12.7 Functional Résumé

Carole A. Greco

61 Stebbins Drive
Mildmay, ON N0G 2V0
(519) 555-5555
cagrec@email.net

<u>Objective</u>

A permanent position in financial services.

<u>Competencies</u>

Financial

- Interpreted financial investment data
- Assisted with disbursement of trust accounts
- Administered $300 000 budget

Leadership and Management

- Participated in policy making
- Addressed client/customer concerns

Research and Organization

- Researched financial investment data
- Organized trust account data
- Coordinated funding for 35 organizations

<u>Education</u>

Applied degree (Accounting), May 2012, Conestoga College, Kitchener, ON; 86% average; Condors soccer team captain

<u>Experience</u>

Intern (Fall 2011), Sterling Insurance Company, Kitchener, ON

Administrative Assistant (Summers 2009–2010), RBC, Walkerton, ON

Student Council Treasurer (Fall 2010–Spring 2011), Conestoga College, Kitchener, ON

omitted. This style is most appropriate for applicants wishing to emphasize their actual proficiencies rather than their work history.

As the term suggests, the **combination résumé** is a blend of the chronological and functional approaches, featuring a relatively brief skills section at the outset followed by a chronological detailing of work experience. The combination approach is most appropriate for applicants whose experience is relatively diversified and whose skills span a range of functional areas. Figure 12.8 depicts a résumé prepared in the combination style.

Besides the variations in the ways the three styles of résumés present the candidate's credentials, there are also *layout* differences. In Figure 12.6, the category headings are in capitals and are flush with the left margin; in Figure 12.7, they are underlined and centred; and in Figure 12.8, they are capitalized and centred. These differences do not derive from the fact that the three résumés are in chronological, functional, and combination style, respectively. Rather, the variations simply reflect the open-ended nature of résumé design.

For many applicants this flexibility is liberating, allowing them to experiment and exercise creativity. But for others it can pose problems. Someone who is not visually oriented, for example, may find it difficult to choose among the many possible options that present themselves. For this reason some applicants prefer to use the predesigned résumé templates that accompany most word-processing programs. Figure 12.9 depicts one such template available in Microsoft Word. To use it, you'd simply highlight each section of text and replace it with yours, changing Max Benson to your own name, and so forth. Another template provided by Microsoft Word, called Resume Wizard, allows for a high degree of customization by offering choices of styles and headings. In the 2003 version, you can access Word's résumé templates by opening the File menu, clicking New, Templates on my Computer, and then selecting the Other Documents tab. In Word 2007, go to the Word logo (top left), click on New, and choose Resume from the list on the left.

Scannable Résumé

Rapid advances in computer technology have greatly changed every aspect of workplace communications. The hiring process is an obvious example. Many companies now advertise job openings on the internet, inviting applicants to submit résumés electronically to be read on the screen rather than as hard copy. One problem with this development is that, depending on which software is used, a creatively formatted résumé may appear confusingly jumbled or downright illegible on the receiving end. Format enhancements, such as bold print, italics, underlining, bullets, and the like, can dress up a résumé on paper, but in the online environment they can create havoc. For this reason, many career counsellors now urge

Figure 12.8 Combination Résumé

Carole A. Greco

61 Stebbins Drive
Mildmay, ON N0G 2V0
(519) 555-5555
cagrec@email.net

OBJECTIVE

A permanent position in financial services.

COMPETENCIES

- Strong account management and financial analysis skills
- Effective leadership and management capabilities
- Well-developed research and organizational skills

EXPERIENCE

Intern (Fall 2011), Sterling Insurance Company, Kitchener, ON:
Contacted and met with prospective clients, answered client inquiries,
performed general office duties.

Administrative Assistant (Summers 2009–2010), RBC, Walkerton, ON:
Researched financial investment data, organized trust account information, screened and answered customer inquiries, composed business correspondence.

Student Council Treasurer (Fall 2010–Spring 2011), Conestoga College,
Kitchener, ON: Maintained $300 000 budget funding 35 campus
organizations, approved and verified all disbursements, administered
Student Council payroll.

EDUCATION

Applied degree (Accounting), May 2012, Conestoga College,
Kitchener, ON; 86% average; Condors soccer team captain

SERVICE

Volunteer of the Year (2009), Canadian Red Cross, Walkerton, ON

Figure 12.9 "Professional" Résumé

Max Benson

123 Rose Court   (250) 555-1333
Victoria, BC V8Z 3C3   maxbenson@sympatico.ca

Objective   To obtain a full-time sales position that builds on my many skills.

Experience   1990–1994   Arbor Shoe   Southridge, BC
National Sales Manager
- Increased sales from $50 million to $100 million.
- Doubled sales per representative from $5 million to $10 million.
- Suggested new products that increased earnings by 23%.

1985–1990   Ferguson and Bardell   Southridge, BC
District Sales Manager
- Increased regional sales from $25 million to $350 million.
- Managed 250 sales representatives.
- Implemented training course for new recruits — speeding profitability.

1980–1984   Duffy Vineyards   Southridge, BC
Senior Sales Representative
- Expanded sales team from 50 to 100 representatives.
- Tripled division revenues for each sales associate.
- Expanded sales to include mass market accounts.

1975–1980   LitWare, Inc.   Southridge, BC
Sales Representative
- Expanded territorial sales by 400%.
- Received company's highest sales award four years in a row.
- Developed Excellence in Sales training course.

Education   1971–1975   Southridge University   Southridge, BC
- B.A., Business Administration and Computer Science.
- Graduated Summa Cum Laude.

Interests   SR Board of Directors, running, gardening, carpentry, computers.

applicants to greatly simplify the design of their résumés by adopting a no-frills, flush-left format. An online résumé should always be sent as a Word document or RTF file, not as a compressed (zip) or PDF file, which might create problems for the recipient. To enable the employer to quickly locate your résumé, the file name should begin with your last name, like this: Smith_2011_apr.19.doc. Also, resist the urge to attach pictures, graphics, or URLs. Most employers will not bother with these. Figure 12.10 depicts the same résumé as shown in Figure 12.6 but in a readily scannable format.

Streamlining for the computer's sake is probably a positive development. Simpler is generally better in workplace communications, and the trend toward a less complicated résumé layout serves to counterbalance the tendency to overbuild such documents. Indeed, most people who have created scannable versions of their résumés eventually tone down their hard-copy originals as well. An incidental benefit of the simpler format is that more information can be included because limited space is used more effectively. Since scannable résumés are rapidly becoming the norm, many employers now use a strategy called the keyword search. Computerized scanning programs check all résumés received to identify those that include certain terms (that is, keywords) that the employer considers particularly relevant. Of course, the computer can detect keywords wherever they may appear in a résumé, but many job-seekers are now creating a separate, keyword-loaded section—sometimes called the profile—in place of the job objective. Notice that the scannable résumé in Figure 12.10 includes this feature.

Since the mid-1990s, innumerable websites have appeared that can be quite helpful if you're looking for employment. These enable you to post your résumé online in the hopes that prospective employers will seek you out. More realistically, you can inspect job announcements posted by the employers. Most of these sites enable you to focus efficiently, searching by job title, geographical location, company name, keyword(s), and other considerations. The sites often boast company profiles, online job fairs and newsletters, various forms of job search and career development advice, chat rooms and bulletin boards, links to other sites, and even online résumé tutorials. Here are seven such sites:

■ Best Jobs Canada	www.bestjobsca.com
■ CareerBuilder	www.careerbuilder.ca
■ Canada Job Search	www.careerpath.ca
■ Monster	www.monster.ca
■ Public Service Commission of Canada	http://jobs-emplois.gc.ca
■ Service Canada Job Bank	www.jobbank.gc.ca
■ Workopolis	www.workopolis.com

Figure 12.10 Scannable Résumé

CAROLE A. GRECO

61 Stebbins Drive
Mildmay, ON N0G 2V0
(519) 555-5555
cagrec@email.net

PROFILE: Experienced financial services professional with
accounting degree and expertise in customer service, data retrieval,
and budget, payroll, and investment analysis and management.
Administrative and research skills, along with computer proficiency
in Microsoft Word, Adobe Photoshop, and PowerPoint.

EDUCATION: Applied degree (Accounting), May 2012, Conestoga
College, Kitchener, ON; 86 percent average; Condors soccer team
captain

EXPERIENCE: Intern (Fall 2011), Sterling Insurance Company,
Kitchener, ON: Contacted and met with prospective clients,
answered client inquiries, performed general office duties.

Administrative Assistant (Summers 2009–2010), RBC, Walkerton, ON:
Researched financial investment data, organized trust account
information, screened and answered customer inquiries, composed
business correspondence.

Student Council Treasurer (Fall 2010–Spring 2011), Conestoga College,
Kitchener, ON: Maintained $300 000 budget funding 35 campus
organizations, approved and verified all disbursements, administered
Student Council payroll.

SERVICE: Volunteer of the Year (2009), Canadian Red Cross,
Walkerton, ON.

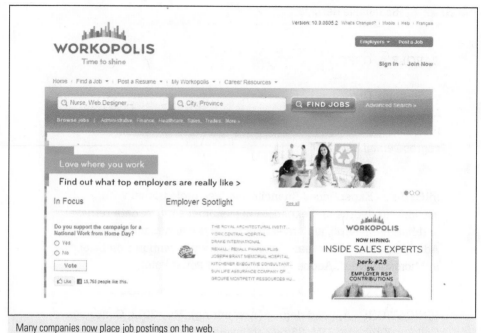

Many companies now place job postings on the web.

If you are looking for a career in a specific area, you can use the following websites to help guide you in your decision making:

- Canadian Careers: www.canadiancareers.com
- Human Resources and Skills Development Canada: www.hrsdc.gc.ca
- Looking Ahead: A 10 Year Outlook for the Canadian Labour Market (2006–2015): www.hrsdc.gc.ca/eng/publications_resources/research/categories/labour_market_e/sp_615_10_06/page00.shtml
- National Occupation Classification: www5.hrsdc.gc.ca/NOC/English/NOC/2006/Welcome.aspx

 ## Tech Tips

For optimal results, you should create and save a résumé only as a Word document, not online such as with Google docs. Save the document in hypertext markup language (HTML) so you can easily post your résumé to the web. But you should adhere to several important rules:

- Create the résumé as plain text, using a conventional font in 12-point size throughout.
- Set 1.2" (3 cm) side margins.
- Position all text flush with the left margin.
- Enter your name and the category headings in uppercase letters.

- Insert only one space after periods and other end punctuation.
- Do not use the ampersand (&), bold print, centring, indentations, italics, line justification, the percent sign (%), ruling lines, the slash (/), bullets, or underlining.
- Limit each line to 6" (15.2 cm) on your computer screen, and advance down the screen by hitting the Enter key before reaching the end of the line, rather than allowing the lines to wrap around automatically.

Some employers will want your résumé in the body of the email. If so, open the document you created, copy the text, and paste it into your email window.

Other employers may want you to attach your résumé. If so, from your email screen,

click Add Attachments (or a similar button, depending on your email program). Search through your computer directories until you find your file, highlight it, and press Open (or Choose or Attach, depending on your program). The file should then attach. Always check to make sure the attachment is there before you send off your résumé.

If you have posted your résumé to the web, reference the URL in the body of your message so employers can click on it and go directly to your site. Whatever you do, follow the same three-part approach recommended for the traditional job application letter but without the inside addresses. For a subject line, use the job title or posting number.

INTERVIEW

If your letter and résumé result in an interview, you can assume that you're in the running for the position; no personnel office deliberately wastes time interviewing applicants who are not. But now you must outperform the other finalists by excelling in the interview. For this to happen, you must have three assets going for you: preparation, composure, and common sense.

To prepare, find out everything you can about the position and the workplace. Read any existing literature about the employer (website, annual reports, promotional materials, product brochures, and so on). Consult some of the employment-related websites mentioned earlier in this chapter. If possible, talk to past and current employees or to persons in comparable jobs elsewhere. For generic information about the job title, consult some of the websites listed earlier on page 308. By familiarizing yourself with the nature of the job and the work environment, you'll better equip yourself to converse intelligently with the interviewer. You'll *feel* more confident, a major prerequisite to successful interviewing.

If possible, locate the interview site beforehand and determine how much time you'll need to get there punctually. Be sure to get enough sleep the night before. Take a shower. Eat breakfast. Dismiss from your mind all problems or worries. All this may seem like obvious and rather old-fashioned advice, but it goes a long way toward ensuring that you'll be physically and mentally at ease and ready to interact smoothly. Of course, you should not be *too* relaxed; an employment interview is a fairly formal situation, and you should conduct yourself accordingly. Stand up straight, shake the interviewer's hand firmly, establish eye contact, and speak in a calm, clear voice. Sit down only when invited to or when the interviewer does. Do not smoke or chew gum, and—needless to say—*never* attend an employment interview with alcohol on your breath or while under the influence of any controlled substance. Also, turn off your pager and your cellphone. No interviewer enjoys being interrupted by an applicant's incoming calls.

Whether you have applied by mail or online, be sure to have several copies of your résumé with you.

Anticipate key questions. As mentioned earlier, the interviewer might begin by asking you about your interests and hobbies, or perhaps by remarking about the weather or some other lightweight topic. From there, however, the conversation will become more focused. Expect discussion of your qualifications, your willingness to work certain hours or shifts, your long-range career plans, your desired salary, your own questions about the job, and so on. Here's a list of 20 typical questions often asked by interviewers:

1. Tell me about yourself. (A common variation is, If you had to describe yourself in just one word, what would it be?)

2. What do you do in your spare time?

3. Why did you choose your particular field of study?

4. What do you think you've learned in college/university?

5. How much do you know about computers?

6. Why aren't your grades higher?

7. Do you plan to further your education?

8. What are your long-range goals?

9. What kind of work do you like best? Least?

10. What was the best job you ever had? Why?

11. How do you explain the gaps on your résumé?

12. Can you provide three solid references?

13. Why do you think you're qualified for this position?

14. Why do you want to work for this particular company?

15. Are you willing to work shifts? Weekends? Overtime?

16. Are you willing to relocate?

17. If hired, when could you start work?

18. How much do you expect us to pay you?

19. Why should we hire you?

20. Do *you* have any questions?

Interviewers ask questions such as these partly because they want to hear your answers but also because they want to determine how poised you are, how clearly you express yourself, and how well you perform under pressure. Try to formulate some responses to such queries beforehand so you can reply readily, without having to grope for intelligent answers. Just as important, try to settle on several good questions of your own. Gear these to matters of importance, such as the employer's training and orientation procedures, the job description and conditions of employment, performance evaluation policies, likelihood of job stability, opportunities for advancement, and the like. You want the employer to know you're a serious candidate with a genuine interest in the job. But don't talk *too* much or attempt to control the interview. Answer questions fully—in three or four sentences—but know when to stop talking. Stay away from jokes or controversial topics. Avoid excessive slang. Don't try to impress the interviewer with big words or exaggerated claims. Maintain a natural but respectful manner. In short, just be yourself, but be your *best* self.

Many applicants are unsure about how to dress for an interview. The rule is actually quite simple: wear approximately what you would if you were reporting for work. If you are applying for a "dress-up" job, dress up. For a "jeans and sweatshirt" job, dress casually. Some employment counsellors advise applicants to dress just a step above the position for which they are interviewing. In any case, make sure your interview clothing fits properly, is neat and clean, and is not too outlandishly stylish. Minimize jewellery. Small earrings are acceptable (two or three for a woman, one for a man), but nose and eyebrow rings, tongue studs, chains, or any other such adornments are better left at home, as are shower flip-flops, sweatpants, hats, and any clothing imprinted with crude or tasteless slogans. Just as the physical appearance of your letter and résumé will influence whether you're invited to an interview, your *own* appearance will influence whether you get hired. As mentioned at the beginning of this section, *common sense* is a major factor in interviewing well.

FOLLOW-UP

The follow-up to an interview is another exercise in common sense. Although it requires very little effort, many applicants neglect it. This is unfortunate because a timely follow-up (within a day or two) can serve as a tiebreaker among several comparably qualified candidates. Every employer wants to hire someone willing to go a bit beyond what's required. Your follow-up is evidence that you are such a person, so it can enable you to get a step ahead of the other applicants.

In the form of a simple letter or email, the follow-up expresses gratitude for the interview and assures the employer that you're still interested in the job. There's no need to compose anything elaborate; a brief note will do. For an example, see Figure 12.11.

Figure 12.11 Follow-up Letter

55 Cortland Avenue
Vancouver, BC   V6F 6T2

April 15, 2011

Ms. Maria Castro
Director of Human Resources
The Senior Citizens' Homestead
666 Grand Avenue
Vancouver, BC V6B 4A2

Dear Ms. Castro:

Thank you for meeting with me to discuss the electrician position.

Having enjoyed our conversation and the tour of the Senior Citizens'
Homestead, I am still very interested in the job and am available to
start work immediately after my graduation from college next month.
I can also start sooner (on a part-time basis) if necessary.

Please contact me if you have any further questions about my background or credentials, and thanks again for your time.

Sincerely,

James Carter

James Carter

✓ Checklist   Evaluating an Application Letter, Résumé, and Follow-up

A good application letter

___ follows a standard letter format (full block is best);

___ is organized into paragraphs:

   ☐ First paragraph asks for the job by name, and indicates how you learned of the opening

   ☐ Middle paragraphs briefly outline your credentials and refer the reader to your résumé

   ☐ Last paragraph closes on a polite note, mentioning that you would like an interview

___ does not exceed one page;

___ uses simple language, maintains appropriate tone, and contains no typos or mechanical errors in spelling, capitalization, punctuation, or grammar.

A good résumé

___ looks good, making effective use of white space, capitalization, boldface type, and other format features;

___ includes no irrelevant personal information;

___ includes separate, labelled sections for education, experience, and other major categories of professional qualifications;

___ maintains a consistent approach to abbreviation, spacing, and other elements;

___ does not exceed one page;

___ contains no typos or mechanical errors in spelling, capitalization, punctuation, or grammar.

A good follow-up letter

___ follows a standard letter format (full block is best);

___ is organized into paragraphs:

   ☐ First paragraph thanks the employer for the interview and mentions the job by name

   ☐ Middle paragraph restates your interest and availability

   ☐ Last paragraph politely invites further contact

___ does not exceed one page;

___ uses simple language, maintains appropriate tone, and contains no typos or mechanical errors in spelling, capitalization, punctuation, or grammar.

Exercises

Exercise 12.1

Read the classified advertisements in a recent issue of your local newspaper and write a memo report about what you find there. Include information not only about what kinds of jobs are listed but also about the qualifications required. Provide a breakdown of how many jobs require written responses as opposed to telephone or personal contact. Indicate whether there appears to be any correlation between the type of job and the likelihood that a written response will be requested.

Exercise 12.2

Using the websites listed on page 308, explore the employment-related websites Workopolis and Monster.ca and write a report about what you discover. Compare and evaluate these sites. Which one is best for your purposes? Why? Which is the *least* useful to you? Why?

Exercise 12.3

Using the internet along with print resources, research a particular job title, and write a report discussing your findings. What are the principal responsibilities of the position? What qualifications are typically required? What is the salary range? Are there more openings for this job in certain geographical areas?

Exercise 12.4

Using the internet along with print resources, research a particular employer and write a report discussing your findings. What are the employer's main products or services? How long has the employer been in business? Where is the corporate headquarters? How large is the workforce? What kinds of skills or credentials are required to work for this company?

Exercise 12.5

Interview someone currently employed in a job related to your field of study, and write a report summarizing the conversation. Why did the person choose this kind of work? How long has the person been in the position? What kind of education and other qualifications does the individual possess? What was said about the best and worst features of the job? Does he or she find the work challenging, interesting, and rewarding?

Exercise 12.6

Using the websites listed on pages 293–294, find an actual classified advertisement for an opening in your field that specifically requests a written response. Compose a job application letter and a chronological résumé. Pretend you have been successful in getting an interview and have met with the personnel director. Compose a follow-up letter.

Exercise 12.7

Find an actual classified advertisement for an opening in some field unrelated to your own that specifically requests a written response. Compose a job application letter and a functional résumé. Pretend you have been successful in getting an interview and have met with the personnel director. Compose a follow-up letter.

Exercise 12.8

Find an actual classified advertisement for an opening in some field other than your own but related to it that specifically requests a written response. Compose a job application letter and a combination résumé. Pretend you have been successful in getting an interview and have met with the personnel director. Compose a follow-up letter.

Exercise 12.9

Design scannable versions of the chronological, functional, and combination résumés you created in response to Exercises 12.6–12.8.

Exercise 12.10

Three application letters accompanied by résumés follow on the next few pages. For a variety of reasons, all are badly flawed. Rewrite each to eliminate its particular weaknesses.

mycanadiantechcommlab

Visit www.mycanadiantechcommlab.ca for everything you need to help you succeed in the job you've always wanted! Tools and resources include the following:

- Composing Space and Writer's Toolkit
- Document Makeovers
- Grammar Exercises—and much more!

Exercise 12.10 (Continued)

Carla Zogby
2400 Front St., Apt. 32
Toronto, ON M6P 1Y8

February 23, 2011

Diversified Services, Inc.
500 Tower Street
Toronto, ON M6H 2A6

Dear Sirs:

I am writting this letter in reply to your recent add in the *Toronto Star*.

As you can see from the enclosed resume, I have all the qualifications for which you are looking for.

Thank you for your time.

Your's Truely,

Carla Zogby

Carla Zogby

Exercise 12.10 (Continued)

NAME: Carla Zogby
ADDRESS: 2400 Front St., Apt. 32, Toronto, ON   M6P 1Y8
TELEPHONE MUMBER: 416-555-4370
DATE OF BIRTH: October 1, 1983
RELIGION: Cathoilc
MARITAL STATUS: Single
HEIGHT: 160 cm (5′ 3″) WEIGHT: 50 kg (110 lbs)

EXPERIENCE

9/2009–2/2010 Receptionist	St. Aedan's Church Answered phones, greeted visitors, handled weekly collection deposits, prepared and distributed weekly bulletin.
3/2009–8/2010 Store Trainer, Waitress	Friendly's Corporation Trained all new waitstaff, took food orders, cleared tables, washed dishes, helped cook.
11/2009–present Insurance Processor	Scotia Bank Process disability and death claims, work with insurance companies to pay accounts.

EDUCATION

9/2005–6/2009	St. Aedan's High School ■ Honor Roll 3, 4 ■ Student Council 2
8/2009–present	George Brown College Secretarial Science

SKILLS
Personal computer systems, software proficiency with spreadsheets, word processing and database programs.

Exercise 12.10 (Continued)

Thomas Logan
105 Lincoln Ave.
Canmore, AB T1W 1P4
July 17, 2010

Conklin's Department Stores, Inc.
1400 West Carroll Street
Calgary AB T2P 3K7

Gentlemen,

I am responding to an employment ad of yours that I found via the internet for the Store Security postion. I am sure that you will find that I am highly qualified for this job.

As a military policeman in the Canadian Armed Forces from July 2004 until April 2010 I had over six years experience in law enforcement. My job responsibilities included public relations, emergency vehicle operations, weapons handling, equipment maintenance and personnel management. My training included interpersonal communication skills, radio communications procedures, weapons safety, police radar operations, unarmed self-defense and riot and crowd control operations. I enforced traffic regulations by monitoring high traffic areas, being visible to the public, and issuing citations as necessary. I performed law enforcement investigations as needed, as well as prepared, verified, and documented police reports to include sworn statements and gathering and processing evidence. I conducted foot and motorized patrols of assigned areas and applied crime prevention measures by maintaining control and discipline through ensuring that all laws and regulations were obeyed at all times.

I also performed basic first aid as first responder when needed.

Earlier I served as a parachute rigger, rigging, assembling, and repairing several of the military parachutes used in Airborne operations. I rigged various vehcles, weapons, and supplies to be air-dropped as well as hold airborne status for the duration. I also trained in combat operations.

At present I have just enrolled in the Criminal Justice program at Bow Valley College, and I have also completed a Human Relations course at Sprott Shaw Community College, a Combat Lifesaver course, a 10-week course at the Canadian Armed Forces Police School, as well as studies at the Canadian Armed Forces Airborne and Pararigger Schools and the Canadian Armed Forces Basic Training and Infantry Schools.

Additional Skills include knowledge of first aid, knowege of conversational French, an accident-free driving record (nine years (civilian and military), and a Canadian Armed Forces Secret Security Clearance.

Sincrely,

Thomas Logan

Exercise 12.10 (Continued)

Résumé of

Thomas Logan, Jr.

105 Lincoln Avenue
Canmore, AB T1W 1P4

Career Objective
Full-time position in law enforcement or security.

Education
Dickinson High School
Canmore, AB (Class of 2004)

Bow Valley College
Canmore, Alberta (Currently enrolled)

Armed Forces
Canadian Army (2004–2010)

Interests
Fishing, Hunting, Snowmobiling

References
Professor John Dhayer
Sgt. Warren Landis
Mr. Thomas Logan, Sr.

Exercise 12.10 (Continued)

July 17, 2010

Superior Steel, Inc.
c/o Manitoba Department of Labour
121 North Main Street
Winnipeg, MB R3A 0J5

Dear Superior Stell;

I am applying for the machinist/production assembler position you
have posted with the Depratment of Labour. I have been a machinist
at the Curtis Arms Co. for two years with experience in the manufacture of low tolerance parts from blueprints. I also have eight years
experience as a self-employed general contractor, and additional
experience as a tree service worker. I am now continuing my education at Red River College. I have completed 12 credits towArd a
diploma and have maintained straight A's. I am looking forward to
meeting with you for an interview as soon as possible. Thank you for
your consideration.

Sincerely;

Roland Perry

Roland Perry

Exercise 12.10 (Continued)

Roland Perry
30 East Street
Winnipeg, MB R0G 0X0
(204)555-3806
email: rolper30@sympatico.ca

OBJECTIVE

To obtain a full-time position as a machinist with Superior Steel.

WORK HISTORY

Curtis Arms Company, Inc., Winnipeg, MB

Machine operation/set-up on CNC, Pratt-Whitney bore reamers,
NAPCO black oxide colour line, neutral and hardening furnaces.
(January 2008–present)

DUTIES
- machining gun parts to tolerances of +/– .005 inch
- metal fabricating from blue prints
- hardening parts to Rockwell hardness specifications
- maintaining quality standards

Larry's Tree Service, Winnipeg, MB

Ground crew member. (July 2007–January 2008)

DUTIES
- operated chain saws, chippers, stump machine
- controlled lowering lines and climbers lifeline
- operated and maintained trucks and machinery

Exercise 12.10 **(Continued)**

-page 2-

Perry Construction, Inc., Winnioeg, MB

Self-employed general contractor. (August 1997–February 2007)

DUTIES

- carpentry, masonary , plumbing, electrical work
- contracts, book-keeping, customer service

EDUCATION

Red River College, Winnepeg, MB (August 2008-present)

COURSES COMPLETED

- Air Conditioning Technology 101–A
- Technical English 101–A
- Technical Math 101–A
- Public Speaking 101–A

COMMUNITY ACTIVITIES

Volunteer Fire Department
Canadian Legion Post Secretary
Community Band (Tuba Player)

PHOTO CREDITS ·

INDEX